New Casebooks

JANE EYRE

EDITED BY HEATHER GLEN

Introduction, selection and editorial matter
© Heather Glen 1997

All rights reserved. No reproduction, copy or transmission of
this publication may be made without written permission.

No paragraph of this publication may be reproduced, copied or
transmitted save with written permission or in accordance with
the provisions of the Copyright, Designs and Patents Act 1988,
or under the terms of any licence permitting limited copying
issued by the Copyright Licensing Agency, 90 Tottenham Court
Road, London W1P 9HE.

Any person who does any unauthorised act in relation to this
publication may be liable to criminal prosecution and civil
claims for damages.

The author has asserted her rights to be identified as the author of this
work in accordance with the Copyright, Designs and Patents Act 1988.

 First published 1997 by
MACMILLAN PRESS LTD
Houndmills, Basingstoke, Hampshire RG21 6XS
and London
Companies and representatives
throughout the world

ISBN 0–333–62245–6 hardcover
ISBN 0–333–62246–4 paperback

A catalogue record for this book is available
from the British Library.

This book is printed on paper suitable for recycling and
made from fully managed and sustained forest sources.

10   9   8   7   6   5   4   3   2   1
06   05   04   03   02   01   00   99   98   97

Typeset by EXPO Holdings, Malaysia

Printed in Hong Kong

 Published in the United States of America 1997 by
ST. MARTIN'S PRESS, INC.,
Scholarly and Reference Division
175 Fifth Avenue, New York, N.Y. 10010

ISBN 0–312–16580–3

Contents

Acknowledgements

The editor and publishers wish to thank the following for permission to use copyright material:

Elisabeth Bronfen for material from *Over Her Dead Body: Death, Femininity and the Aesthetic* (1990), pp. 219–23, by permission of Manchester University Press; Penny Boumelha for material from *Charlotte Brontë* (1990), ch. 3, by permission of Harvester Wheatsheaf, an imprint of Prentice-Hall; Karen Chase for material from *Eros and Psyche: The Representation of Personality in Charlotte Brontë, Charles Dickens and George Eliot* (1984), Methuen & Co, pp. 52–65, by permission of Routledge; Peter Allan Dale for 'Charlotte Brontë's "Tale Half-Told": the Disruption of Narrative Structure in *Jane Eyre*', *Modern Language Quarterly*, 47:1 (1986), 108–29. Copyright © University of Washington 1986, by permission of Duke University Press; Margaret Homans for material from *Bearing the Word: Language and Female Experience in Nineteenth-Century Women's Writing* (1986), ch. 4, by permission of University of Chicago Press; Susan Meyer for 'Colonialism and the Figurative Strategy of *Jane Eyre*', *Victorian Studies*, 33:2 (1990), by permission of the Trustees of Indiana University; Jini Politi for '*Jane Eyre* Class-ified', *Literature and History*, 8:1 (1982), 56–66, by permission of the University of Greenwich; Mary Poovey for material from *Uneven Developments: The Ideological Work of Gender in Mid-Victorian England* (1988), pp. 126–48, by permission of University of Chicago Press; Doreen Roberts for '*Jane Eyre* and "the Warped System of Things"' in *Reading the Victorian Novel: Detail Into Form* (1980), Vision Press, by permission of the author; Elaine Showalter for material from *A Literature of Their Own: British Women Novelists from Brontë to Lessing* (1977), pp. 112–22. Copyright © 1977 by Princeton University Press, by permission of Princeton University Press; Carolyn Williams for material from 'Closing the Book: the Intertextual End of *Jane Eyre*' from *Victorian Connections*, ed. Jerome McGann (1989), by permission of University Press of Virginia.

Every effort has been made to trace the copyright holders but if any have been inadvertently overlooked the publishers will be pleased to make the necessary arrangement at the first opportunity.

General Editors' Preface

The purpose of this series of New Casebooks is to reveal some of the ways in which contemporary criticism has changed our understanding of commonly studied texts and writers and, indeed, of the nature of criticism itself. Central to the series is a concern with modern critical theory and its effect on current approaches to the study of literature. Each New Casebook editor has been asked to select a sequence of essays which will introduce the reader to the new critical approaches to the text or texts being discussed in the volume and also illuminate the rich interchange between critical theory and critical practice that characterises so much current writing about literature.

In this focus on modern critical thinking and practice New Casebooks aim not only to inform but also to stimulate, with volumes seeking to reflect both the controversy and the excitement of current criticism. Because much of this criticism is difficult and often employs an unfamiliar critical language, editors have been asked to give the reader as much help as they feel is appropriate, but without simplifying the essays or the issues they raise. Again, editors have been asked to supply a list of further reading which will enable readers to follow up issues raised by the essays in the volume.

The project of New Casebooks, then, is to bring together in an illuminating way those critics who best illustrate the ways in which contemporary criticism has established new methods of analysing texts and who have reinvigorated the important debate about how we 'read' literature. The hope is, of course, that New Casebooks will not only open up this debate to a wider audience, but will also encourage students to extend their own ideas, and think afresh about their responses to the texts they are studying.

John Peck and Martin Coyle
(*University of Wales, Cardiff*)

Introduction

HEATHER GLEN

Jane Eyre is, and has been since its first publication, an unambiguously popular novel. Its earliest reviewers hailed it as 'a book to make the pulses gallop and the heart beat, and to fill the eye with tears';[1] one whose 'high and headlong course [was] calculated to rivet attention, to provoke sympathy, to make the heart bound, and the brain pause'.[2] 'The popularity of *Jane Eyre*', remarked one, disapprovingly, 'is a proof how deeply the love of illegitimate romance is implanted in our nature':[3] but no less a bastion of middle-class morality than Queen Victoria herself was to deem it 'a wonderful book'.[4] 'I wish you had not sent me *Jane Eyre*. It interested me so much that I have lost (or won if you like) a whole day in reading it at the busiest period with the printers I know waiting for copy', wrote Thackeray, to its publisher, four days after the novel appeared.[5] 'People still sit up into the night with *Jane Eyre*', declared Mrs Humphry Ward, over half a century later, in an Introduction to the novel for the sumptuous seven-volume Haworth Edition of the Brontës' works.[6] Half a century later yet, the American poet Adrienne Rich tells of reading *Jane Eyre* in childhood and returning to it 'over and over in adolescence, in my twenties, thirties, now in my forties': 'I have never lost the sense', she says, 'that it contains ... some nourishment I needed then and still need today.'[7] 'It remains the most durable of melodramas, angry, sexy, a little crazy, a perennial bestseller', writes Angela Carter, in 1992, 'one of the oddest novels ever written, a delirious romance.'[8] And that to which these voices testify is – as Jane herself might have put it – simply what 'millions' have felt. Generations of girls (especially) have empathised with Jane's sufferings, succumbed, ingenuously, to Mr Rochester's dark allure, thrilled to the mysteries of Thornfield, rejoiced at that famous assertion, 'Reader, I married him'. If the readership for many major novelists is now largely created, through teaching, by the academy, *Jane Eyre*, one suspects – far more than *Middlemarch*, *A Portrait of a Lady* or *Nostromo* – would, without any such sponsorship, still be discovered and read.

A novel so much loved, so intimately compelling, presents a peculiar challenge to academic criticism – a challenge which is indeed registered, again and again, in the records of its readers' response. 'We took up *Jane Eyre* one winter's evening, somewhat piqued at the extravagant commendations we had heard, and sternly resolved to be ... critical', an early reviewer recalled, in 1849. 'But as we read on we forgot both commendations and criticism, identified ourselves with Jane in all her troubles, and finally married Mr Rochester about four in the morning.'[9] 'Even while the head condemns, the heart is taken by surprise, and compelled, sometimes against its will, both to sympathise, and to respond', admits the conduct-book writer Sarah Ellis, in 1850, in a review which deplores the novel's 'glaring violations of good taste', its failure to 'elevate' or to 'improve': 'this style of writing', she concludes, 'is as unhealthy as it is absorbing'.[10] 'We cannot stifle the suspicion that we shall find her world of imagination as antiquated, mid-Victorian, and out of date as the parsonage on the moor', Virginia Woolf was to write of re-reading Charlotte Brontë, over 70 years later.

> We open *Jane Eyre*; and in two pages every doubt is swept clean from our minds ... Nor is this exhilaration short-lived. It rushes us through the entire volume, without giving us time to think, without letting us lift our eyes from the page.[11]

'The power of *Jane Eyre* ... needs no further adjectives', says Raymond Williams, in 1970. 'Readers still respond ... and critics follow them; sometimes critic following reader a bit uneasily in the same personality.'[12] The sense is of an intensity of identification which threatens to overwhelm the critical faculties: indeed, one recent critic, in a manner oddly reminiscent of that of Mrs Ellis, has for this reason dubbed *Jane Eyre* a 'dangerous' book.[13]

Yet critics have hardly been slow to pronounce upon *Jane Eyre*. Early reviewers, whilst concurring in recognition of the novel's power, engaged in passionate argument as to the morality or otherwise of its effect. Twenty years after Charlotte Brontë's death, this hotly evaluative dispute entered a different phase, with Swinburne's eulogistic monograph of 1877, *A Note on Charlotte Brontë*, and Leslie Stephen's more soberly critical essay of reply. To Swinburne, Charlotte Brontë's 'genius' outshone even the ascendant star of George Eliot: but Stephen took the opposite view, criticising her for the 'feverish disquiet' which disrupted her writing and showed, he felt, that her mind had 'never worked itself clear by reflection, or developed a harmonious and consistent view of life'.[14] And it was Stephen's view which prevailed – amongst critics, if not amongst readers – during the following 80 years. Certainly, the qualities for which he looked in a great work of literature – objectivity, balance, detachment – were hardly to be found in *Jane Eyre*. Perhaps, it was felt, they were more evident in the once less-valued *Wuthering Heights*. The next 50 years saw a remarkable rise in Emily Brontë's reputation and a corresponding decline in Charlotte's: by 1907, when the Haworth Edition of the Brontës' works appeared, Mrs Humphry Ward was to declare unreservedly that 'Emily's genius was the greater of the two'.[15] Where her sister was now admired as the mature practitioner of a sophisticated narrative art, Charlotte Brontë, even when praised, had come to be viewed as a passionate outpourer of personal feeling: her novels were seen as narrow in scope, distorted by anger or need. Thus, Virginia Woolf, in *A Room of One's Own* (1929), deplores the 'rancour which contracts those books, splendid as they are, with a spasm of pain'.[16] Thus, five years later, Lord David Cecil, in an influential 'revaluation', finds Charlotte Brontë's 'range confined' to 'the world of her own inner life'.[17] Thus, in a yet more influential study, published in 1948, F. R. Leavis, defining a 'great tradition' of moral seriousness in the English novel, remarks in a footnote that there is 'only one Brontë' worthy of consideration – and that one, of course, is not Charlotte.[18]

But by 1977, when the earliest essay in this collection (that by Elaine Showalter) appeared, the tide of critical opinion was beginning to turn. A series of New Critical and formalist analyses was gradually replacing what one critic called 'The Purple Heather School of Criticism and Biography', and beginning to point to the conscious artistry of *Jane Eyre*.[19] Concomitant with this, there had begun to be a new kind of exploration of unrealistic elements in the novel;[20] and a new attention to the historical specificity of the issues with which it engaged.[21] And an emerging generation of feminist critics had begun to revalue the 'anger' that Virginia Woolf found so disabling in the novel, and to hail *Jane Eyre* as a central feminist text.[22] This process of revaluation was to continue throughout the next 20 years: it is still continuing today. Indeed, this New Casebook, which reprints essays written between 1977 and 1992, may in one sense be seen as a contribution to it. Each of the approaches outlined above is represented and developed here, often in ways undreamt of in the 1970s. But the aim of this collection is not simply to illustrate the impressive diversity of contemporary critical approaches, or to show how they have issued in a series of powerful re-readings of what is now, apparently, an indisputably 'canonical' text. The intention, rather, is to pose a more open-ended question: one which *Jane Eyre* itself seems, indeed, to provoke.

More directly, perhaps, than any other to which a New Casebook has been devoted, this enduringly popular novel raises questions about the gulf between the passionate response of the ordinary reader and the cold abstractions of critical theory: questions which have become more, rather than less, pressing as it has been incorporated into the canon as an academically respectable text. For the years which have seen the institutionalisation of *Jane Eyre* have seen also the rise of an increasingly professionalised academic criticism and the development of an increasingly sophisticated critical metalanguage – which sometimes seem designed, implicitly or explicitly, to patronise and denigrate the unsophisticated intensities of popular response. Often, these developments are presented as a history of progress away from naïvety and toward enlightenment, in a narrative in which complacent liberal humanism and unexamined 'common sense' are shown to have been undermined by structuralist, poststructuralist, deconstructionist, Marxist, feminist and psychoanalytic modes of thought, and the eternal verities presumed by traditional aesthetic criticism challenged by a more developed sense of the historicity of texts once hailed as 'timeless' works of art. Yet, as the case of *Jane Eyre* quite sharply suggests, that narrative might be rather more critically viewed.

On the simplest level, the rapid growth of an increasingly sophisticated critical industry has provoked, in many, a very real concern about the thickets of 'secondary reading' through which students now have to hack to 'approach' even the most apparently accessible of texts. To point to this is not necessarily to hark back to a golden age of theoretical innocence, in which the 'common reader' had unmediated access to 'the realms of gold': it has, indeed, been one of the achievements of literary theory to show categorically that there was never, in fact, such a time. But it is to acknowledge that the proliferating academic criticism of the last 20 years has, in practice, often seemed more mystifying than enlightening, more intimidating than enlivening, to the students for whom it is presumably designed. Part of the purpose of this New Casebook is, indeed, to try to counter that sense of intimidation: to encourage the reader to think critically about the critical approaches represented here, by directing attention to the differences between them and to the ways in which each is shaped by the circumstances of a particular historical moment and a specific set of theoretical concerns. Yet the aim is not merely to provoke thought of this kind. For most readers of this volume will come to it not merely, or even mainly, to reflect on the relative merits of the critical essays it contains, but to look through them, to the work with which they deal – a work which 'millions' have urgently, if often incoherently, felt to be speaking of and to their own most intimate concerns. And that work and its popularity pose a sharper challenge to an increasingly professionalised criticism than it has, perhaps, always been prepared to meet: one which the reader of this collection is urged to keep in mind as he or she reads. Is *Jane Eyre* – once so ardently extolled, so vehemently condemned – simply being safely academicised, as the passionate partisanship of an earlier evaluative criticism (such as one finds in the previous Casebook) is replaced by a 'cooler', more sophisticated mode of analysis, and as that which is most unsettling, most stirring in the novel is theorised and explained? Or do the essays which follow suggest that *Jane Eyre* is indeed being read within the academy in a way which does full justice to the significance, and potential significance, of that still-continuing history of passionate response?

I

If *Jane Eyre* does not invite, it may seem in many ways hardly to require academic criticism. Jane's satisfying story of dangers survived and desire fulfilled presents far fewer problems of interpretation than the more sombre, more obviously crafted, apparently more sophisticated *Villette*. Unlike that later novel, *Jane Eyre* does not draw attention to silences and inconsistencies in its narrator's story: Jane speaks with apparently trustworthy directness, taking the reader into her confidence from the opening page. And her narrative, as it develops, has the unambiguous logic of childish wish fulfilment fantasy: the deserving succeed, and the undeserving are appropriately punished, in the black-and-white manner of the fairy-tales to which the novel again and again alludes.[23] Jane's is a world not of considered judgement, but of identification and revulsion, of violent oppositions, of life-and-death struggle: of prejudice rather than reasoned argument, of intense partisanship rather than subtle moral discrimination. As Doreen Roberts observes, 'the reader knows all too well what he is meant to think about the heroine and the subsidiary characters':[24] there is nothing here of the nuanced moral analysis of a Jane Austen or a George Eliot. It is of this, one imagines, that F. R. Leavis was thinking, when he pronounced, influentially, that Charlotte Brontë's interest was 'of a minor kind':[25] it is to this that Angela Carter points, when she remarks, not at all disapprovingly, that 'of all the great novels in the world, *Jane Eyre* veers the closest towards trash'.[26] And like 'trash', *Jane Eyre* seems to present no bar to the reader's absolute empathy. 'Is not that vivid, real, picturesque? It reads like a page out of one's own life and so do many other pages in the book', declared G. H. Lewes of the portrait of Jane's childhood, in an early review:[27] 'I was convinced that it was by some friend of my own, who had portions of my childish experience in his or her mind', recalled Harriet Martineau, in her *Autobiography*.[28] Nineteenth-century voices such as these are echoed, again and again, in the twentieth century. 'The writer has us by the hand, forces us along her road, makes us see what she sees', says Virginia Woolf;[29] 'The descriptions of Jane Eyre's ill-treatment at the hands of the Reeds, and the sufferings of the pupils at Lowood, revive a whole series of associations in the readers' minds which the more imaginative and intellectually developed among them will hate to recall', observes Rebecca West;[30] 'Like Jane, I was a rebel, a chronic bad girl ... and Jane exploded my life into reality', declares the contemporary American feminist, Jane Lazarre.[31]

Yet arguably, it is precisely a work such as this, which appears so artless, so accessible, which compels such unquestioning identification in its readers, which seems so easily assimilable to contemporary concerns, that can most be illuminated by the kinds of criticism which have been developing in the academy over the last 20 years. For one of the most important functions of that criticism has been to prompt a renewed recognition of the otherness of the cultural artefact which the critic confronts; a sharper sense of its distinctive particularity; a less immediate, more reflective understanding of the feelings it inspires. Such 'estrangement' (as we might call it) has, in practice, been effected in a number of different ways. Structuralists and practitioners of the 'new stylistics' have paid close attention to the text as linguistic artefact, viewing it not as a transparent window on a pre-existing reality, but as a fiction, made of language, engaging with generic and cultural conventions and expectations of sharply particular kinds. Historicist critics of differing persuasions – Marxists, feminists, new historicists, cultural materialists – have pointed to the historical specificity of that language, the ideological assumptions it embodies and engages with, the ways in which the meanings the text invokes might be subtly different from 'ours'. And in their attempts to reconstruct the original contexts of the literary works they discuss they have enabled not merely a clearer sense of the difference of those contexts from our own, but also of the ways in which those works may question as well as confirm 'our' presuppositions – question as well as confirm, indeed, the confidence of that first person plural whereby we seek to appropriate them to 'our' own concerns. Feminist and psychoanalytic critics have turned their attention in a rather different direction – on the powerful feelings called forth by the literary work: they have sought to consider the precise nature of the fantasies it seems to evoke and engage with, and to chart the psychic or cultural purposes those fantasies serve. The analytic distancing involved in such critical approaches is rather different from the passionate intensity of immediate, uncritical response. But it is by no means diametrically opposed to it. For in preventing too easy, too unreflective, an appropriation of the literary work it opens the way for a genuine dialogue with it: a more challenging, more enriching and far from dispassionate realisation of its potential to enlarge or disrupt, rather than simply corroborate, that which we already know.

The first of the essays in this volume provides a peculiarly striking example of this process of 'estrangement' at work. Drawing eclectically on the insights of the new stylistics and of reader-response criticism, Doreen Roberts addresses herself to the question, what is it that the reader responds to in responding to *Jane Eyre*? Roberts' opening words, indeed, invoke the 'unanalysed' immediacy of popular response. But she quickly moves beyond impressionism to point, in a sharply specific way, toward that in the text which she sees as producing the 'mixed and restless reading experience' which its readers appear to share. That apparently artless prose turns out, when closely examined, to be highly idiosyncratic – full of Latinate and Miltonic locutions, passive constructions and syntactic inversions, antithetical clauses and unexpected personifications; heavily marked off by frequent pauses between sense-units; to be thick with allusions to the Bible and to Bunyan, and to have a metaphoric concreteness and vividness which threatens to subvert the surface sense. As Roberts' analysis proceeds, many of the clichés of conventional response are destabilised and challenged: this exploration of that to which the reader is responding – perhaps subliminally – in reading, throws into question much that standard accounts of the novel assume. We see that the character Jane Eyre, whom readers seem so unproblematically to abstract, is in fact constructed in the prose as an oddly divided entity. Those readings which figure her progress as in some sense a growth to maturity begin to appear less plausible: as Roberts points out, the narrative method means that this heroine's view of the others in her world 'cannot change or deepen in any essential respects'. And this seemingly uncrafted 'autobiography' appears less as as that naïve attempt at realism (albeit marred by 'improbabilities') which its earliest critics saw, than as embodying a distinctive, imaginatively coherent, movement from realism to fantasy, as 'elements that were initially visible mainly in the style, and also in the world of Jane's reading and dreaming, become concretised as characters and plot events'.[32] Roberts does not pursue the implications of her insights in any of the directions sketched out by later contributors to this volume. She does not analyse the sociohistorical significance of that which she notes, or consider possible differences between what the present-day 'reader' notices and what the early Victorian reader might have seen. Nor does she attempt a psychoanalytic interpretation of the peculiarities she notes in the text. But, perhaps partly *because* she does not seek to harness her insights to any single explanatory theory, she offers an extraordinarily varied and illuminating account of that which she calls the novel's 'eccentricity' – those features of the text which seem to have led its early reviewers to speak of the 'intensity' and 'absence of perspective' in *Jane Eyre*. And in doing so, she anticipates much that later contributors to this volume explore.[33]

If Roberts' essay challenges the simplistic categories of earlier thematic accounts, so, too, does that by Karen Chase (essay 2), which takes as its subject the constructed nature of the 'character' most such accounts assume. Like Roberts, Chase pays close attention to the text's stylistic peculiarities, but her concern, more centrally than Roberts', is with the historicity of the discourses within which Charlotte Brontë's representation of her heroine is framed.

Reminding her reader that nineteenth-century novelists 'did not inherit a supple and illuminating picture of the mind, but that they had to construct it for themselves, taking insights where they found them', she examines the ways in which, in *Jane Eyre*, Brontë reworks the abstractions of contemporary psychological explanation – the faculty psychology of the Enlightenment, the fashionable 'pseudo-sciences' of phrenology and physiognomy – to articulate a more finely nuanced sense of her heroine's interior world.[34] Again, this is an estranging reading: like the reader of Roberts' essay, though in a very different way, the reader of this essay is struck by a sense of the foreignness of this familiar text – the difference (for example) of its analyses of motives and feelings from those which twentieth-century modes of psychological understanding might produce. Yet the novel which emerges from Chase's account is of more than merely historical interest. For she is concerned not simply with the presence within it of particular, early nineteenth-century languages of psychological explanation, but also with the critically creative ways in which those languages are deployed. In *Jane Eyre*, she argues, some of the central, apparently neutral concepts of early nineteenth-century psychology – its notion of the self as a constellation of differing faculties, its precise physical location of 'the most immaterial of mental traits' – become pivotally shaping metaphors, which configure subjectivity in striking and distinctive ways. Thus, Jane Eyre's inner life is envisioned, above all, in spatial terms; and her psyche becomes the arena wherein a charged and complex drama is played out. And this drama is echoed throughout the whole symbolic structure of the novel, in its shaping images of exposure and confinement, of architectural and geographical space. The result, Chase suggests, is a picture of psychic experience far subtler, more intricate than any that early nineteenth-century psychology could provide: a powerful and innovative 'expressive organisation' of feeling, which explains not merely why *Jane Eyre* so moved its original readers, but also its continuing, distinctive power.[35]

II

Elaine Showalter, too, has a sophisticated sense of the symbolic structure of *Jane Eyre*, but the patterns of imagery she notes (essay 3) are intriguingly different from the spatial metaphors traced by

Chase. For the latter, the red-room in which Jane is locked up is part of that dialectic of confinement and exposure which organises the novel's depiction of psychic life. But for Showalter, its association of death and of blood and 'its Freudian wealth of secret compartments, wardrobes, drawers, and jewel chest' are evocative of 'the adult female body': Jane's imprisonment there is like an 'adolescent rite of passage' which marks a significant stage in that growth toward womanhood which it is the central project of the novel to portray. For to Showalter, Jane is above all else a woman, and *Jane Eyre* a 'classic feminine novel', in which enduring questions of female development are confronted and explored.[36] In this account, Helen Burns and Bertha Mason loom large, as opposing Victorian stereotypes of womanhood – the self-denying Angel in the House, the devil-woman of unbridled animal passion: each, Showalter says, is 'an aspect of Jane's personality', which she must confront and reject. And in doing so, she becomes her 'own mistress' – a new kind of 'feminine heroine', whose 'full and healthy womanhood' *Jane Eyre* triumphantly affirms.[37] Yet the significance of Showalter's discussion lies not merely in her identification of a specifically 'female symbolism' in *Jane Eyre*, but in her location of the novel within a specifically female tradition of writing and reading. Others, of course, had noticed the novel's feminism. Indeed, in a famous passage in *A Room of One's Own*, Virginia Woolf, speaking of the distorting effects of anger on the woman writer's imagination, had taken *Jane Eyre* as her example, finding in Jane's passionate plea for her sex evidence that Charlotte Brontë wrote 'of herself, where she should write of her characters': 'she left her story, to which her entire devotion was due, to attend to some personal grievance'.[38] Yet Showalter (who later in *A Literature of Their Own* – the influential book from which her essay comes – condemns Virginia Woolf's criticism of Brontë as part of her 'flight into androgyny'),[39] offers a rather different valuation of the 'feminine' project of *Jane Eyre*. The 'feminine heroine' of her title is in fact not Jane Eyre, but Charlotte Brontë, the novelist against whom (along with George Eliot) all other nineteenth-century women novelists were measured, and measured themselves.[40] And what they found in her fiction, Showalter suggests, was by no means simply the ingenuous expression of a 'personal grievance'. The Charlotte Brontë of her account is neither artless nor naïve, but an innovative and experimental writer, whose 'use of structure, language, and female symbolism has been misread and underrated by male-oriented criticism',[41] in ways which Showalter's analysis seeks to redress.

Showalter's reading of *Jane Eyre* presents a powerful challenge to the still often articulated view that what the novel offers is merely 'escape reading for girls'.[42] It is not merely that, like Adrienne Rich, writing three years earlier,[43] she sees in Jane's narrative an analysis of woman's oppression, a model for feminine fulfilment, which speak not of escape from but of engagement with the world. More crucially, perhaps, the 'we' of Chase's commentary ('We value [*Jane Eyre*], I think, for its powerful implicit presentation of certain emotional tensions and resolutions...') is for Showalter emphatically gendered: part of a continuing tradition of female readers for whom the novel offers a compelling vision of the determining conditions, the transformative possibilities of their own lives. This discussion of *Jane Eyre* is, indeed, part of a larger study, in which Showalter traces the ways in which women writers since the late eighteenth century have responded to one another's achievements, and in doing so have created a developing 'literature of their own'. And the revaluing of the woman reader that is implicit in this argument points (though she does not discuss this) to an issue with which *Jane Eyre* itself is quite centrally concerned.

For if, in the novel's opening pages, Jane's sufferings compel the reader's sympathy, her first independent act evokes, also, a more intimate identification: she, like that reader, sits turning the pages of a book, escaping from the actual into another, imaginary world. And this image signals not merely that 'secret sharing' between 'the "I" of the novel and the subjective position ... of the reader' which is assumed by this 'urgent' narrating voice,[44] but also the novel's critical engagement with an early Victorian stereotype of womanhood as suggestive, in its way, as those other stereotypes of idealised self-denial and unbridled passion so central in Showalter's account. For the female reader, carried in fantasy far from the restrictions of everyday life, was, by the time of *Jane Eyre*'s publication, a familiar and much-disparaged figure.[45] From Charlotte Lennox's 'female Quixote' to Jane Austen's Catherine Morland to Charlotte Brontë's own Caroline Vernon (heroine of an unpublished novelette written nearly ten years before *Jane Eyre*)[46] she was portrayed, usually, from the perspective of a more knowing, more disillusioned realism, as one whose book-induced day-dreams were destined to be corrected, ironically or tragically, by experience of the world. Ten years after the publication of *Jane Eyre* the trope found perhaps its most powerful literary expression in Flaubert's *Madame Bovary*: it can still be traced, more than 70 years later, in Joyce's Gerty McDowell.[47] Yet at the beginning of *Jane Eyre* the female reader appears in a very different light. Here, she is not a captive of fashionable cliché, but one who enters unknown realms and 'form[s] an idea of [her] own'; not the deluded victim of a disabling, narcissistic fantasy, but 'drawing parallels in silence' which inspire her, decisively, to act (ch. 1). And she is evoked again, suggestively, at the two moments in the novel where Jane most extensively seeks to connect her own singular story to that of a wider world. Thus, remembering how, as a governess, she gazed out to distant horizons, listening to a 'tale' her 'imagination created, and narrated continuously' of the 'incident, life, fire, feeling' so absent from her own 'sequestered' life, she speaks of the 'millions' who share such desires, and aligns their 'silent revolt' with all the unknown 'rebellions' which 'ferment in the masses of life which people earth' (ch. 12).[48] Thus, as she portrays herself 'eagerly glancing at the bright pages of *Marmion*' – 'one of those genuine productions so often vouchsafed to the fortunate public of those days' – she asserts that, even now, in the world of her maturity, 'poetry' and 'genius' 'not only live, but reign and redeem' (ch. 32). Such passages as these in the novel are very different from Flaubert's coolly detached portrait of the naïvely susceptible Emma Bovary, turning herself in fantasy into the object rather than the owner of the gaze: they are certainly provocatively different from other early Victorian characterisations of the day-dreaming girl. And in this they seem, quite strikingly, to underwrite and confirm Showalter's pioneering effort to show how the passionate responses of generations of women readers might feed into a tradition more subversive, more empowering than that of those conventional narratives within which patriarchy has sought to confine them: how *Jane Eyre* for 'millions' of women might be part of 'a literature of their own'.

Showalter's *A Literature of Their Own* (published, in England, by one of the new women's publishing houses) was part of a burgeoning feminist criticism, which by 1977 was beginning to be acknowledged and incorporated within the academy: alongside it, we might place such other early feminist readings of *Jane Eyre* as Adrienne Rich's 'Jane Eyre: The Temptations of a Motherless Woman' (1973) and Sandra Gilbert's 'A Dialogue of Self and Soul: Plain Jane's Progress'.[49] Yet if by the 1980s, as Gayatri Spivak disapprovingly noted, *Jane Eyre* had become 'a cult text of feminism', feminist criticism since then (partly because of Spivak's own example)[50] has been more concerned to place the text ideologically than to speak of its utopian power. The disarming intimacy of Jane's autobiographical voice, the fact that it seems unquestioned by other perspectives within the narrative, the way in which Jane's judgements are surrealistically confirmed and vindicated throughout, have, it seems, led to unease in some, at least, of the novel's readers, and prompted them to examine the presuppositions of this heroine's stance from a less laudatory, more critical point of view. And a growing concern within the academy with issues of class, gender, and race – no less, of course, than the novel's own problematic evocation of each of these issues – has inflected the questions they ask in quite particular ways. Thus, Jina Politi's powerful reading of the novel (essay 4) is implicitly pitted against that notion of a universal femininity which seems to underwrite such accounts as those of Showalter and Rich. To Politi, Jane is not everywoman, but a figure of social contradiction: one whose subordination as child, as woman, as propertyless dependant, is complicated by the fact that her allegiances, ultimately, are those of a privileged class. And so, Politi suggests, are Charlotte Brontë's: in miraculously transforming her heroine from marginalised outcast to lady of the house, she glosses over those issues of inequality which her story initially seemed to raise. If the novel begins by seeking 'to shatter the comforts of the first-person plural and with it the myth of a common humanity', it ends, Politi argues, by celebrating 'the very ideology which it set out to expose'.[51] What she finds in the novel is not the clear voice of that 'untamed ferocity perpetually at war with the accepted order of things' which provoked Virginia Woolf's unease,[52] but an altogether more insidious narrative: one by which the social arrangements and dominant ideological assumptions of early nineteenth-century England are, in the end, not questioned, but endorsed.

The originality of Politi's essay lies not merely in the sharpness with which it argues that Jane's is a story not of rebellion, but of 'quiescent socialisation', but also in its concern with the way in which that which is other, foreign, non-English, is represented and rejected in her tale. Jane's Protestant, self-disciplined integrity is, Politi points out, defined against the frivolity of the French child, Adèle, the immorality of Rochester's foreign mistresses, and the florid insanity of Bertha Mason, the Creole. Briefly but suggestively, Politi connects this strategy with what were, in 1847, still recent memories of the French revolution, and with fears of social revolution at home.[53] She points to the way in which, in the novel, rebellion against social codes is associated with foreignness: in *Jane Eyre*, as she puts it, 'revolution, sexuality, insanity, belong "abroad"'.[54] The Jane of this reading is very similar to that 'fiercely Protestant, chauvinistic and self-righteous heroine' of whom Roberts speaks.[55] And Politi, like Roberts, is centrally concerned with the novel's movement from realism to fantasy, from a plot 'grounded on grim, social determination' to one full of miraculous accidents, by which Jane's problems are magically resolved. Yet she sees that movement in a rather different way. To her, *Jane Eyre's* departures from realism signal the abandonment of the revolutionary thrust with which Jane's story began. For to Politi the entry of fantasy into the novel is a mark of its ideological complicity: the point at which it becomes an 'erotic fable', in which oppressive inequalities are rendered desirable, and in which revolutionary acts – the burning of Thornfield, the ripping of the marriage veil – are performed by another, who is grossly embodied, un-English, insane.

To Politi, Bertha is not, as for Showalter, an aspect of womanhood which Jane must reject, but distinctively and emphatically *Other*. Yet Bertha is not part of that French/English opposition which Politi sees as central to *Jane Eyre*. She is, significantly, a Creole: a native of the West Indies, from which not merely Rochester's wealth, but also, ultimately, the legacy which makes Jane 'an independent woman' come. In the next essay in this volume, Susan Meyer (essay 5) pursues the implications of this fact. Central to the characterisation of the swarthy, savagely violent Bertha, with her 'pigmy intellect' and 'giant propensities' is, she argues, a peculiar racial ambiguity. Imprisoned out of sight in an elegant English mansion, 'a crime ... incarnate' which can 'neither be expelled nor subdued by the owner' (ch. 20), she becomes in the novel a figure for that repressed history of imperialist oppression on which the prosperity of early nineteenth-century England was built. For Meyer is not concerned merely with Bertha: the pivotal presence of this darkly menacing figure within this narrative of English domestic life points, she argues, to its much more pervasive deployment of a highly charged, historically specific discourse and imagery of race. Like Politi she registers the way in which *Jane Eyre* asserts British superiority by figuring oppression as something foreign and alien to true English ways; like Politi, she notes that the utopia to which the novel points is a partial one – for the privileged, white,

English domestic middle class; more extensively than Politi, she shows how such strategies are enabled and underwritten by an imperialist rhetoric whose racism can hardly be denied. Yet that rhetoric is also, Meyer suggests, at work within the novel in rather more subversive ways. Thus, she traces the ways in which, both as subjugated child and as prospective wife, Jane is metaphorically linked to those racial others who were experiencing European imperialism in these years: her 'determined revolt' against oppression evokes, says Meyer, an image of considerable contemporary resonance – that of the rebellious slave. Thus, rather differently, the allusions to non-white races which attend the novel's presentation of such 'dark and imperious' figures as Blanche Ingram and her mother, Mrs Reed and her son, no less than Jane's figuring of Rochester as an Eastern sultan, hint, Meyer argues, at similarities between the ruling class at home and the racial other abroad: implicit in such images is the suggestion that imperialism corrupts and contaminates the dominant race.

For what Meyer traces in the novel is not the covert but unambiguous inscription of ideology of which Politi speaks, but a complex and subtle 'figurative strategy', in which imperialism is both reaffirmed and questioned in intricate and unsettling ways. And her rather different sense of the novel's relation to ideology is signalled by her very different reading of its close. Here, she finds not 'consolidation', but a question mark: not complicity, but 'unease'. For this ending, she suggests, is marked by traces of that suppressed history of violence and oppression which again and again has surfaced in the novel's metaphors of race. Thus, against the 'virtual consensus' of previous readings, she argues that the missionary imperialism, the 'icy racial superiority' of St John Rivers, which here assume such prominence, are not unqualifiedly endorsed. Thus, she finds an image of the tainting effect of imperialism on those who profit by it in the insalubrious atmosphere of the house in which Jane and her husband live, apparently on the proceeds of her uncle's West Indian wealth. And most hauntingly, most tellingly, inscribed within the novel (as Meyer points out in a brilliant reading of the scene in which St John Rivers recognises his cousin) is the ineradicable awareness that Jane's triumphant narrative of 'independence' is in fact radically dependent upon a colonial ink. It is an image which seems, Meyer suggests, to point to a 'lingering anxiety' on Charlotte Brontë's part as to the implications of her own 'figurative tactics' in *Jane Eyre*.

Readings such as those by Politi and Meyer offer an important challenge to that uncritical identification with its heroine's perspective which *Jane Eyre* appears to invite. In exploring the ways in which specific nineteenth-century discourses of class, of gender, of nationhood, of race, may be traced within Jane's narrative, they point not merely toward the historical otherness of this familiar text, but also to the class- and race-blindness of those earlier feminist readings which saw it, simply, as 'an epic of self-determination',[56] 'a distinctively female *Bildungsroman* in which the problems encountered by the protagonist are symptomatic of difficulties Everywoman in a patriarchal society must meet and overcome'.[57] *Jane Eyre*, which its earliest readers found so radical, appears, in these new readings, as – at best – not quite radical enough: its author, once seen as a 'moral Jacobin', is now exposed as the mouthpiece of a 'repressive ideology', or as 'anxious' about her own complicity in the exploitative structures of power which shape the world of which she speaks. But such readings as these also leave some questions open. What, in face of them, is one to make of the excited intensity of the ordinary reader's identification with Jane Eyre? Should that reader simply be dismissed as another Emma Bovary, too easily enchanted, too naïvely susceptible; or seen as one whose ideological complicity must be exposed? It is something like this that Penny Boumelha implicitly asks, in her thought-provoking reading of *Jane Eyre* (essay 6). Like Politi and Meyer, Boumelha is interested in 'those other women whose stories are occluded by Jane's tale':[58] she, too, is concerned with the novel's handling of issues of class, gender and race. For her, also, Jane is a problematic figure, whose trajectory seems to lead towards an acceptance, even embrace, of those divisions within the society which her story has exposed: indeed, she offers a detailed account of the ways in which ideas of kinship, of Nature and of Providence are invoked in the novel to this end. But Boumelha is concerned less simply with exploring the ideological assumptions which shape Jane's narrative than with trying also to find (as she puts it) a way of 'honouring' the 'female heroism' to which generations of readers have 'thrilled' in *Jane Eyre*. In the final section of her essay, she implicitly challenges Politi's assumption of an identity between Jane's voice and her creator's, by suggesting that Jane's own unitary, providential interpretation of her story need not, necessarily, be shared by the reader: that her narrative gives evidence of a rather wider range of needs and desires, of more varied (real or fantasised) possibilities

for fulfilment, than its ending in the ostensible 'bliss' of quiet domesticity can in fact subsume. She points, too, to the violence inscribed in the novel, both in the 'intense and startling physicality' of
its imagery, and in the peculiar narrative power of that controlling
autobiographical 'I'. *Jane Eyre* appears in this reading, briefly but
suggestively, as altogether stranger – more exploratory, more
threatening, more open-ended in its imaging of feminine desire –
than can quite be accounted for by considering its handling of
questions of class, or gender, or race.

III

As the conscious provocativeness of Politi's essay perhaps most
sharply suggests, these readings which seek to expose the ideological implications of Jane's narrative are, in a sense, readings
against the grain. *Jane Eyre* certainly does not invite its readers to
make judgements of this nature: there is nothing in the novel of the
moralising or aesthetic or critical distancing of a George Eliot, a
Henry James. Moreover, as each of these critics – Politi, Meyer,
Boumelha – rather differently registers, much of the narrative is
shaped less by the conventions of realism than by those of the more
archaic forms of fairy-tale and romance – forms which work on the
reader's fantasies and feelings with a peculiar intimacy and directness, and which seem to require analysis of a rather different kind.
Such forms as these, Angela Carter remarks, are 'so close to dreaming [that] they lend themselves readily to psychoanalytic interpretation':[59] and indeed many twentieth-century critics of *Jane Eyre* have
tried to account for these aspects of the novel in psychoanalytic
terms – seeing them sometimes as offering insights into the psyche
of its author,[60] sometimes as symbolically expressive of its heroine's
inner life.[61] More recently, however, critical theorists have begun
to argue that readings such as these 'displace the object of analysis
from the text to some person',[62] and beg the question of the larger
cultural significance of the configurations they seek to explain. The
influence of such thinking is evident in the three following essays in
this volume, each of which, very differently, addresses itself to what
one early critic[63] called the 'melodrama and improbability' in *Jane
Eyre*. Each draws, quite centrally, on psychoanalytic theory. But
unlike many earlier psychoanalytic readings, which tended to speak
either of the author Charlotte Brontë or of the character Jane Eyre,

each focuses on the text itself – its tropes and figures, its narrative evasions or inconsistencies, its distinctive rhetorical texture. And unlike many earlier psychoanalytic readings, each, in a very different way, is concerned with the historicity of *Jane Eyre*: with the ways in which even (or perhaps especially) its more fantastic elements may be seen as configuring significant aspects of the world of early nineteenth-century England, and articulating a 'cultural unconscious' which realism could not contain.

Margaret Homans' discussion of *Jane Eyre* (essay 7) is taken from a longer study, in which she seeks to revise Lacanian psycholinguistic theory by exploring the nineteenth-century woman writer's problematic relation to the symbolic order of culture. Her concern is not merely with the constant objectification of the feminine – as matter, as nature – within the culture of which she writes (particularly during and just after the romantic period), but also with the creative ways in which women writers were able to exploit the 'literal' to which they were relegated by this dominant cultural myth. The strength of her approach, from our point of view, lies, however, less in its proof or disproof of the theory which underpins it than in the light it sheds on some of the strangest and least remarked features of *Jane Eyre*. Like several earlier critics,[64] Homans relates the novel to the literary convention of the Gothic, which she sees as 'literalising' the romantic imagination by projecting subjective states as objective features of a world. *Jane Eyre*, she argues, plays with this convention in self-conscious and sceptical ways, evoking Gothic possibilities only to undercut them by a dampening appeal to 'the plain truth', and then finding in 'the plain truth' realities more threatening than the most fantastic fears. Homans connects these strategies in the novel to what she sees as a central preoccupation: that other material process of 'literalisation' in which 'what was once internal acquires its own objective reality' – the process of childbearing, in fact and in fantasy so central to a nineteenth-century woman's life. For childbearing, as she shows, is evoked within *Jane Eyre* in striking and pivotal ways: not merely in those dreams of children which punctuate Jane's narrative, bringing her intimations of 'what it would be like to become other than herself', but also in the images of childbirth which recur throughout, figuring the potentially devastating 'uncontrollability of real things'.[65] To find this 'brightest, happiest' of Charlotte Brontë's novels (as one critic has called it)[66] 'full of a horror of childbirth'[67] may seem, at first, surprising. Yet Homans' reading is both suggestive and persuasive, and not as far from that of the ordinary reader as might at first appear. For in charting these figurative under-currents in the novel she is beginning, I think, to bring into focus something to which most readers have responded, but which few critics have managed to explain: that urgent sense of a threat to very existence which attends Jane's narrative of success and survival, and which charges even repeated re-readings of the novel with a peculiarly cliff-hanging suspense. And in suggesting that the 'feverish disquiet' to which she points is less a failure of balance or of realism than a meaningful dimension of the text, she offers a significant challenge to those earlier, patronising judgements of Charlotte Brontë as one who never managed to develop a 'harmonious and consistent view of life'.[68] For what she finds in these once-despised 'improbabilities' is not merely a powerful imaginative articulation of the experiental realities of the nineteenth-century woman's life (she points, tellingly, both to actual and figurative maternal mortality in nineteenth-century England, and also to twentieth-century psychoanalytic discussion of the significance of childbirth for the mother), but also a powerful imaginative riposte to that romantic myth of a benign Mother Nature which enabled the male romantic poets to form a 'harmanious' view of their world.

Like Homans', Mary Poovey's reading of *Jane Eyre* (essay 8) is part of a larger project, but hers is a project of a very different kind. *Uneven Developments*, from which the extract in this volume is taken, explores the 'unevenness' with which notions of gender shaped ideology in a variety of spheres in mid-nineteenth-century England: it is in the context of a discussion of the debate over the employment of women as governesses that this analysis of *Jane Eyre* appears. Like Homans, Poovey uses insights drawn from psychoanalysis to explore the significance of non-realist elements of the text, but unlike Homans, she sees these elements as 'hysterical' symptoms, contradicting what she calls its 'explicit design'. For unlike Homans', her work is shaped also by Marxism, which sees cultural texts as involved in the production and interrogation of ideology, in both acknowledged and unacknowledged ways. In some ways, indeed, her concerns seem closer to Politi's. She, too, focuses on the figure of Jane as governess; she, too, points to the novel's invocation of a normative 'Englishness'; she, too, explores the ways in which the threat of a subversive female sexuality seems through Jane's narrative to be evoked and contained. But unlike

Politi's, Poovey's reading is not intended as a comprehensive account of *Jane Eyre*. Her interest is, rather, in the novel's participation in a particular mid-nineteenth-century cultural debate. Indeed, her essay begins not with *Jane Eyre*, but with a detailed account of the ways in which the plight of the governess was being addressed in other writings of these years. The governess, she argues, became a pivotal, problematic and much discussed figure because, as one enjoined to self-suppression and self-control, yet compelled to competitive self-exertion, she appeared to epitomise two quite contradictory stereotypes: that of the domesticated woman, dependent on and devoted to others, and that of the independent labourer for wages in the public sphere. Prominent amongst the anxieties this figure provoked was, she suggests, a fear of female sexuality: the spectres of lunacy and immorality recur again and again in the writings which discuss her plight. It is in the context of such discussions that Poovey positions *Jane Eyre*, with its central, apparently exemplary governess-figure, and its warning images of Rochester's discarded mistresses and lunatic wife. Yet within this context, *Jane Eyre* emerges as a rather less straightforwardly conservative text than might initially appear. For if, at first, Poovey seems to be pointing toward a reading like Politi's, in which the fairy-tale resolution of Jane's story is the expression of 'a logic that eroticises economics so that class and financial difficulties are overcome by the irresistible and (and inexplicable) "sympathy" of romantic love', she differs from Politi in the way in which she complicates her reading by considering the dreams of children which are at the centre of Homans' account. To her, those dreams signify not danger, but anger – an anger which is displaced from the character Jane and enacted through the narrative itself. The fact that 'Jane ... appears to grow strong, because those around her diminish or die', noted by Karen Chase as a peculiarity of characterisation[69] interpreted by earlier critics in crudely Freudian terms,[70] and by Jina Politi as a straightforward narrative expulsion of all that threatens the '*ethos* upon which bourgeois capitalism and its ideology rest',[71] is here seen as expressive of 'a rage that remains implicit at the level of character but materialises at the level of plot':[72] a rage whose source not merely in the anomalous situation of the governess, but in 'every middle-class woman's life' is signalled by those images of dependence and impotence which recur in Jane's attendant dreams.

The *Jane Eyre* of this account is rather different from Homans' – speaking not of dread and danger, but of subversive anger, of a 'restless' passion which threatens to destabilise the ideology which sought to keep the mid-nineteenth-century woman in her place. Elisabeth Bronfen's *Jane Eyre* (essay 9) is different again. Like Homans' and like Poovey's, Bronfen's reading is part of a larger argument: one in which she traces – through a whole series of nineteenth-century artefacts – that 'conventional association of femininity with death' of which, she argues, *Jane Eyre* is a paradigmatic text. Like several other contributors to this volume, she focuses on those other women who figure so prominently in Jane's narrative – the passionate, violent Bertha Rochester and the saintly, self-denying Helen Burns. For her, as for others, they represent opposing stereotypes of mid-Victorian womanhood – that of the sexually licentious demon and that of the passionless, angelic domestic ideal. But the significance she finds in these figures is rather different from that to which others point. For each, she argues, exposes the deathly implications of the stereotype she embodies in a peculiarly striking way. The ideal of womanly self-sacrifice is fuelled, Bronfen suggests, by 'fantasies of a masochistic turning inward of the death drive':[73] and *Jane Eyre* draws attention to this by its depiction of the self-abnegating Helen Burns, who actively embraces death. Conversely, the fact that the image of the destructive, fatal demon-woman represents 'a sadistic turning outward of the same drive' is underlined by the monstrous, murderous Bertha Rochester, dashed to her own death after making attempts on both Jane's and her husband's life. In one sense, Bronfen argues, the project of Jane's 'autobiography' is to point to a middle way between these extremes: for her, to repudiate the extremes of self-denial and self-assertion which these figures represent is, very exactly, to *survive*. But *Jane Eyre* is, in Bronfen's reading, very far from that tale of successful self-fashioning which critics such as Showalter and Politi (each rather differently) find. For the resonance of these expelled figures within the text leaves the reader, she suggests, with more disturbing questions than Jane's own view of her trajectory can quite encompass. They point not merely to what must be discarded for successful womanhood to be achieved within the society the novel depicts, but to a disruptive violence, a haunting anxiety, at the heart of the world to which Jane eventually makes her triumphant accommodation: the presence of death in life, which can never be entirely repressed. Indeed (one might add), this sense is underlined by the novel's closing image of one who – determinedly masculine – nevertheless, in his deliberate self-immolation, his aggressive ambition, embodies something of each of these contradictory feminine stereotypes: the troubling, enigmatic figure of St John Rivers, whose open-ended final words disrupt the satisfactory closure of Jane's story and point most tellingly toward death.[74]

IV

The next essay in this volume, that by Peter Allan Dale (essay 10), is very different in its emphases from Bronfen's, and sheds a quite different kind of light on the 'restless' experience of reading *Jane Eyre*. Yet like Bronfen, Dale, too, points toward the ways in which the novel resists closure; and in doing so he, too, suggestively speaks of death. Drawing on structuralist narrative theory, he finds within Jane's apparently unambiguous story of a movement from exclusion to acceptance two competing narrative paradigms, each of which evokes rather different expectations, and each of which works against the other's resolution in a peculiarly unsettling way. That which is more usually noted today is the 'romantic' story of Jane's successful search for earthly fulfilment: this is the narrative structure which underwrites feminist 'heroic' readings of the novel such as Showalter's – and, indeed, more ideologically critical readings such as those by Politi and Meyer. But it is toward the other, a religious paradigm of spiritual pilgrimage, which Dale – against the grain of most contemporary criticism – seeks most centrally to point. For it is this, he argues, which the novel's earliest readers would have expected to find in *Jane Eyre*. Coming to the novel with a set of expectations shaped by religion in ways almost lost to us today, they would have sought for that straightforward narrative of a soul's journey toward salvation which much in Jane's story seemed to promise, and found their expectations frustrated in several significant respects. The moment of conversion pivotal to such narrative, in which the erring protagonist acknowledges and submits to God's power, is oddly absent here. And that confession of faith on the part of the protagonist to which such a story conventionally led is likewise, disquietingly, withheld. For in *Jane Eyre* that confession comes not from the narrator, but from another, whose end is very different from hers. 'No fear of death will darken

St John's last hour', says Jane (my italics), in a penultimate paragraph which stresses the third person pronoun as insistently as the
preceding narrative has stressed the first: she is eloquently silent
about her own spiritual fate. Indeed, Dale suggests, the Biblical
resonances which attend her account of her wedded bliss are less
signs of a 'providential' reconciliation of spiritual and fleshly des-
tinies (as some commentators have claimed)[75] than 'blasphemous'
indications of a disjunction between romantic fulfilment and religious salvation which the novel cannot resolve. And this 'unsolved
discord' points, he argues, less to incompetence on Charlotte
Brontë's part than to her sensitivity to her own historical moment:
her imaginative recognition of uncertainties which she and her
readers shared.[76]

In taking the religious questions raised by the novel seriously
Dale is, as I have suggested, writing against the grain of much contemporary criticism of *Jane Eyre*. Certainly, it has become more
customary for historicist critics to consider its dealings with issues
of class or gender or race. Yet in showing how *Jane Eyre* seems to
be engaging with this structure of expectations Dale poses a real
challenge to such readings: for all their attempts at historical
specificity, do they still miss some of the most significant nuances in
the novel, by viewing it too exclusively through the prism of twentieth-century concerns? The difficulty, it seems, is to find a way of
being alert to the text's past meaning, whilst still remaining alive to
the ways in which it seems to speak of urgent contemporary concerns. In the final essay in this volume, Carolyn Williams attempts
to negotiate just this difficulty, by exploring not merely the historical specificity of the discourses which may be traced in Jane's narrative, but also what has, for contemporary feminist theorists, become
a central question: what does it mean for a woman to negotiate a
world of men's words? Like Dale, Williams examines the indeterm-
inacies of the novel's ending: like him, she points to the way in
which Jane's voice and Jane's story are replaced by those of
another, and to the echoes of the Bible and of Bunyan which enter
to counterpoint and complicate her tale. Yet her interest in these
features of the text is rather different from Dale's. Why, she asks,
does this ending still continue to evoke such a powerful response in
its readers? What is the effect of the appearance of this authoritative – indeed, canonical – discourse at the conclusion of a woman's
autobiography such as Jane's? She, like Dale, notes the fact that the
novel has failed to register anything like a religious conversion in

Jane: she, too, ascribes this failure to a deliberate narrative choice. But unlike Dale, she sees that choice in psychoanalytic terms – as part of a complicated oscillation between the gendered poles of Mother Nature and God the Father through which the narrating Jane defines her own 'production of meaning and voice'. For to Williams, institutionalised religion, as it is presented in *Jane Eyre*, is above all, emphatically male. The novel's evocation of the authoritative voices of St Paul and St John the Divine must be linked, she argues, to its portrayal of such figures as the Reverend Mr Brocklehurst and St John Rivers – phallic, coercive figures of patriarchal authority and power. Jane's rejection of the path to which such voices and figures point is part of that logic of contradiction whereby she defines herself: her 'Protestant, romantic, feminist' protest against the masculine line of mediated authority they represent. Thus, in the novel's closing paragraphs, the traditional authority of *Pilgrim's Progress* and the Bible are evoked, Williams suggests, *in order* to be distanced; marked as other, rather than blended with Jane's narrating voice. What she finds in the novel's conclusion is less that equivocation between romantic and religious possibilities to which Dale points than a radical gesture of narrative self-definition – one in which Jane seeks at once to reject and to appropriate these authoritative masculine voices which speak of a power elsewhere.

Yet as Williams admits, this is a boldly *ambivalent* narrative gesture. Like Dale's, her account issues less in a straightforward, 'heroic' reading of Jane's story than in a sense of the ways in which, even as it moves towards it, *Jane Eyre* resists closure, and allows other possibilities of meaning to come flooding into the text. And in this, perhaps, hers is an appropriate essay with which to end this volume. For if there is any single theme which can be extracted from the essays collected here, it is that the *Jane Eyre* they configure is an altogether more ambiguous, less univocal work than that which the contributors to the original Casebook defined. Where those earlier critics found (or looked for) coherence, resolution, containment – 'a profound, spiritual experience, expressed in the most adequate symbolism', and ending 'on a note of calm'; 'a triumph of structure and emphasis', in which Charlotte Brontë 'was able to accept and keep in due subordination material from her fantasy world'[77] – the readings in this New Casebook offer a very different view. The sense that emerges, both from each individual essay and from the differences between them, is of something strange, disturbing, inassimilable in *Jane Eyre*. What these critics find is not unity, but contradiction; not balance, but eccentricity; not calm, but – frequently – violence; not resolution, but open-endedness and unease. Of course, in one way these emphases may be seen as expressive of changing critical fashion: where once New Critics looked for 'organic unity', now deconstructionists value the 'aporias', or radical uncertainties, of the text.[78] Yet the essays collected here do not, I think, either individually or cumulatively, suggest that *Jane Eyre* is *simply* being made to fit contemporary theoretical preoccupations, *simply* being appropriated to contemporary concerns. For in their differing ways – and this is one of the most striking differences between this and the previous Casebook – most of the essays in this volume are quite centrally concerned with the historical otherness of the text with which they deal. Those earlier debates about the novel's 'truth to life', its sense of, or departures from, an unproblematically assumed 'reality', have now been replaced by an awareness that the sense of 'reality' itself is always historically shaped – an awareness that is manifested, for instance, in Chase's analysis of the historical specificity of the discourses within which its representation of character is framed and in Dale's of the narrative paradigms which shape Jane's tale, no less than in Showalter's, Boumelha's, Bronfen's, of the stereotypes of womanhood it invokes, or in Politi's, Meyer's, Poovey's very different discussions of the operations of ideology within the text. The *Jane Eyre* of this volume may be more problematic than of that earlier Casebook: but it is, I would argue, more sharply, because more historically, seen.

Yet the essays which follow by no means rule a line under *Jane Eyre*. Indeed, they are quite explicitly less conclusive, more open in their acknowledgement of that in the text which baffles or escapes them, than were those collected in 1974. What they offer is less a series of definitive readings or confident evaluations than a sense of questions focusing, of areas of exploration being mapped out. And in this they point, perhaps, to one way through that dilemma posed by the professionalisation of criticism with a discussion of which this Introduction began. Certainly, the increasing amount and sophistication of such criticism might seem to present an intimidating obstacle to the novice critic: what more can there be left to say? But the contention of this New Casebook (as of the series of which it is a part) is that this need by no means be so: that this collection should be seen as offering a starting-point for thinking, rather than a series of examples for the reader to follow or admire. It is not merely that each of these essays, rather differently, opens up questions which it does not neatly resolve; not merely, even, that the implicit or explicit disagreements between them point toward cruces in the novel which the reader might fruitfully explore. Most crucial, perhaps, is the fact that, in drawing together some of the best studies of its subject published in the last 20 years, a volume such as this is designed to prompt the reader familiar with the text which they discuss to notice what they do not deal with, as well as what they do. And for this reason it seems proper to end, like *Jane Eyre*, in open-endedness: by posing some of the questions with which future work might engage. If historicist criticism has alerted us to the ways in which issues of class and gender and race are raised in Jane's story, what of those other issues to which generations of unprofessional readers have responded so centrally in *Jane Eyre*: those apparently 'universal' themes of childhood suffering and romantic love? Should these be more closely examined, seen in more historical particularity? How might seeing them so alter or complicate our reading of the text? Has the last word indeed been said on the novel's ending – that peculiar abrogation of Jane's autobiographical voice, the prominence of another at the close of her tale? Above all, and most urgently, perhaps, how might the intellectual rigour, the historical reach of a sophisticated analysis be brought to bear on the energy, the passion, with which ordinary readers still respond to Brontë's text? How might we – even as we see the novel as belonging to its time – show how and why it can still speak forcefully for our own? It is toward such a reading – a *Jane Eyre*, if you like, for the year 2000 – that this New Casebook seeks to point.

NOTES

1. From an unsigned review, *Atlas*, 23 October 1847, in Miriam Allott (ed.), *The Brontës: The Critical Heritage* (London, 1974), p. 68.

2. From an unsigned review, *People's Journal*, November 1847, in Allott (ed.), *Critical Heritage*, p. 80.

3. Elizabeth Rigby, in an unsigned review, *Quarterly Review*, December 1848, in Allott (ed.), *Critical Heritage*, p. 107.

4. In her diary, 23 November, 1880:

Finished *Jane Eyre*, which is really a wonderful book, very peculiar in parts, but so powerfully and admirably written, such a fine tone in it, such fine religious feeling ... The description of the mysterious maniac's nightly appearances awfully thrilling ... (G. E. Buckle and A. C. Benson [eds], *The Letters and Journals of Queen Victoria* [1926–7], III, p. 259)

Queen Victoria had 22 years previously read *Jane Eyre* aloud to her 'dear Albert': this reading, unlike Thackeray's, seems to have taken five months. (See the portions of her journal for March–August 1858 reproduced in *Brontë Society Transactions*, 13:3 [1968], p. 296, and reprinted in Miriam Allott [ed.], *Jane Eyre and Villette: a Casebook* [London, 1973], pp. 140–1).

5. Letter to W. S. Williams, 23 October 1847, in Allott (ed.), *Casebook*, p. 43.

6. *The Life and Works of Charlotte Brontë and her Sisters*, in Seven Volumes, with Introductions to the Works by Mrs Humphry Ward (London: Smith Elder & Co., 1906), Vol. I, *Jane Eyre*, p. x.

7. Adrienne Rich, 'Jane Eyre: The Temptations of a Motherless Woman' (1973), in *On Lies, Secrets and Silence: Selected Prose 1966–1978* (London, 1980), p. 89.

8. 'Charlotte Brontë: *Jane Eyre*', in *Expletives Deleted* (London, 1992), p. 161.

9. Unsigned review in *Fraser's*, December 1849, in Allott (ed.), *Critical Heritage*, p. 153.

10. Mrs Ellis (ed.), *The Morning Call, A Table Book of Literature and Art* (London, 1850–2), Vol. I, 1850, pp. 34–5, 42, 36.

11. '*Jane Eyre* and *Wuthering Heights*' (1916), in *The Common Reader: First Series* (London, 1925), pp. 196–7.

12. *The English Novel from Dickens to Lawerence* (London, 1970), p. 63.

13. 'Like Jane', she suggests, 'the reader is seduced by a compelling narrative', and hence fails to 'interrogate' the ideologically suspect nature of the 'pleasure' it provides (Bette London, 'The Pleasures of Submission: *Jane Eyre* and the Production of the Text', *English Literary History*, 58 [1991], pp. 204, 209–10). In a curious reversal of Mrs Ellis's arguments about the novel's failure to 'improve' its readers, London – explicitly drawing on and developing Nancy Armstrong's *Desire and Domestic Fiction: A Political History of the Novel* (New York, 1987) – reads *Jane Eyre* as a 'nineteenth-century deportment book, offering its readers ... lessons in the proper forms

of feminine conduct': the 'rapturous response' of 'the modern feminist reader' fails, she argues, to take account of this dimension of the text.

14. Stephen's essay was published in the *Cornhill Magazine* for December 1877, and reprinted in the third edition of his *Hours in a Library* (1987). Extracts from both are reprinted in Allott (ed.), *Casebook*, pp. 144–8, 148–56.

15. Introduction to *Wuthering Heights*, in Allott (ed.), *Critical Heritage*, p. 454.

16. Virginia Woolf, *A Room of One's Own* (1929), ed. Hermione Lee (London, 1991), p. 68.

17. *Early Victorian Novelists: Essays in Revaluation* (1934), in Allott (ed.), *Casebook*, p. 174.

18. F. R. Leavis, *The Great Tradition* (London, 1948; rpt. Harmondsworth, 1962), p. 37.

19. Robert Martin, in *The Accents of Persuasion: Charlotte Brontë's Novels* (London, 1966). Other formalist analyses from this period include an important essay by David Lodge, 'Fire and Eyre: Charlotte Brontë's War of Earthly Elements', in *The Language of Fiction* (London, 1966); Wendy Craik, *The Brontë Novels* (London, 1968); Earl A. Knies, *The Art of Charlotte Brontë* (Athens, OH, 1969); Karl Kroeber, *Style in Fictional Structure: the Art of Jane Austen, Charlotte Brontë, George Eliot* (Princeton, NJ, and London, 1971); Margot Peters, *Charlotte Brontë: Style in the Novel* (Madison, WI, 1973).

20. See, for example, Robert B. Heilman, 'Charlotte Brontë's "New" Gothic' in *From Jane Austen to Joseph Conrad*, ed. Robert C. Rathburn and Martin Steinmann, Jr (Minneapolis, 1958), pp. 118–32; repr. Allott (ed.), *Casebook*, pp. 195–204.

21. The first sustained analysis of *Jane Eyre* along these lines was Kathleen Tillotson's enduringly valuable chapter on the novel in her *Novels of the 1840s* (London, 1954). Other, rather differently 'historicist' studies dating from the 1970s include Richard Benvenuto, 'The Child of Nature and the Child of Grace and the Unresolved Conflict of *Jane Eyre*', *English Literary History*, 39 (1972), 620–38; Nancy Pell, 'Resistance, Rebellion and Marriage: the Economics of *Jane Eyre*', *Nineteenth-Century Fiction*, 31 (1977), 397–420; and, most extensively, Terry Eagleton's influential *Myths of Power: a Marxist Study of the Brontës* (London, 1975).

22. See, for example, Inga-Stina Ewbank, *Their Proper Sphere: A Study of the Brontë Sisters as Early Victorian Female Novelists* (London, 1966); Harriet Björk, *The Language of Truth: Charlotte Brontë and the Woman Question* (Lund Studies in English, 1974); Helene

Moglen, *Charlotte Brontë: The Self Conceived* (New York, 1976); Maurianne Adams, '*Jane Eyre:* Woman's Estate', in *The Authority of Experience: Essays in Feminist Art*, ed. Arlyn Diamond and L. R. Edwards (Amherst, MA, 1977); and the suggestive remarks by Ellen Moers in *Literary Women* (London, 1977).

23. On this subject see Robert K. Martin, '*Jane Eyre* and the World of Faery', *Mosaic*, 10 (Summer 1977), 85–95.

24. See p. 41 below.

25. *The Great Tradition*, p. 37. Queenie Leavis, however, was later to interpret the novel, in her introduction to the still-in-print Penguin Classics edition, as a straightforward moral fable, in which the 'embittered little charity child finds the way to come to terms with life and society' (Charlotte Brontë, *Jane Eyre*, ed. Q. D. Leavis [Hardmondsworth, 1966], p. 16).

26. Carter, *Expletives Deleted*, p. 162.

27. G. H. Lewes, 'Recent Novels: French and English', *Fraser's Magazine*, 36 (1847), 686–95, reprinted in Allott (ed.), *Casebook*, p. 55.

28. Harriet Martineau, *Autobiography* (1877), ed. Gaby Weiner (London, 1983), Vol. II, p. 324.

29. Woolf, *The Common Reader*, p. 197.

30. Rebecca West, 'Charlotte Brontë', *The Great Victorians*, ed. H. J. Massingham and Hugh Massingham, Vol. I (London, 1938), p. 68.

31. Jane Lazarre, 'Charlotte's Web: Reading *Jane Eyre* Over Time', in *Between Women: Biographers, Novelists, Critics, Teachers, and Artists Write about Their Work on Women*, ed. Carol Ascher et al. (Boston, 1984), p. 223.

32. See pp. 44, 49 below.

33. One might, for example, compare her discussion of the novel's use of phrenological language with that which Chase offers in the following essay (p. 55), her exploration of the relations between 'realistic' and 'romantic' elements in the text with the very different accounts given by Politi (p. 88) and by Poovey (pp. 183–4), and her brief analysis of Jane's dealings with 'foreigners' with Politi's and Meyer's much fuller elaborations of this theme (pp. 84–5, 96–123).

34. See pp. 55–9 below.

35. Thus, in her conclusion to *Eros and Psyche*, Chase argues that *Jane Eyre*, along with the other novels she discusses, still 'provides a training for the sensibility ... disciplines the emotions ... renews the moral sense' (p. 192).

36. See pp. 69, 70 below.

37. See p. 75 below.

38. Virginia Woolf, *A Room of One's Own* (1929), ed. Hermione Lee (London, 1991), pp. 65, 68.

39. Elaine Showalter, *A Literature of Their Own* (London, 1978), p. 285.

40. Showalter, *A Literature of Their Own*, pp. 103–12. Showalter goes on, in the portion of her chapter which follows this extract, to discuss the 'revolutionary' influence of *Jane Eyre* in the nineteenth century, and the continuing inspiration the novel has provided for women writers up to and including Margaret Drabble.

41. The paragraph from which these remarks are taken immediately precedes that with which this extract begins. See *A Literature of Their Own*, p. 112.

42. This, says Patricia Meyer Spacks, is how her husband was taught to regard the novel (*The Female Imagination* [New York, 1975], p. 228). Joanna Russ, in *How To Suppress Women's Writing* (London, 1983), tells of

    > a young professor I met at a cocktail party in 1970 who, upon hearing that I was teaching *Jane Eyre*, said, 'What a lousy book! It's just a lot of female erotic fantasies', as if female erotic fantasies were *per se* the lowest depth to which literature could sink. (p. 46)

43. See Adrienne Rich, 'Jane Eyre: The Temptations of a Motherless Woman' (1973), in *On Lies, Secrets and Silence: Selected Prose 1966–1978* (London, 1980).

44. These phrases are taken from Raymond Williams' suggestive account of 'the connecting power of Charlotte Brontë's fiction' in *The English Novel from Dickens to Lawrence* (London, 1970), p. 69.

45. Most discussion of this subject has centred on women as novel readers. On eighteenth-century opposition to women's novel-reading, see Jane Spencer, *The Rise of the Woman Novelist: from Alphra Behn to Jane Austen* (Oxford, 1986), ch. 6, and Peter de Bolla, *The Discourse of the Sublime: Readings in History, Aesthetics and the Subject* (London, 1989), pp. 252–78: on the longer history of such opposition, see Kate Flint, *The Woman Reader, 1837–1914* (Oxford, 1993), ch. 2. For a suggestive discussion of feminist opposition to 'romance' in the early nineteenth century see Cora Kaplan, 'The Thorn Birds', in *Sea Changes: Essays on Culture and Feminism* (London, 1986), pp. 121–5.

46. 'Caroline Vernon', in Charlotte Brontë, *Five Novelettes*, ed. Winifred Gérin (London, 1971).

47. On the connected pejorative modernist construction of 'mass culture' as essentially feminine, and on *Madame Bovary* as one of the 'found-

ing texts' of this view, see Andreas Huyssen, 'Mass Culture as
Woman: Modernism's Other', in Tania Modleski (ed.), *Studies in
Entertainment: Critical Approaches to Mass Culture* (Bloomington,
IN, 1986).

48. It has become almost a commonplace of criticism of *Jane Eyre* to
find, in these references to a 'revolt' amongst 'masses', a rhetoric of
class rebellion which in 1847 might have seemed – as it did to
Elizabeth Rigby – to point toward 'chartism and rebellion at home'.
See, for example, Cora Kaplan, 'Pandora's Box', in *Sea Changes*,
p. 173. Yet this passage, with its emphasis on an enforced
'tranquillity' (rather than a compulsion to labour) and a desire for
'action' (rather than a demand for rights) far more centrally evokes
the 'bored leisure', the escapist dreams, of those women of the
polite classes whose frustrations posed no such obvious political
threat: its challenge to contemporary readers lies precisely in its
insistence that this, too, is a 'rebellion' of a widespread and
significant kind.

49. Adrienne Rich's 'Jane Eyre: The Temptations of a Motherless
Woman' was originally written for *MS.* magazine. 'A Dialogue of Self
and Soul' (drafted by Sandra Gilbert) appears as a chapter in Sandra
Gilbert and Susan Gubar, *The Madwoman in the Attic: The Woman
Writer and the Nineteenth-Century Literary Imagination* (New
Haven, CT, 1979). *Jane Eyre* indeed provided the central metaphor,
and the title, for the central (and influential) argument of this volume:
that nineteenth-century women's texts present a surface which conceals 'less accessible (and less socially acceptable) levels of meaning',
of which Bertha Mason, 'bloody, envious, enraged', is a potent figure:
'as if the very process of writing had itself liberated a madwoman, a
crazy and angry woman, from a silence in which neither she nor her
author can continue to acquiesce' (p. 77). Both Rich's and Gilbert's
essays, less historicist in their emphases than Showalter's, seek, like
her, to conscript the energies of the reader's response to the cause of a
contemporary feminism.

50. Gayatri Chakravorty Spivak, 'Three Women's Texts and a Critique of
Imperialism', *Critical Inquiry*, 12 (1985), p. 244.

51. See pp. 78, 79 below.

52. Virginia Woolf, *The Common Reader*, p. 200.

53. It is suggestive also to compare this reading of *Jane Eyre* as an anti-
French, nationalistic fable with Mary Ward's observation, in her
Introduction to the Haworth Edition of 1906, that whilst 'Charlotte
Brontë's main *stuff* is English, Protestant, law-respecting, conven-
tional even', it was the 'French romantic movement' (and most parti-
cularly George Sand) which 'quickened and fertilised her genius':
'One may almost say of [*Jane Eyre*], indeed, that it belongs more to

the European than to the special English tradition' (*The Life and Works of Charlotte Brontë and her Sisters*, in Seven Volumes, with Introductions to the Works by Mrs Humphry Ward [London: Smith Elder & Co., 1906], Vol. I, *Jane Eyre*, pp. xxxv–xxxviii).

54. See p. 90 below.

55. See p. 47 below.

56. Hermione Lee, 'Emblems and Enigmas in *Jane Eyre*', *English*, 30 (Autumn 1981), 223.

57. Gilbert and Gubar, *The Madwoman in the Attic*, p. 339.

58. See p. 132 below.

59. Carter, *Expletives Deleted*, p. 162.

60. See, for example, Helene Moglen, *Charlotte Brontë: the Self Conceived* (New York, 1976); Maurianne Adams, 'Family Disintegration and Creative Reintegration: the Case of Charlotte Brontë and *Jane Eyre*', in *The Victorian Family: Stress and Structure*, ed. Anthony Wohl (London, 1978); Robert Keefe, *Charlotte Brontë's World of Death* (Austin, TX, 1979).

61. See, for example, Ruth Bernard Yeazell, 'More True than Real: Jane Eyre's Mysterious Summons', *Nineteenth-Century Fiction*, 29 (1974), 127–43; Sandra Gilbert, 'A Dialogue of Self and Soul'; John Maynard, *Charlotte Brontë and Sexuality* (Cambridge, 1984), pp. 93–144.

62. Peter Brooks, 'The Idea of a Psychoanalytic Literary Criticism', in *Discourse in Psychoanalysis and Literature*, ed. Shlomith Rimmon-Kenan (London, 1987), p. 2.

63. G. H. Lewes, in Allott (ed.), *Critical Heritage*, p. 85.

64. The pioneering essay was that by Robert Heilman, 'Charlotte Brontë's "New" Gothic in *Jane Eyre* and *Villette*' in *From Jane Austen to Joseph Conrad*, ed. Robert C. Rathburn and Martin Steinmann, Jr (Minneapolis, 1958), pp. 118–32. For a later, feminist reading of *Jane Eyre* in relation to the Gothic, see Eugenia C. De Lamotte, *Perils of the Night: A Feminist Study of Nineteenth-Century Gothic* (Oxford, 1990), ch. 6.

65. Homans, *Bearing the Word* (Chicago, 1986), p. 112.

66. Thomas Vargish, *The Providential Aesthetic in Victorian Fiction* (Charlottesville, VA, 1985), p. 58.

67. Homans, *Bearing the Word*, p. 113.

68. Leslie Stephen in Allott (ed.), *Casebook*, p. 153.

69. Karen Chase, in *Eros and Psyche* (London, 1984), ch. 4 (the chapter which succeeds the one reprinted here).

70. Thus, Richard Chase, 'The Brontës: A Centennial Observance', *Kenyon Review*, 9 (Autumn 1947), p. 495:

> The universe conspiring against Jane Eyre, like the circumstances which so often conspired against the [Brontë] sisters, must be chastened by an assertion of will, catastrophic if necessary. And so Charlotte sends Rochester's house up in flames and makes him lose his eyesight and his left hand in a vain attempt to save Bertha. Rochester's injuries are, I should think, a symbolic castration.

71. See p. 90 below.

72. See p. 184 below.

73. See p. 196 below.

74. His emphatic masculinity indeed stresses the fact that (as Bronfen elsewhere puts it) 'notions of domination and inferiority based on gender difference are ... secondary to a more global and non-individuated disempowerment before death' (*Over Her Dead Body* [Manchester, 1992], p. 35).

75. For a powerful statement of this view, see Thomas Vargish, *The Providential Aesthetic in Victorian Fiction*, pp. 58–67.

76. 'We are left with the sense of an unsolved discord', wrote Leslie Stephen, in 'Hours in a Library', of the ending of *Jane Eyre* (Allott [ed.], *Casebook*, p. 154). Although Stephen does not explicitly speak of religion, his reading, in its closeness to Dale's, confirms the latter's sense that the conflict he identifies would have been much more evident to Victorian readers than it is today:

> At one moment in *Jane Eyre* we seem to be drifting towards the solution that strong passion is the one really good thing in the world, and that all human conventions which oppose it should be disregarded. This was the tendency which shocked the respectable reviewers of the time. Of course they should have seen that the strongest sympathy of the author goes with the heroic self-conquest of the heroine under temptation. She triumphs at the cost of a determined self-sacrifice, and undoubtedly we are meant to sympathise with the martyr. Yet it is also true that we are left with the sense of an unsolved discord. (Allott [ed.], *Casebook*, pp. 153–4)

77. M. H. Scargill, 1950, *Casebook*, p. 176; Kathleen Tillotson, *Casebook*, p. 183. Even David Crompton, who considered the novel 'relatively immature in conception and execution' found that 'the more one goes into *Jane Eyre* the richer the structural unity of the book becomes' (*Casebook*, pp. 213, 211).

78. For a discussion of the importance of the concept of 'aporia' in deconstructionist thought see Christopher Norris, *Deconstruction: Theory and Practice* (London, 1982), p. 49.

1

Jane Eyre and 'The Warped System of Things'

DOREEN ROBERTS

The first unanalysed impression that most readers receive from *Jane Eyre* is that it has a very violent atmosphere. If this were simply the effect of the plot and the imagined events then sensation novels like Walpole's *The Castle of Otranto* or Mrs Radcliffe's *The Mystery of Udolpho* ought to produce it even more powerfully. But they do not. Nor do they even arouse particularly strong reader responses. Novelists like Charlotte Brontë or D. H. Lawrence, on the other hand, are able quite quickly to provoke marked reactions of sympathy or hostility from readers. The reason, apparently, is that the narrator's personality is communicating itself through the style with unusual directness. It is for reasons deriving from this one that I do not re-read middle and late Lawrence with pleasure, and find the opening of *The Rainbow* hard to get past. Those who do not admire the fifth paragraph for instance, can find its incantatory quality irritating, even faintly embarrassing.

A number of Charlotte Brontë's nineteenth-century readers, including Matthew Arnold, reacted to her work in a comparably personal (sometimes immoderate) way. And it does indeed offer a mixed and restless reading experience – on one page a striking psychological insight, on the next, a piece of fiercely self-righteous invective charged with an evidently real yet (in fictional terms) obscure emotion. We may be successively impressed by the conscious and penetrating registering of oddnesses or weaknesses in the heroine, and staggered by the apparent authorial obliviousness to others. We encounter a minutely analysed psyche moving through a world of shadowily adumbrated or else luridly poster-coloured figures. Brontë is a writer who can be as irritating, even maddening, as she is interesting and often fascinating. The power of her work seems to depend on the way it bulldozes through our notions of decorum and stylistic restraint, our respect for balance and a sense of proportion and – at a quite radical level – our notions of fairness. The narrative method being, to my mind, the central issue, I would like to approach *Jane Eyre* initially by way of the style. The dangers of generalising about a whole novel from a single extract are real ones and are often pointed out. But, the appropriate caveats accepted, looking at a passage in detail does seem to be one of the obvious ways of making the point that in this novel there is a particularly close connexion between the medium and the message, and again, that the tone of the book is an especially important influence on the reader's response. Apart from this, it is the case that less stylistic variation is felt in *Jane Eyre* than in, say, *Villette*. Indeed the strangeness that we frequently note about the dialogue is traceable to the relative constancy of the style, one peculiarly unadapted to conveying idiomatic conversation. The example chosen is a striking but representative passage that comes at the end of Chapter 26 and describes Jane's feelings just after the interrupted marriage ceremony and ensuing revelation of the existence of the first Mrs Rochester.

> I was in my own room as usual – just myself, without obvious change: nothing had smitten me, or scathed me, or maimed me. And yet where was the Jane Eyre of yesterday? – where was her life? – where were her prospects?
>
> Jane Eyre, who had been an ardent expectant woman – almost a bride – was a cold, solitary girl again: her life was pale; her prospects were desolate. A Christmas frost had come at midsummer; a white December storm had whirled over June: ice glazed the ripe apples, drifts crushed the blowing roses; on hayfield and cornfield lay a frozen shroud: lanes which last night blushed full of flowers, to-day were pathless with untrodden snow; and the woods, which twelve hours since waved leafy and fragrant as groves between the tropics, now spread, waste, wild, and white as pine-forests in wintry Norway. My hopes were all dead – struck with a subtle doom, such as, in one night, fell on all the first born in the land of Egypt. I looked on my cherished wishes, yesterday so blooming and glowing; they lay stark, chill, livid corpses that could never revive. I looked at my love: that feeling which was my master's – which he had created;

it shivered in my heart, like a suffering child in a cold cradle: sickness and anguish had seized it; it could not seek Mr Rochester's arms – it could not derive warmth from his breast. Oh, never more could it turn to him; for faith was blighted – confidence destroyed! Mr Rochester was not to me what he had been; for he was not what I had thought him. I would not ascribe vice to him; I would not say he had betrayed me; but the attribute of stainless truth was gone from his idea, and from his presence I must go: that I perceived well. When – how – whither, I could not yet discern; but he himself, I doubted not, would hurry me from Thornfield. Real affection, it seemed, he could not have for me; it had only been fitful passion: that was balked; he would want me no more. I should fear even to cross his path now: my view must be hateful to him. Oh, how blind had been my eyes! How weak my conduct!

My eyes were covered and closed: eddying darkness seemed to swim round me, and reflection came in as black and confused a flow. Self-abandoned, relaxed, and effortless, I seemed to have laid me down in the dried-up bed of a great river; I heard a flood loosened in remote mountains, and I felt the torrent come; to rise I had no will, to flee I had no strength. I lay faint, longing to be dead. One idea only still throbbed lifelike within me – a remembrance of God: it begot an unuttered prayer: these words went wandering up and down in my rayless mind, as something that should be whispered, but no energy was found to express them.

'Be not far from me, for trouble is near: there is none to help.' It was near; and as I had lifted no petition to Heaven to avert it – as I had neither joined my hands, nor bent my knees, nor moved my lips – it came: in full heavy swing the torrent poured over me. The whole consciousness of my life lorn, my love lost, my hope quenched, my faith death-struck, swayed full and mighty above me in one sullen mass. That bitter hour cannot be described: in truth, 'the waters came into my soul; I sank in deep mire: I felt no standing; I came into deep waters; the floods overflowed me.'

This is typical of many of the strange effects of Charlotte Brontë's style, an extremely uncolloquial and un-modern one beside that of, say, Mrs Gaskell in *Wives and Daughters*. It is highly literary and consciously rhetorical, yet at the same time vehement and perfervid. It keeps setting up formal, stylised sentence-patterns and then disrupting them with rhetorical questions, exclamations, exhortations, appended clauses and appositional phrases. It loves word-runs of two or three, like 'waste, wild, and white', 'stark, chill, livid', or 'self-abandoned, relaxed, and effortless', the linkage often reinforced by alliteration or assonance. It builds up structures of echoing serial phrases or clauses, again in twos or threes and often arranged with crescendo force, like 'nothing had smitten me, or scathed me, or maimed me. And yet where was the Jane Eyre of yesterday? – where was her life? – where were her prospects?' Here the harmony of the pattern is characteristically dissolved in the effect of staccato abruptness produced by the frequent and insistent pauses between sense-units and the heaviness of the punctuation. (Charlotte Brontë makes unusually lavish use of the dash, and often has a punctuation mark where a conjunction might have been expected, and in general, despite the apparent length and complexity of her sentences, tends to work in rather short sense-units and to like paratactic clausal or phrasal arrangements.) Such a style cannot possibly flow. Nor is there any of the effect of rising and falling emphasis normal in narrative prose. It is more like a sustained series of small explosions.

Again, the narrator has a marked fondness for balanced or antithetical clauses and various forms of isocolon: 'Mr Rochester was not to me what he had been; for he was not what I had thought him!' or (rather biblically) 'to rise I had no will, to flee I had no strength'. But the patterns are not repeated constantly enough to establish them as guiding syntactic principles (as they are in some eighteenth-century prose). Expectancy is defeated by the abrupt shifts and staccato sharpness.

In another respect the eighteenth-century mannerisms fail of an eighteenth-century effect. One important use of personification for the Augustans was to universalise individual crises, and statements of antitheses like Wit and Judgement, Fancy and Reason, Taste and Genius, the Beautiful and the Picturesque or Sense and Sensibility were current because they believed in universally recognisable categories. Through these, individual conflicts, dilemmas or problems of choice could be brought into the realm of public debate, where they could be analysed in a more general and objective context, according to received ethical principles. Thus they also became amenable to rhetorical treatment, and it is notable that Charlotte Brontë adopted the more rhetorical of those stylistic habits that we associate particularly with the century before her own. Most modern readers take *Jane Eyre* to be dramatising a psychological conflict between opposing impulses in the self, at a level which precedes (but may lead to) the moral. But apparently the book believes itself to be debating a general and familiar moral issue, in the received 'Sense and Sensibility' terms. The 'public' element in the style seems to be trying to distract attention from the personal and idiosyncratic element. It might be interesting, from this point of view, to examine the problems of terminology in the ambiguous 'temptation' scene of Chapter 27, where Jane seems unsure whether she is defending her God-commanded chastity, her status in Rochester's eyes, or her self-image.

Another almost obsessional stylistic device is syntactic inversion: the object, predicate or adverb of the sentence is often found in an abnormal place, as in the last two quotations above, or in 'from his presence I must go'. This is, of course, a device for isolation and emphasis. The style also leans towards archaistic or obsolescent words like 'smitten', 'scathed', and 'lorn'. A small sample of this vocabulary (much of it eighteenth-century Miltonese) elsewhere in the book would be ''ere', 'e'n', 'ire', 'ireful', 'front [forehead]', 'viewless', 'jetty [black]', 'ebon', 'trackless', 'shrilly', 'gore', 'drear' and 'curbless'. There are many Latinistic or Miltonic locutions like 'his idea [the idea of him]', 'my view [the sight of me]' and 'I doubted not'. Unusual, often double-barrelled, adjectives abound: 'rayless', 'self-abandoned', 'death-struck'. There are also many participial or gerundive adjectives, again sometimes used in a quasi-Miltonic way: 'the whole consciousness of my life lorn' (for 'of my life being lorn', plus 'of my forlorn life'), and this goes with a liking for the use of the ablative absolute construction.

Still more noticeable is the recurrent and weird use of passive constructions where one would have expected active ones: 'these words went wandering up and down in my rayless mind, as something that should be whispered; but no energy was found to express them' (for 'as something that I should whisper; but I found had no energy to express them'). This is only one of many dissociation techniques in the style. It gives the effect of someone behaving compulsively, or being acted upon by external forces. That is, the self is presented as object, not subject (I believe this is also common in the thinking of schizophrenics). Thus Jane does not *think* disconnected words – words go wandering up and down in her mind, as if it were a place, full of independent entities. Related to this is the trademark of personification or semi-personification, especially of the heroine's feelings. I have already mentioned a major traditional use of personification, but the more personal use is different in its effect. Jane visualises her emotions as separate agents, and the style sets them to work in very physical, indeed violent ways. She energises the old metaphor of dead hopes by describing them as 'struck dead' and sees her love as a suffering child in a cold cradle over which she is helplessly watching. Reflection and, by implication, tears, come in a black confused flow; Jane *hears* her own feelings approaching her. The black confused flow becomes a flood that threatens to drown her, and the stricken faith sways sullenly above her (like an avalanche threatening to fall?).

The consciousness is stretched and so hyperactive that it splits into parts and the observer-self sits in the middle, registering all this activity around it. The narrator tries to numb herself, and to regain objectivity, by describing herself in the third person, as if she were somebody else: 'Jane Eyre, who had been an ardent expectant woman – almost a bride – was a cold, solitary girl again: her life was pale; her prospects were desolate.' Or one part of the consciousness addresses another in the second person.

So sustained is the dissociation-projection technique, so strong the sense of a drama going on not just within but around the heroine, that it takes a second for the reader to register that the 'Christmas frost' which has 'come at midsummer' bringing the 'white December storm' is part of an inner landscape, not an external scene.

The stage on which the psychic struggle is enacted is progressively expanded in space and time till it reaches cosmic proportions. The metaphor extends outwards to the pine-forests of Norway and backwards in time to the plagues of Egypt. The naturalness of that allusion reveals how readily the heroine thinks of herself as an object specially marked out by divine providence. From here, after a brief echo of *Macbeth*, the passage moves into a series of overt biblical references: 'Self-abandoned, relaxed, and effortless, I seemed to have laid me down in the dried-up bed of a great river; I heard a flood loosened in remote mountains, and I felt the torrent come' unites an image of spiritual lassitude from the Book of Job (14: 11–12) with a cry of panic from Lamentations (3:54) and the end of the passage is a loose quotation of the opening of the sixty-ninth Psalm. The heroine boldly identifies herself through, and finally with, the great paradigms of suffering.

The novel implies a reader very familiar with the Old Testament, and with Bunyan. But its use of the Bible is idiosyncratic. Unlike, say, George Eliot, Charlotte Brontë blurs the dividing line between a quotation and her heroine's 'own' words. She uses a close, or only close-ish, quotation and works it intimately into the text, on two occasions unannounced even by quotation marks. She uses the Bible less as the source of ideas about God or moral conduct than as a way of defining her own experience. Bunyan of course does the latter, but in a specifically religious context, whereas Charlotte Brontë's narrator projects herself dramatically into the situation of the Old Testament speaker and rapidly adapts it to fit her own (a reverse of the usual practice). The biblical situation is removed from its original context into an erotic one. It is used 'blasphemously' in that a comparison is being made between a soul cut off from its God and a woman cut off from her lover.

However we read it, the passage sounds febrile and highly charged. But taken on its own like this, of course, it seems a good deal wilder, even madder, than when it is encountered in context. Naturally this is partly because we then have the whole story to date to assist us in interpreting the passage and in judging whether the heroine's reactions are excessive. But equally importantly, what in isolation might be seen as a congeries of purely stylistic features (lurid ones at that) turn out not to be used at random. A lot of them, in fact, turn out to provide some of the book's recurrent images and motifs, a substantial part of the 'detail' of the fictional world, miniature versions of events in it, and a microcosmic reflection of its dialectical structure. The ice and fire contrast has already emerged as a pattern in the book at both the literal and the metaphoric level, the white December storm reminds us of the 'real' one that has blasted the Thornfield chestnut tree, the image of the suffering child relates both to the young Jane – and one of her recent dreams – and to Helen Burns, and the world of Jane's childhood reading provides the nordic imagery.

But still, everything in the passage, as in the book, has a tremendously centripetal, egocentric reference, though this is partly disguised by the concreteness of the imagery. The effect is of nervous intensity cutting weirdly through a formal, literary style and a syntax that has a marked tendency to the stilted and the pedantic. The style of the Age of Reason meets and clashes with the style of the romance and its assimilations from the Bible and Bunyan. There is a double effect of repression and violence. The style itself enacts the struggle which is the theme of the plot: between Id and Superego, reaction and quiescence, private and public.

In one way the style, with its intense and unremitting concentration on the heroine and her feelings, is a highly self-conscious one. But in its uninhibited honesty and its lack of detachment it is unselfconscious in a manner now impossible to the post-Jamesian, post-Freudian English novel, aware that the House of Fiction has many windows and that the most significant glimpses of the author are the ones that are not intended. Charlotte Brontë has paid the price of this in the amount of biographically or psychoanalytically slanted criticism that her writing has attracted.

The loudness of tone in *Jane Eyre* is undoubtedly effective in communicating tension and frustration, but the style does of course have its related limitations. It precludes the use of the small suggestive detail or the quiet but telling observation that Mrs Gaskell and George Eliot are so good at. In such a fortissimo performance as this, the pianissimo gets drowned out, or noted only as an incongruity (which helps to account for the book's moments of unintended comic bathos). Again, it makes the whole question of modulation of tone a difficult one, and it is also hard to manage irony elegantly, as the Brocklehurst and Ingram portraits show. There is unconscious ambiguity but little deliberate irony in *Jane Eyre*. Hence the remarkable unity of critical interpretation of the book – the reader knows all too well what he is meant to think about the heroine and the subsidiary characters. The novel does not merely request our judicious sympathy for the heroine, it demands that we see with her eyes, think in her terms, and hate her enemies, not just intermittently (as in *David Copperfield*) but *in toto*. It was, incidentally, because James Joyce recognised the similar tendency of *Stephen Hero* that he reshaped his autobiographical material as *A Portrait of the Artist as a Young Man*, retaining the 'first-person effect' but building in stylistic and structural irony that would guard against the appearance of wholesale authorial endorsement of Stephen.

There is not much of the middle or neutral narrative style in *Jane Eyre* – the sort of unremarkable style whose function is simply to get the plot along or the characters established for the reader. That the lurid style is not reserved for maximising the impact of the most sensational narrative events is evidenced by the above passage, which is analysing Jane's feelings *after* such an event. In fact one of the novelties of the Brontë method is that she manages to cast a unique aura of excitement around even the most superficially ordinary or bread-and-butter events, like Jane's decision to apply for a job as a governess (ch. 10). This comes to us as a dramatic dialogue between the heroine and herself, with all the momentousness of the conversion of a St Paul on the road to Damascus; and apparently the same divine agency is involved. It is at points like this that the reader is most struck by the book's intensity of treatment because the event is intrinsically so much less sensational than, say, the locking in the red-room, not to mention the doings at Thornfield, so that the air of drama here is more obviously a function of the personality of the narrator. The red-room description, in fact, has its companion-piece in the description of Thornfield drawing-room (ch. 11), a lavish and arresting study in the 'blending of snow and fire'. But in this drawing-room there takes place nothing more (or less) *tressaillant* than Jane's first extended cross-examination by Rochester. On the other hand it is the events that are sensational enough in themselves not to need a lot of stylistic intensification that offer a few surprises in the way of downbeat, deliberately humorous treatment. There is, most notably, the episode in which Jane saves Rochester from the maniac's bonfire. I am not sure whether Charlotte Brontë intended this symbolically, but the image of Jane pouring cold water on her 'master's' fiery bed is pleasingly reminiscent of Jane's habit, in the courtship scenes, of damping him down (verbally) whenever his behaviour becomes too amorous.

But it is the prevalent intensity of treatment that establishes the book's atmosphere. It is also responsible for the absence of perspective. Since the scale of values is supplied by the heroine's feelings, it is difficult to make any useful distinction between 'major' and 'minor' events. If feeling is involved at all it is stirred to its depths. If not, the treatment is, on examination, unmistakably perfunctory, as in the way the novel presents (or fails to present) Jane's relationships with Mrs Fairfax and Adèle. Here there is a thinness of detail, and the reader, subconsciously missing the dramatic style, senses that he can relax his attention.

This absolutism is the stylistic equivalent of the all-or-nothing approach that Jane admits apropos St John Rivers (ch. 34): 'I know no medium: I never in my life have known any medium in my dealings with positive, hard characters, antagonistic to my own, between absolute submission and determined revolt. I have always faithfully observed the one, up to the very moment of bursting, sometimes with volcanic vehemence, into the other.' And of course this dialectic between absolute and violently opposed polarities is the essence of the book. Even the two Reed sisters make such a pair – an ascetic one with a mania for order and a hatred of the flesh, and a flighty sensualist. The reason why Helen Burns cannot function for the reader as the pattern of true Christian resignation that the author evidently intended her to be is that this exaggerative imagination has created her instead as the image of morbid stoicism, whose answer to the problem of suffering is to cultivate an exterior indifference to pleasure or pain, and whose death is the logical culmination of her effort to detach herself from the world. Her natural anti-type is of course mad Mrs Rochester, the fictional vandal of all time, who would like to tear the world apart with her teeth and then burn up the remnants.

The strain of Calvinism in Charlotte Brontë's writing curiously reinforces the Romanticism with which it competes. It can be seen doing so in the long passage already quoted. Just as the style lacks a middle ground, so there is no middle ground – such as a sense of society would provide – between the individual self and the cosmos at large. This self-absorption is characteristic of both tempers, and Charlotte Brontë offers an unmediated confrontation between the self and its world, or the soul and its God. By the same token the fortissimo tone and the lack of rising and falling emphasis is a feature not only of the style but of the book's whole rhythm. It lives on its nerves, from crisis to crisis, and the pauses in the plot are not moments of quiet but bursts of mental activity.

I think this lack of middle ground or middle-distance detail can be related to the all-or-nothing feeling towards most of the subsidiary characters in Jane Eyre (apart from the one or two like Mrs Fairfax, for whom Jane feels a tolerant contempt). Usually the heroine either loves people intensely or is instantly repelled by them, deeply admires them or scathingly scorns them. (One catches the idiolect as one discusses the book.) Occasionally the heroine does both; her feelings may be mixed but they are seldom moderate. The lack of casual acquaintanceships and ordinary daily contacts in the *Jane Eyre* world increases the reader's sense of the heroine's psychic isolation, her orphanhood.

A pertinent case to cite here would be the revisit by the adult Jane to the Reed household. To be sure it corrects the child's sense of the phantasmagoric awe-fulness of her aunt. But Jane's claimed forgiveness of her does nothing to render her less unpleasant or more understandable and hence pitiable (though her instinctive, irrational hatred of Jane is convincingly rendered). But the heroine's newfound patience and tolerance is the measure less of a deepening view of her old foe than of the distance Jane has travelled on the road to external self-command, and of her new superiority to rejection and insult, which is mostly Rochester's doing. Indeed, she relishes the new challenge to 'subdue' Mrs Reed 'in spite of her nature and her will'. And her forgiveness has, as it were, no fictional outcome as the woman dies horribly and her children all go to the dogs.

Mrs Reed will stand for the pattern of all the dislikable characters in the book. All the nasty characters dislike or despise the heroine (Miss Abbot, the Reeds, Mr Brocklehurst, the Ingrams and so on), while all the good and nice characters admire or respond to her (Bessie, Helen Burns, Miss Temple, Mr Rochester of course, the Rivers sisters – their brother is a special case).

This fits entirely with the way the minor figures in the book are presented; though 'minor' is perhaps a misleading term in the context of autobiographical narrative, and certainly in the context of this book. The narrator's response to them is visual-intuitive. She studies their appearance, their faces and figures and often their voices too, and then makes a leap into a reading of their inner selves. This method has affinities with Bunyanesque allegorical portraiture, reinforced by phrenology.[1] But since both allegory and phrenology have to assume that character is fixed and given, not contingent and developing, the implication is that people do not change. More important in *Jane Eyre* is that the heroine's *view* of them cannot change or deepen in any essential respects; though we find that she herself resents the way other characters jump to conclusions about her, on the mere external evidence of her small plain appearance and lowly status. Again, the persistence of the phrenological method reveals the very real continuity of the adult with the childhood sections of the book. The child's vision persists, and the qualities that were strengths in the child (her imagination, her fighting spirit, and her will to survive) remain in the adult Jane as mixed blessings. It is for this reason that I remain admiring but doubtful about Q. D. Leavis's energetic attempt to read *Jane Eyre* as a realistic novel and to discuss it in terms of what Jane learns.

At all events, by the same token that it is non-developmental, the phrenological method precludes gradual revelation of character, because all the evidence is there from the outset. Because of this, and also because the effect is so concentratedly vivid, the part that the characters will play later on is quite unpredictable from the mode of their introduction. There is no gradation of detail to indicate the characters' 'rank' in the book, little sense of a scale as between a full portrait and a light sketch (such as we can find in most Victorian fiction apart from that of Dickens). The method of presenting John Reed, Mrs Reed, Miss Temple, Lady Ingram and her daughter, and Mr Mason is essentially the same. Here is

Mr Mason (whose failure to reappear significantly in the book in a villain's role would be bound to surprise a child reader) –

> His manner was polite; his accent, in speaking, struck me as being somewhat unusual – not precisely foreign, but still not altogether English [always a bad sign in a Brontë novel]: his age might be about Mr Rochester's – between thirty and forty; his complexion was singularly sallow: otherwise he was a fine-looking man, at first sight especially. On closer examination, you detected something in his face that displeased; or rather, that failed to please. His features were regular, but too relaxed: his eye was large and well cut, but the life looking out of it was a tame, vacant life – at least so I thought.
> The sound of the dressing-bell dispersed the party. It was not till after dinner that I saw him again: he then seemed quite at his ease. But I liked his physiognomy even less than before: it struck me as being at the same time unsettled and inanimate. His eye wandered, and had no meaning in its wandering: this gave him an odd look, such as I never remembered to have seen. For a handsome and not an unamiable-looking man, he repelled me exceedingly: there was no power in that smooth-skinned face of a full oval shape; no firmness in that aquiline nose and small cherry mouth; there was no thought on the low, even forehead; no command in that blank, brown eye.
>
> (ch. 18)

In a similar fashion Lady Ingram's features and deportment all bespeak patrician pride, fierceness, hardness, pomposity and dogmatism. She has not one redeeming feature. She is Mrs Reed writ even larger, just as Bertha Rochester is Blanche Ingram gone crazy, and the confrontation between Jane and Bertha in Chapter 26 is a kind of re-working in reverse of the 'look upon this picture and on this' episode in which Jane tortures herself by drawing and comparing the portraits of herself and her imagined rival (ch. 16). In their address to servants, the Ingrams actually say things like 'Cease that chatter, blockhead, and do my bidding' and the mother calls her daughter 'My queenly Blanche'.

By contrast, benignant light shines from the irids of Miss Temple, and her sensitivity cannot be mistaken in her 'fine pencilling of long lashes'. It is eminently in keeping that Jane Eyre likes to paint people. She tends to represent them in terms of flashing eagle glances, sea-blue eyes, ivory or 'jetty' brows, and carrion images. But the main point is that this kind of presentation suggests no scale. That Miss Ingram should elicit hostile reactions is understandable, given her lofty station and supposed position as rival.

There is some reason for the book's attention to her effect on Jane. But the extraordinary floodlighting of a character so microscopic as Mr Mason is quite unnecessary to the plot, and makes its real contribution to the understanding of the heroine's preferences and needs. It also reveals how, in the end, she confuses people's temperamental characteristics with their moral qualities. As in the case of St John Rivers, an emotional reaction from the heroine is also a moral judgement.

Characters in Brontë's work respond to each other immediately, intuitively and demonstratively. If they dislike each other, they radiate vibrations of antipathy and contempt. If they attract each other, it is straight away. Even Jane's accidental meeting with Rochester, before she knows who he is, strangely excites her and at once revives her dormant discontent with her useful, easy, secure but drab existence at Thornfield. When the pair have their first social introduction they get straight to the point and establish a personal, intimate, self-consciously suggestive tone of exchange, with Rochester laying on thick his image of aggressive, gruff, pouncing abruptness and Jane counterpointing it with demure caginess.

The method is dramatic and strange even in the context of quite natural encounters. St John Rivers does not introduce himself to Jane by walking straight up his own garden path and inviting her into his house: he lurks around in the darkness listening in on her plea to the servant for help, till he overhears her say to herself 'I can but die, and I believe in God. Let me try to wait his will in silence.' Whereupon his disembodied voice sepulchrally replies 'All men must die, but all are not condemned to meet a lingering and premature doom, such as yours would be if you perished here of want.' And Jane, naturally, is startled. But the reader is by this time so inured to the strange atmosphere that he hardly notices St John's behaviour is odd. At least, it is not one of the incidents in the book that gets pointed out. Again St John, who seems to have some kind of an ancestor in Angelo in *Measure for Measure*, before he launches into a very Jane-ish declaration of passion for Miss Oliver, takes out his watch and puts it on the table to ensure that he will not indulge himself for longer than fifteen minutes. The ensuing discussion makes it clear that he is very angry with Miss Oliver for attracting him when she is such an unsuitable mate for him.

The attitudes throughout the novel are not balanced or compromised, but polarised. Jane Eyre's own violence emerges equally as passionate love, bitter hate, masochistic self-mockery and (when turned on society) as moral censoriousness. Since there is, for instance, no means offered for seeing past the heroine's vision of the Ingram family, it is more useful to take it as evidence about the narrator rather than as the social criticism she imagines it to be. It is part of that unbuttoned confessional honesty – honesty because it so unblushingly includes crabbed bigotry – which is one of the reasons why this novel is so original. We get the heroine fully, warts and all. Her prejudices are plain to see. On five separate occasions Jane indicates that all the child Adèle's failings stem from her continental heritage. In the final chapter it is claimed that 'a sound English education corrected in great measure her French defects'. And of course the improvement is accelerated by the fact that Adèle is now removed from the influence of Rochester's mistresses, of whom all are foreigners: Bertha is a Creole, Céline is French, Clara German, Giacinta Italian and, as it were, Blanche is also Angrian.

All this is really part of the characterisation of the fiercely Protestant, chauvinistic and self-righteous heroine, with her need to feel justified even if she cannot feel happy or socially accepted. Even her erotic drives include an element of conflict and pain that no English novelist apart from Richardson had ever recognised before as part of the experience of love. We need only consider the house-party at Thornfield, during which Rochester, with characteristic sadism, torments Jane by studiously ignoring her and paying attentions to Miss Ingram. 'I looked, and had an acute pleasure in looking – a precious yet poignant pleasure; pure gold, with a steely point of agony: a pleasure like what the thirst-perishing man might feel who knows the well to which he has crept is poisoned, yet stoops and drinks divine draughts nevertheless' (ch. 17). But Jane gets her own back at Ferndean when, under pretence of rousing him out of his melancholy (as she claims), she prolongs as long as she can his painful suspense about her relationship to St John Rivers, just as she punishes him for his cruel teasing of her in Thornfield garden by allowing him to suppose that he has only imagined her back at his side. Charlotte Brontë cannot imagine a love that does not include a powerful strain of violence and aggression – best exemplified, of course, in mad Mrs Rochester with her lust to attack the man she once loved, and her unerring knack of identifying the new object of his affections.

We are always sure that the heroine is fiery and passionate, which is quite an achievement when the plot has had to keep her passive, inactive and loveless for long stretches. Up to the point when Jane's

love declares itself, the novel establishes the passion largely by nega-
tives – a method very prophetic of that of D. H. Lawrence, who
was in many ways influenced by Charlotte Brontë. Before we see
the heroine in love, we are persuaded that she is a good hater. But
the hatred has to be used as an oblique way of measuring her
capacity to love. So it has both a cathartic function and a function
in suggesting the heroine's affirmative side. She usually claims to
dislike characters like Mr Mason on account of their lack of a
quality she holds dear. In Mason it is the lack of that decisiveness
and fiery courage that Rochester (and she) so conspicuously
possess. The heroine's capacity for love has no channel until the
lover presents himself, so it emerges as its opposite and continues to
imply it. And meanwhile the characters she hates are magnified into
pseudo-objective symbols of that which is hateful. It is a 'wound
and bow' process, à la Edmund Wilson.

At this point I would like to return to the question of the plot
movement and the different narrative levels of the book. David
Lodge raises a crucial issue when he asks 'how Charlotte Brontë
created a literary structure in which the domestic and the mythical,
the realistic world of social behaviour and the romantic world of
passionate self-consciousness, could co-exist with only occasional
lapses into incongruity'. As far as the plot and setting go, however,
this states the question rather misleadingly, for in fact at Thornfield
there begins a progressive plot movement from realism to fantasy.
By 'realism' I do not mean the predominance of the every day and
commonplace, or an authorial objectivity of treatment, but simply
the use of material that the reader can accept as existing in the ordinary world as well, or of events of a kind that might happen in it
without being viewed as extraordinary. That is, things that have a
face-value currency of meaning prior to any concealed meaning
they may hold or suggest. Thus while Gateshead and Lowood
School fit neatly into, and contribute importantly to, the symbolic
pattern of the book, they are perfectly believable places in their own
right. Even the heavy-handed and obvious satire of Mr Brocklehurst
and his family does not invalidate him as a credible conception. But
with the beginning of the mystery of the Thornfield attic the plot
starts moving away from this face-value actuality. The Ingrams
belong to the Angrian world; there is the coincidence of Uncle Eyre
in Madeira happening to know the Masons in Jamaica, and alerting
them to the bigamous marriage; the still more remarkable coincidence that Jane, wandering aimlessly around England, should

stumble first go on her unknown cousins; then come the handy legacy, the still more convenient conflagration (after umpteen abortive attempts by the culprit), and the final telepathic communication that rescues Jane from St John Rivers at the eleventh hour.

Why do not more readers notice this drastic and quite sudden shift in plotting? They certainly notice the changes of gear in Dickens, Melville or Twain. It must be because there is no marked change of atmosphere. Charlotte Brontë may have a divided consciousness but she has a remarkably unified sensibility and this holds the book together even when the 'story-line' starts shooting off in strange directions. The reason it does so is that it has become increasingly difficult to continue the plot in the realistic vein because this would necessitate a modification of Jane's characteristic sensibility and vision. On the other hand, once the actual childhood is past, the book has to produce concrete 'evidence' to justify this way of seeing and relating to the world. So increasingly these elements that were initially visible mainly in the style, and also in the world of Jane's reading and dreaming, become concretised as characters and plot events. It is the early stages of this process that we can see in the passage from Chapter 26, in the dramatisation of Jane's emotions. But meanwhile, starting with the child's magnified vision has established the dominant viewpoint and prepared the reader for the persistent distortion which is the essence of the book's method. This is really only a way of saying that the book moves increasingly closer to expressionism, and this can, in a way, be measured in the progression from Mrs Reed to Blanche Ingram to the first Mrs Rochester.

Reading Mrs Gaskell's *Life of Charlotte Brontë* after *Jane Eyre* is a curious experience. The subject of the biography is recognisably the same person who wrote the novel, but the effect of the two books is utterly different. The biography is indeed depressing and painful reading. It captures better, I believe, than any subsequent biography the introverted and puritan pessimist side of Charlotte Brontë, and conveys the real dreariness of the world of privation, critical discouragement and limited opportunity that so often made her complain in her letters that she felt marked out for suffering.

Jane Eyre, on the other hand, is exhilarating reading, partly because the reader, far from simply pitying the heroine, is struck by her resilience, and partly because the novel achieves such an imaginative transmutation of the drab. Unlike that of Jane Austen's

Fanny Price or Dickens's Arthur Clennam or John Harmon, Jane Eyre's response to suffering is never less than energetic. The reader is torn between exasperation at the way she mistakes her resentments and prejudices for fair moral judgements, and admiration at the way she fights back. Matthew Arnold, seeking 'sweetness and light' was repelled by the 'hunger, rebellion and rage' that he identified as the keynotes of the novel. One can see why, and yet feel that these have a more positive effect than his phrase allows. The heroine is trying to hold on to her sense of self in a world that gives it little encouragement, and the novel does put up a persuasive case for her arrogance and pugnacity as the healthier alternatives to patience and resignation. That the book has created a world in which the golden mean seems such a feeble solution is both its eccentricity and its strength.

From *Reading the Victorian Novel: Detail Into Form*, ed. Ian Gregor (London, 1980), pp. 131–49.

NOTES

[This essay originally appeared in a collection of essays by a group of colleagues at the University of Kent at Canterbury, which undertook to explore some of the most basic yet most intractable questions raised by their shared experience of reading, discussing and teaching the Victorian novel – how do we actually read a novel? where does our sense of the novel come from? how do the individual details of the reading process cohere into a sense of the form of the whole? In engaging with these questions, this essay seeks both to characterise the peculiar experience of reading *Jane Eyre* and to offer a detailed analysis of those features of Charlotte Brontë's style which might account for the reader's response. Doreen Roberts' essay belongs to no obvious school or grouping, though in its close attention to the details of the text her work has some affinities with 'the new stylistics' and 'linguistic criticism' developed in the 1970s by such critics as David Lodge and Roger Fowler, and in its concern with the process of reading, with that of such reader-response critics as Stanley Fish, Wolfgang Iser and H. R. Jauss. Textual references are to the Penguin edition of *Jane Eyre*, ed. Queenie Leavis (Harmondsworth, 1966). Ed.]

1. Direct references to phrenology would include the following:

    'I suppose I have a considerable organ of veneration.' (ch. 5, p. 79)

    'And Helen obeyed, my organ of veneration expanding at every sounding line.' (ch. 8, p. 105)

'He lifted up the sable waves of hair which lay horizontally over his brow, and showed a solid enough mass of intellectual organs, but an abrupt deficiency where the suave sign of benevolence should have risen.' (ch. 14, p. 163)

'Really, your organs of wonder credulity are easily excited.' (ch. 18, p. 222)

'You who have an eye for natural beauties, and a great deal of the organ of Adhesiveness?' (ch. 23, p. 278)

Serious uses of the concept that the whole character and inner life can be deduced or 'read' in the 'physiognomy' are a vital part of the method of characterisation throughout the novel.

After Jane's formal introduction to Rochester she gives a portrait of him based on a reading of his 'broad and jetty eyebrows, his square forehead, ... his full nostrils, denoting... choler; his grim mouth, chin and jaw' (ch. 13, p. 151). In ch. 14 Rochester achieves a lengthy divination of Jane's character, all based on what he 'reads' in her 'eyes', having already guessed her unspoken thoughts simply from her 'glance' (pp. 166–7). He follows this up, of course, with more of the same in the famous gipsy scene. Jane says that he 'had sometimes read [her] unspoken thoughts with an acumen to [her] incomprehensible' (ch. 22, p. 273). This fits in with the instinct he has developed which tells him when Jane is in the offing, without having to look (ch. 23). Even Lady Ingram claims to be 'a judge of physiognomy' who can read in Jane's 'all the faults of her class' (ch. 17, p. 206). St John Rivers has the same powers: 'I trace lines of force in her face which make me sceptical of her [Jane's] tractability' (ch. 29, p. 366). After reviewing only the barest sketch of Jane's history, he discerns that in her nature is an alloy as detrimental to repose as his own. His evidence is a leisurely reading of her face, 'as if its features and lines were characters on a page' (ch. 30, pp. 380–1). Jane intuits the characters of the Rivers trio with the same immediacy, and has even less difficulty in understanding Miss Oliver: 'I had learnt her whole character' (ch. 32, p. 394). And St John also has a Rochesterian 'instinct' which 'seemed to warn him of her [Miss Oliver's] entrance, even when he did not see it' (ch. 32, p. 393). I have not even given a complete list here of such phenomena.

2

Jane Eyre's Interior Design

KAREN CHASE

When Brontë set out to write *Jane Eyre* she boldly promised her sisters 'a heroine as plain and as small as myself, who shall be as interesting as any of yours'.[1] As claimed, Jane appears decidedly plain: 'so little, so pale' with 'features so irregular and so marked', 'sensible, but not at all handsome', 'queer', a 'little toad'. Rochester is scarcely more prepossessing with his 'massive head', 'unusual breadth of chest, disproportionate almost to his length of limb'. In the novel's final pages, the two have the following exchange:

> 'Have you a pocket-comb about you, sir?'
> 'What for, Jane?'
> 'Just to comb out this shaggy black mane. I find you rather alarming, when I examine you close at hand: you talk of my being a fairy; but I am sure, you are more like a brownie.'
> 'Am I hideous, Jane?'
> 'Very, sir: you always were, you know.'
>
> (ch. 37)

The exaggerated insistence on the unloveliness of her protagonists must be seen as part of Brontë's calculated withdrawal from her previous conventions. In an inversion of the Angrian formula, the innocents are 'hideous' while the threatening figures (Blanche Ingram, for example, or St John Rivers) are often of great beauty.

If a protagonist can be 'plain' and yet 'interesting', indeed if the protagonist seems to be more interesting the plainer she is (with *Villette*'s Lucy Snowe as a kind of apotheosis of plainness), then clearly interest lies elsewhere than on the surface of the body. And if Brontë has such exaggerated contempt for the bodily surface, it is because of her new interest in psychological depth, an interior space that will serve as a highly charged dramatic arena. Her early work had consistently neglected an inner world. In Angria inclinations were simple; only circumstances were complex. But through the course of her later career, Brontë attempts to mark out an intricate private realm, attentive to emotional nuance and self-division. As will become evident, the task is fraught with ambiguity: it is one thing to posit an inner space; it is quite another to give it fictional expression.

Brontë had before her the Enlightenment tradition of philosophical psychology which had represented the human mind in terms of a few leading faculties: reason, judgement, conscience, memory, feeling, imagination. These terms appear frequently in *Jane Eyre*, often with upper-case authority, and Jane depends on them whenever she attempts to give a thorough exposition of her state of mind. They provide the discursive scaffolding of the novel; when *explanation* is in order, these terms come forth to explain. For instance, when Jane first feels herself giving way to an infatuation with Rochester, she holds a private tribunal:

> Arraigned at my own bar, Memory having given her evidence of the hopes, wishes, sentiments I had been cherishing since last night – of the general state of mind in which I had indulged for nearly a fortnight past; Reason having come forward and told in her own quiet way, a plain, unvarnished tale, showing how I had rejected the real, and rabidly devoured the ideal; – I pronounced judgement to this effect:–
> That a greater fool than Jane Eyre had never breathed the breath of life: that a more fantastic idiot had never surfeited herself on sweet lies, and swallowed poison as if it were nectar.
>
> (ch. 16)

In the course of the novel, this play of faculties resolves into a familiar Romantic dualism, the opposition between Feeling and Judgement, or, as it is also expressed, between Passion and Reason. Rochester at one point impersonates a gypsy come to read the fortunes of the guests at Thornfield Hall. He demands that Jane, too, appear before him, and when she obliges he offers this reading of her personality:

> Reason sits firm and holds the reins, and she will not let the feelings burst away and hurry her to wild chasms. The passions may rage furiously, like true heathens, as they are; and the desires may imagine

all sorts of vain things: but judgement shall still have the last word in every argument, and the casting vote in every decision.

(ch. 19)

Clearly, if Brontë's work is so often submitted to the Passion–Reason dichotomy, it is because Brontë herself depends so heavily on the formulation. But here we need to be careful. For, while it is certainly true that these discursive categories punctuate *Jane Eyre*, their force is by no means as great as a casual reading might suggest. On what would have been her wedding day, when Jane learns the secret of Rochester's marriage to Bertha, she recognises that she must leave Thornfield, and then she undergoes new agonies as she attempts to decide whether she ought to depart without seeing him once more:

> I wanted to be weak that I might avoid the awful passage of further suffering I saw laid out for me; and conscience, turned tyrant, held passion by the throat, told her tauntingly, she had yet but dipped her dainty foot in the slough, and swore that with that arm of iron, he would thrust her down to unsounded depths of agony.
>
> (ch. 27)

If we extract too quickly the concepts that Brontë employs – reason, judgement, passion, then we miss a telling feature of all three examples: the extravagant *figural* presentations that dominate each of the passages. Reason first appears as a steady-minded advocate, then as a determined charioteer holding against the untamed feelings, which appear as horses, then change to heathens. The figures become most elaborate in the last example, where conscience and passion are not only identified by gender but become associated with parts of the human body, conscience as an 'arm of iron', passion as a 'throat' and 'dainty foot', and where the struggle between them carries hints of sexual sadism.

Jane invokes traditional faculties in order to explain some oddity in her behaviour, but her explanations, one is obliged to say, become more inscrutable than the actions that they mean to illuminate. Some of Brontë's most elaborate conceits occur when she employs this apparently neutral vocabulary of philosophical psychology. Reason and passion, offered as instruments for interpreting people, are themselves personified; the interpretive terms are further interpreted. And one might regard this habitual and marked tendency in Brontë – the tendency to transform concepts into con-

ceits – as a tacit recognition of the limits of her technical vocabulary. Traditional faculty psychology has, after all, relatively few
terms with which to describe the infinite gradations of human feelings, and Brontë's imaginative reworking of these terms reflects a
straining after finer discriminations.[2]

Only in this light can we make adequate sense of that curious
minor interest: Brontë's fascination with phrenology and physiognomy, to which she refers in all of her major fiction.[3] Occasionally
the allusions are playful, but most often Brontë turns the theories to
practical advantage, using them to provide terse assessments of
character. During one of Jane's early conversations with Rochester,
'He lifted up the sable waves of hair which lay horizontally over his
brow, and showed a solid enough mass of intellectual organs, but
an abrupt deficiency where the suave sign of benevolence should
have risen' (ch. 14). When Rochester, in the guise of the gypsy,
offers to read her future, Jane scoffs at the notion that her destiny
lies in the palm of her hand. Rochester agrees; it is rather 'in the
face: on the forehead, about the eyes, in the eyes themselves, in the
lines of the mouth'. 'Ah! now you are coming to reality,' says Jane,
'I shall begin to put some faith in you presently' (ch. 19). Rochester,
in fact, goes on to provide a convincing assessment of Jane's character. In *Villette*, Lucy Snowe has her first meeting with Paul
Emanuel, when he is summoned to read her countenance. His im-
pressions are fateful; based on his assessment of her physiognomy,
Madame Beck hires Lucy as governess.

Certainly, Brontë was not alone in her interest. In the decades
after the Napoleonic Wars, phrenology had its great flowering,
when, like many another system, it migrated from the continent to
England. Franz Josef Gall had elaborated the fundamental principles during the last years of the eighteenth century; Johann Gaspar
Spurzheim became a convert to Gall's ideas and brought them to
England where George Combe became the great proponent of the
theory. The Phrenological Society was founded in 1823, and a host
of journals sprang up, with such engaging titles as *The Zoist* and
The Phreno-Magnet. Brontë submitted her skull to phrenological
examination; George Eliot had a cast of her head made. From our
perspective such fascination with 'pseudo-science' might seem mere
extra-literary dalliance, the frivolous amusement of unrigorous
minds. But this would be to dismiss the interests too lightly. The
concern of Victorian novelists with heterodox theories of mind –
however inchoate the theories, however suspect their evidence –

reveals an impatience with prevailing notions of personality, and a desire for finer distinctions and deeper explanations than philosophy or medical science offered. We incline to take for granted the literary historical commonplace that the nineteenth century was the great age of literary psychology, and we tend to forget that these novelists did not inherit a supple and illuminating picture of the mind, but that they had to construct it for themselves, taking insights where they found them.

In founding his system of phrenology, Gall had begun with a plausible physiological assumption that many subsequent researchers would share: that the brain is the site of the personality. From here, however, he took a more controversial step, holding that the brain was not a single organ but a congeries of many organs, each responsible for a distinct mental function, and each, as is well known, indicated by a protuberance on the surface of the skull. Other factors being equal, size provided the measure of an organ's power (Rochester's 'massive head' may have been inspired by this claim). But this stipulation ought not to suggest a high precision in phrenological calculations: Combe depended on such classifications as 'small', 'rather small', 'full', 'rather large'.[4]

No doubt part of the attraction for Brontë was the sheer wealth of affective distinctions which phrenology offered. As the movement gained in strength, the regions of the skull increased in number, until some American adherents of the doctrine held that there were no fewer than forty organs directing the course of the personality.[5] Phrenology, then, insisted on a radical multiplicity of traits; it was pre-eminently a doctrine of the divided self: it presented character as the complex interaction of competing forces. Whereas in Brontë's Angria personality had remained essentially unitary, each character dominated by a single consuming desire, her later work insists on the internal complexity of the psyche. Phrenology offered a ready-to-hand catalogue of potentially warring faculties that range well beyond the simple opposition between feeling and judgement, and Brontë typically has recourse to its terminology when she wants to introduce a new trait of character or a collection of traits. Here is the introduction of Hiram Yorke in *Shirley*:

> Mr Yorke, in the first place, was without the organ of Veneration – a great want, and which throws a man wrong on every point where veneration is required. Secondly, he was without the organ of

Comparison – a deficiency which strips a man of sympathy; and, thirdly, he had too little of the organs of Benevolence and Ideality, which took the glory and softness from his nature, and for him diminished those divine qualities throughout the universe.

(ch. 4)

Apart from furnishing such a battery of descriptive epithets, phrenology and physiognomy offer a solution to a potential narrative dilemma. If Brontë's interest, as I have argued, moved from bodily surface to inner depth, then the question arises how a limited first-person narrator can have access to the private recesses of other minds. How can Jane, limited to what she sees, see what most interests her, the underlying dispositions that inform character? Phrenology and physiognomy offer a way out of the difficulty, holding, as they do, that inner states manifest themselves on outer surfaces, that emotional truths do not merely lurk within, but *display* themselves in public form. 'By the aid of Phrenology', one proponent claimed, 'we are enabled to ascertain correctly, at a glance, [the difference] between the fool and the philosopher, between the honest and the dishonest, the light and trifling and the modest and well-conducted, the Animal and the Christian, and lastly, whereby we may hang the mantle on the right shoulder.'[6] Jane can confine herself to what she sees and still make judgements of personality, because personality not only lies within, but lies upon, the visible body. Consider, for instance, this introductory description of the dowager Lady Ingram:

She had Roman features and a double chin, disappearing into a throat like a pillar: these features appeared to me not only inflated and darkened, but even furrowed with pride; and the chin was sustained by the same principle, in a position of almost preternatural erectness. She had, likewise, a fierce and a hard eye: it reminded me of Mrs Reed's; she mouthed her words in speaking; her voice was deep, its inflections very pompous, very dogmatical, – very intolerable, in short.

(ch. 17)

Jane limits herself to a physical exterior, but when we learn that the features are full of 'pride', the eye 'fierce and hard', the voice 'pompous' 'dogmatical' 'intolerable', we feel little need to plumb to further depths of the character.

Brontë's suspicions of beauty and her preference for markedly plain characters ought to make better sense. The ideal of beauty in

Jane Eyre is Grecian. Rivers has a face 'like a Greek face, very pure in outline; quite a straight, classic nose; quite an Athenian mouth and chin', and Jane concedes that, 'He might well be a little shocked at the irregularity of my lineaments, his own being so harmonious' (ch. 29). Blanche Ingram, too, is 'Grecian', but in *Jane Eyre* harmony of features implies a simplicity or severity of character. Rochester and Jane are extravagantly 'irregular', as though a rich mental life depended on an unsightly superabundance of phrenological organs.

As revealing as are Brontë's attractions to phrenology and physiognomy, equally revealing are her hesitations. She never puts the doctrines to systematic use; she remains at a cautious distance; and, as I have indicated, she sometimes assumes a distinctly ironic attitude. When Blanche Ingram wants to discourage questions, she sulkily invokes phrenological jargon: 'Really your organs of wonder and credulity are easily excited' (ch. 18); and Blanche's mother dismisses Jane by remarking, 'I am a judge of physiognomy, and in hers I see all the faults of her class' (ch. 17), a comment that not only disqualifies Mrs Ingram from serious consideration, but casts doubt on physiognomic science. Brontë's ambivalence should not surprise us. The same sensibility that turns 'passion' and 'reason' from concepts into figures naturally hesitates to adopt any scheme with pretensions to a scientific understanding of character. Perhaps the best way to regard Brontë's use of psychological abstractions is to see it as manifesting two contrasting attitudes: on the one hand, the desire to establish fixed markers within the fluidity that is human psychological experience, and, on the other, the recognition of the limits to fixity. To do her justice, we must follow Brontë to her abstractions and then follow her still, when she moves past them.

So far we have relied on Jane's overt attempts to explain behaviour, her direct assessments of feelings, states, and dispositions. However, although these occur at pivotal moments, and although they offer us a preliminary sense of Brontë's vision of personality, we ought not to confuse a preliminary sense with a final understanding. *Jane Eyre* is not a discursive fiction. We do not value it for its disquisitions on the sources and ends of human behaviour, its variations on Enlightenment psychology, or its use of contemporary pseudo-sciences. We value it, I think, for its powerful implicit presentation of certain emotional tensions and resolutions – a complex structure that Jane's own explanations scarcely begin to exhaust.

Before turning away from phrenology and physiognomy, let me suggest one further reason why they held such fascination for Brontë. One of the persistent dilemmas for any theory of mind has been the relation between the mental qualities we want to understand, and the human body that might lead us to understanding. It is one thing to study benevolence; it is quite another to find it in the benevolent body. Physiognomy, and especially phrenology, were particularly aggressive in giving precise physical expression to the most immaterial of mental traits. For Gall and his followers, pride, envy and veneration were not simply dispositions of the soul, or habits of behaviour; they were specific organs of the brain which could be duly located. Phrenology and physiognomy conceive of the mind in terms of size and place; they are spatial theories of character; that is our clue.

Few novels are as spatially *articulate* as *Jane Eyre*. Its houses, of which there are many, abound with gardens, galleries, bedrooms, dining rooms, schoolrooms, libraries, attics, halls, and closets. These spaces are in continual upheaval. Characters seem ceaselessly engaged in the opening and closing of windows and doors, the ascending and descending of staircases, the crossing of thresholds. Houses are full then suddenly deserted; they are devotedly cleaned or savagely burnt to the ground. Moreover, these houses preoccupy their inhabitants. Rochester comes to see Thornfield Hall as 'a great plague-house'; Jane sees Moor House as 'a charm both potent and permanent'. Indeed, as Martin has shown, the succession of buildings furnishes the broad organisation of the plot; Jane's five principal residences mark the five large movements in her career.[7] And within houses, individual rooms come to have distinct personalities. At Thornfield Hall, the schoolroom becomes a 'sanctum', while at Gateshead whole areas of the house have become menacing; 'Restricted so long to the nursery,' reflects Jane, 'the breakfast, dining, and drawing-rooms were become for me awful regions, on which it dismayed me to intrude':

> I now stood in the empty hall; before me was the breakfast-room door, and I stopped, intimidated and trembling. What a miserable little poltroon had fear, engendered of unjust punishment, made of me in those days! I feared to return to the nursery, I feared to go forward to the parlour; ten minutes I stood in agitated hesitation:

the vehement ringing of the breakfast-room bell decided me; I *must* enter.

(ch. 4)

Later, when guests have come to Thornfield, Jane engages in architectural contortions in order to remain the unobtrusive governess:

> And issuing from my asylum with precaution, I sought a backstairs which conducted directly to the kitchen. All in that region was fire and commotion. ... Threading this chaos, I at last reached the larder; there I took possession of a cold chicken, a roll of bread, some tarts, a plate or two and a knife and fork: with this booty I made a hasty retreat. I had regained the gallery, and was just shutting the back-door behind me, when an accelerated hum warned me that the ladies were about to issue from their chambers. I could not proceed to the school-room without passing some of their doors, and running the risk of being surprised with my cargo of victuallage; so I stood still at this end, which, being windowless, was dark.

(ch. 17)

More description is lavished on rooms than on the people who inhabit them. Doubtless, Brontë inherits this devotion to spatial intricacy from her gothic predecessors, but, as I hope to show, her purposes are her own.[8] In her hands the elaborate spatial design is not so much a way to arouse sensation as to organise it.

Containers within containers – let us begin with this recurrent and compelling image. Houses often exist less as domiciles than as outer shells; rooms and passages serve as inner and intricate spaces; within rooms there are pieces of furniture, drawers, and caskets, which mark still more interior rings. *Within* Gateshead Hall, *within* the red-room, *within* a coffin, Mr Reed once lay, and that, says Jane, accounted for the 'spell' of the room, and 'guarded it from frequent intrusion'. During a crisis at Thornfield, when Mason lies bleeding after Bertha's attack, Rochester sends Jane to his room. Inside the room, he tells her, she will find a toilet-table; in its middle drawer lies a glass and a phial; the phial contains a 'crimson liquid', which Mason is to drink. *Villette* includes an even more elaborate example. When Lucy receives the much hoped-for letter from Graham Bretton, her immediate desire is to place it out of sight:

> I procured the key of the great dormitory which was kept locked by day. I went to my bureau; with a sort of haste and trembling lest Madame should creep up-stairs and spy me, I opened a drawer, un-locked a box, and took out a case, and – having feasted my eyes with

one more look, and approached the seal, with a mixture of awe and shame and delight, to my lips – I folded the untasted treasure, yet all fair and inviolate, in silver paper, committed it to the case, shut up box and drawer, reclosed, relocked the dormitory, and returned to class.

(ch. 21)

Despite these precautions, both Madame Beck and Paul Emanuel manage to read the 'triply-enclosed' letters and, accordingly, Lucy takes still more extreme steps. She buys a bottle in which she places the letters and asks the merchant 'to stopper, seal, and make it air-tight' (ch. 26). Then, in a garden, she finds a hollow beneath some ivy, and puts the sealed bottle in the hollow: 'I fetched thence a slate and some mortar, put the slate on the hollow, secured it with cement, covered the whole with black mould, and, finally, replaced the ivy' (ch. 26). In all of these instances, the effect is of a system of Chinese boxes at whose innermost point lies a source of dangerous emotive energy.[9] The danger is greatest when that source is a living, desiring, rebellious human being. In *Jane Eyre* one can reach Bertha only by passing along a 'dark, low corridor' into a 'tapestried room'; behind one of the tapestries stands a second door leading to an 'inner apartment', a room 'without a window', where Bertha moans and shrieks and laughs.

The attempt to represent personality in literature almost invariably takes the form of an effort to visualise the psyche and its contents. Quite often, this involves the personification of emotions, impulses or faculties – thus Dickens personifies abstract desire in Jingle, and Brontë embodies lawless passion in Bertha. But a more interesting, and more difficult, imaginative task is the endeavour to place psychological attributes in relation to one another and in this way portray the dynamics of the inner life: its collisions, compromises, and resolutions. In Dickens and Brontë, this activity is most often implicit and no doubt frequently unconscious, an instinctive response to lively perceptions of psychological diversity. One manifestation, which we have already begun to approach through Dickens, is the elaborate configuration of characters whose alliances and conflicts reflect an attempt to find harmony among rival emotional imperatives. Brontë employs a variant on this method which will soon become pertinent, but what concerns us at the moment is another figure of the mind, an explicitly spatial figure, which expresses the divisions of mental life by attempting to position them relative to one another. The preoccupation with space in the novel gives Brontë a way to confront emotional urgencies by *displaying* them, locating them in terms of high or low, near or far, inner or outer.

Any number of critics (and, no doubt, any number of common readers) have noticed the parallels between Bertha's imprisonment and Jane's confinement in the red-room. In both cases, as Gilbert and Gubar point out, enclosure is the penalty for passion; rooms are asked to contain desires, notably female desires. When Jane thinks of the Reed sisters, Eliza and Georgiana, she pictures 'one the cynosure of a ball-room, the other the inmate of a convent cell' (ch. 22). Jane herself, like Bertha, refuses to accept such imprison-ment, and one of the leading dramatic tensions in the novel assumes the spatial form of a struggle between container and contained, between an enclosure (house, room, body) and an emotional quick-ening at its central core. Gilbert and Gubar go so far as to make the release from confinement the novel's central principle, and in so doing, they identify Jane's aspirations with Bertha's. Although they are right to stress the importance of confinement, they simplify just where the novel complicates.[10]

Confinement is a grave peril in *Jane Eyre*, but no more grave than its spatial antithesis: exposure. When Jane learns of Rochester's marriage, she flees Thornfield Hall, but if we expect this flight to be a saving corrective to her confinement, we, like Jane, are quickly disappointed. Jane, out of doors, is no closer to stability than Jane confined. She wanders for several days, penniless, hungry, and in-creasingly wretched, and though she had first looked to nature for solace, her hope gives way to 'this feeling of hunger, faintness, chill, and this sense of desolation – this total prostration of hope' (ch. 28). She comes to the brink of death, until she finds another house, a new confinement. A similar reversal had occurred early in the work. Enclosed through the winter in the gloom of Lowood school, Jane welcomes 'the gentler breathings' of spring: 'Lowood shook loose its tresses; it became all green, all flowery; its great elm, ash, and oak skeletons were restored to majestic life' (ch. 9). Here, for the first time in the novel, the natural world appears in attrac-tive form, but after a long passage of lavish description, Jane re-verses the expected conclusion:

> That forest-dell, where Lowood lay, was the cradle of fog and fog-bred pestilence; which, quickening with the quickening spring, crept into the Orphan Asylum, breathed typhus through its crowded

school-room and dormitory, and, ere May arrived, transformed the seminary into an hospital.

(ch. 9)

But in *Jane Eyre* even more dreaded than the exposure to careless nature is an exposure to human scrutiny. Although Jane obsessively seeks to 'elude observation', she is continually made to endure the stares of others, which strike her as almost physical assaults. 'Teachers', orders Brocklehurst, 'you must watch her: keep your eyes on her movements, weigh well her words, scrutinise her actions.' To enforce the point he places Jane on a stool and then announces to the assembled class that 'this girl is – a liar!' while Jane stands unprotected against the shocked stares: 'There was I, then, mounted aloft: I, who had said I could not bear the shame of standing on my natural feet in the middle of the room, was now *exposed to general view* on a pedestal of infamy' (ch. 7, my emphasis).

We began by considering a crisis of enclosure, the self separated from the world through a succession of barriers, its range of expression greatly narrowed, its passions severely constrained. But it should now be plain that escape from confinement offers no solution, only a new problem. The absence of barriers leads to a contrary, but no less pressing, crisis: the self stripped of any protective carapace, defenceless before nature and human society. The self exposed thus becomes as vulnerable as the self confined. Indeed, these are the extremes that Jane must avoid, extremes moreover that, though opposed, are closely bound. When Jane recognises that she is drifting toward love of Rochester, she issues herself a stern upbraiding:

> it is madness in all women to let a secret love kindle within them, which, if unreturned and unknown, must devour the life that feeds it; and, if discovered and responded to, must lead, *ignis-fatuus*-like, into miry wilds whence there is no extrication.

(ch. 16)

No statement of the difficulty could be more evocative. Jane warns herself of the agony of love suppressed and the helplessness of love acknowledged – the one depicted as a devouring inner flame, the other as a wilderness.

Part of our ongoing project is to investigate how these Victorian fictions organise passions, sensations, emotions, and dispositions; how such expressive aspects of narrative art constitute a structured whole; not so much how these authors theorise about the self as how they *imagine* it, and how they imagine its parts – with the result that involuntary patterns of imagery become as important as any explicit speculations. Most recently, I have been trying to show how Brontë employs spatial arrangement, in particular the threats of confinement and exposure, as a dominant method for such imaginative organisation. The relations of self and other, love and restraint, wish and fear appear in terms of spatial configuration, and in this regard, Brontë's use of the word 'region' is illuminating. Not surprisingly, it appears first in connection with houses. At Gateshead Hall, the breakfast, dining, and drawing-rooms are 'awful regions' and at Thornfield Jane contrasts the gloom of the third story, 'so still a region', to the 'light and cheerful region below'. The word retains its more familiar use as a general geographic designation – 'I felt we were in a different region to Lowood' (ch. 11) – but it also extends beyond earthly geography. When Helen Burns first speaks of Heaven, Jane wonders to herself 'Where is that region? Does it exist?' (ch. 9) Finally, the word is put to psychological purposes. When Jane becomes apprehensive before the festivities at Thornfield, she finds herself 'thrown back on the region of doubts and portents, and dark conjectures' (ch. 17). This casual movement of the concept among such distinct realms points to the common imaginative structure that underlies them in Brontë's work. Heaven, earth, houses, and minds, all are visualised in terms of regions, and this spatial analogy lets Brontë establish provocative connections among them.

Minds, for instance, assume the aspect of houses. When Rochester views Jane's pictures, he asks where she found her models:

> 'Out of my head.'
> 'That head I see now on your shoulders?'
> 'Yes, sir.'
> 'Has it other furniture of the same kind within?'
>
> (ch. 13)

At Lowood Jane finds that 'better regulated feelings had become the inmates of my mind' (ch. 10), while at Thornfield, 'all sorts of fancies bright and dark tenanted my mind' (ch. 12). Jane startles St John Rivers with her frankness, but explains her attitude thus:

> He had not imagined that a woman would dare to speak so to a man. For me, I felt at home in this sort of discourse. I could never

rest in communication with strong, discreet, and refined minds, whether male or female, till I had passed the outworks of conventional reserve, and crossed the threshold of confidence, and won a place by their heart's very hearthstone.

(ch. 32)

In the well-known concluding sentences of chapter 24 Jane chides herself for worldliness:

My future husband was becoming to me my whole world; and more than the world: almost my hope of heaven. He stood between me and every thought of religion, as an eclipse intervenes between man and the broad sun. I could not, in those days, see God for his creature: of whom I had made an idol.

Thus the awakening of the religious sense, so marked in the last half of the novel, appears as a problem of sight lines: Rochester between Jane and God. Again, the spatial image is striking. But even more striking is the particular choice of simile. Rochester blocks religion the way an eclipse blocks the sun, as though earth and spirit, Rochester and God, belong to the same order of experience, as though they move in the same space and according to similar laws.

At issue is a forceful conjunction of realms. Psychic life, spiritual life, domestic life, all appear as matters of arrangement, of architecture, of spatial relation. Jane suggests that we feel God's presence most strongly when we see his works 'spread before us', but this applies to all of existence in *Jane Eyre*; things possess significance in so far as they are spread before us, displayed, arrayed. Moreover, by passing so rapidly from 'region' to 'region', by employing the same spatial figures in each, Brontë creates the impression of a common space in which mind, body, and spirit all find a place – God just behind Rochester's shoulder, doubts on the third story. Crossing thresholds, descending stairs, opening windows, become therefore extraordinarily resonant acts; one never knows when the threshold will turn out to be social, the stair psychological, the window spiritual.

Still, this ought not to tempt us toward any rigorous symbology; we cannot read Brontë as we might a more programmatic author. If we ask, for instance, what part of the self the kitchen represents, or what stage in spiritual progress the attic marks, then we invite an awkwardly distended paraphrase. 'What my sensations were', Jane writes, 'no language can describe' (ch. 7). No language, one is tempted to reply, only a pattern of images, more finely nuanced than the psychological concepts that Brontë inherits. Passion and reason, feeling and judgement, and the forty organs of the phrenologists, provide only crude distinctions when set against the intricate rhythm of walls and windows, thresholds and compartments, eclipsed suns and unclouded skies. The novel's charged system of spatial relations serves as more than an adornment: it is the imaginative condition of the novel.

From Karen Chase, *Eros and Psyche: The Representation of Personality in Charlotte Brontë, Charles Dickens and George Eliot* (New York and London, 1984), pp. 52–65.

NOTES

[In the book from which this extract is taken Karen Chase explores 'the imaginative endeavour to find a structure for the emotions and a figure for the mind' in the work of three major Victorian novelists – Charlotte Brontë, Charles Dickens, and George Eliot. The Victorian period, she argues, was one in which 'fiction had as strong a claim as psychology to find order in the life of the passions', and the fictional representation of personality made its own powerful contribution to an increasingly sophisticated conception of the inner life. Her concern is not, centrally, with those questions of plot and character which dominate much novel criticism, but with what she calls 'the expressive organisation' of the novels she discusses: the ways in which they draw upon contemporary scientific and pseudo-scientific discourses in order to organise and articulate emotional experience. 'To extend the range of feeling, to give form to the emotions, to express the peculiar tesselations of affective experience – these activities were', she suggests, 'as urgent in Victorian fiction as the striving for a more faithful rendering of social life.' The extract reprinted here is preceded, in *Eros and Psyche*, by a discussion of how *Jane Eyre* differs from Brontë's youthful, 'Angrian' writings, in its newly central emphasis on feminine experience, its greater 'narrative detachment', its new interest in 'psychological depth'; and it is followed by a second chapter on *Jane Eyre*, which develops and extends the argument of this, by exploring the ways in which the essentially spatial sense of inner experience which Charlotte Brontë took from contemporary physiognomy and phrenology informs the whole novel, and 'provides the form that lets complexity appear'. Ed.]

1.   Elizabeth Gaskell, *The Life of Charlotte Bronte* (London, 1874), p. 236.

2. For reference to Brontë's use of abstract personifications and, more generally, the influence of eighteenth-century writers on her work, see Inga-Stina Ewbank, *Their Proper Sphere: A Study of the Brontë Sisters as Early Victorian Female Novelists* (Cambridge, MA, 1966), pp. 179–80, 184–90; Barbara Hardy, *The Appropriate Form* (Evanston, IL, 1971), pp. 62–72; Jane Millgate, 'Jane Eyre's Progress', *English Studies*, 50 (1969), 21–9; Margot Peters, *Charlotte Brontë: Style in the Novel* (Madison, WI, 1973), pp. 41, 98–100, 122–3; Barry Qualls, *The Secular Pilgrims of Victorian Fiction: The Novel as Book of Life* (Cambridge, 1982), pp. 41–69.

3. See Jeanne Fahenstock, 'The Heroine of Irregular Features: Physiognomy and Conventions of Heroine Description', *Victorian Studies*, 24 (1981), 325–50; Ian Jack, 'Physiognomy, Phrenology and Characterisation in the Novels of Charlotte Brontë', *Brontë Society Transactions*, 15 (1970), 377–91; W. M. Senseman, 'Charlotte Brontë's Use of Physiognomy and Phrenology', *Brontë Society Transactions*, 12 (1954), 286–9; Graeme Tytler, *Physiognomy in the European Novel: Faces and Fortunes* (Princeton, NJ, 1982), pp. 191–2, 236–7, 265, 268–9, 275–6.

4. George Combe, *A System of Phrenology* (3rd edn, Boston, 1835), p. 88.

5. David de Giustino, 'Phrenology in Britain, 1815–1855: a Study of George Combe and His Circle', Dissertation, University of Wisconson, 1969, Ann Arbor University Microfilm 32. Gall had identified 27 organs of the mind, Spurzheim and other phrenologists in Britain discovered between 33 and 37 organs. The rapid changes in number and location of the faculties of mind were fuel for critics of phrenology. See David de Giustino, *Conquest of Mind: Phrenology and Victorian Social Thought* (London, 1972), pp. 16, 21.

6. See de Giustino, 'Phrenology in Britain', Appendix A, p. 324.

7. Robert Martin, *The Accents of Persuasion: Charlotte Brontë's Novels* (London, 1966), pp. 60–1.

8. On this point see Robert Heilmann, 'Charlotte Brontë's New Gothic' in Robert C. Rathburn and Martin Steinmann, Jr (eds), *From Jane Austen to Joseph Conrad* (Minneapolis, 1958), pp. 118–32.

9. See Peters's discussion of 'the motif of the buried treasure' in *Villette*, in *Charlotte Brontë: Style in the Novel*, p. 107.

10. Sandra M. Gilbert and Susan Gubar, *The Madwoman in the Attic: the Woman Writer and the Nineteenth-Century Literary Imagination* (New Haven, CT, 1979), pp. 339–71.

3

Charlotte Brontë: Feminine Heroine

ELAINE SHOWALTER

In *Jane Eyre*, Brontë attempts to depict a complete female identity, and she expresses her heroine's consciousness through an extraordinary range of narrative devices. Psychological development and the dramas of the inner life are represented in dreams, hallucinations, visions, surrealistic paintings, and masquerades; the sexual experiences of the female body are expressed spatially through elaborate and rhythmically recurring images of rooms and houses. Jane's growth is further structured through a pattern of literary, biblical, and mythological allusion. Brontë's most profound innovation, however, is the division of the Victorian female psyche into its extreme components of mind and body, which she externalises as two characters, Helen Burns and Bertha Mason. Both Helen and Bertha function at realistic levels in the narrative and present implied and explicit connections to Victorian sexual ideology, but they also operate in an archetypal dimension of the story. Brontë gives us not one but three faces of Jane, and she resolves her heroine's psychic dilemma by literally and metaphorically destroying the two polar personalities to make way for the full strength and development of the central consciousness, for the integration of the spirit and the body. Thus *Jane Eyre* anticipates and indeed formulates the deadly combat between the Angel in the House and the devil in the flesh that is evident in the fiction of Virginia Woolf, Doris Lessing, Muriel Spark, and other twentieth-century British women novelists.

The novel opens at Gateshead, with Jane's transition from the passivity and genderlessness of childhood into a turbulent puberty. This emotional menarche is clearly suggested, despite the fact that Jane is only ten years old, by the accumulation of incident and detail on the psychic level. 'I can never get away from Gateshead till I am a woman,' she tells Mr Lloyd;[1] and, having passed through the gate, she has evidently entered upon womanhood by the end of chapter 4. Her adolescence is marked first by her sudden and unprecedented revolt against the Reeds, a self-assertiveness that incurs severe punishment and ostracism, but also wins her freedom from the family. It is also coloured by her pervasive awareness of the 'animal' aspects of her being – her body, with its unfeminine needs and appetites, and her passions, especially rage. From the undifferentiated awareness of her 'physical inferiority' to the Reed children, Jane becomes minutely conscious both of the 'disgusting and ugly'[2] physical sadism of John Reed, and of her own warm blood and glittering eyes. The famous scene of violence with which the novel begins, John Reed's assault on Jane and her passionate counterattack, associates the moment of rebellion and autonomy with bloodletting and incarceration in the densely symbolic red-room.

It is thus as if the mysterious crime for which the Reeds were punishing Jane were the crime of growing up. The red-room to which Jane is sentenced by Mrs Reed for her display of anger and passion is a paradigm of female inner space:

> The red-room was a spare chamber, very seldom slept in. ... A bed supported on massive pillars of mahogany hung with curtains of deep red damask, stood out like a tabernacle in the centre, the two large windows, with their blinds almost drawn down, were half shrouded in festoons and falls of similar drapery; the carpet was red; the table at the foot of the bed was covered with a crimson cloth. ... This room was chill, because it seldom had a fire; it was silent, because remote from the nursery and kitchens; solemn, because it was known to be so seldom entered. The housemaid alone came here on Saturdays, to wipe from the mirrors and the furniture a week's quiet dust; and Mrs Reed herself, at far intervals, visited it to review the contents of a certain secret drawer in the wardrobe, where were stored divers parchments, her jewel-casket, and a miniature of her deceased husband.[3]

With its deadly and bloody connotations, its Freudian wealth of secret compartments, wardrobes, drawers, and jewel chest, the red-room has strong associations with the adult female body; Mrs Reed, of course, is a widow in her prime. Jane's ritual imprisonment here, and the subsequent episodes of ostracism at Gateshead, where she is forbidden to eat, play, or socialise with other members of the family, is an adolescent rite of passage that has curious anthropological affinities to the menarchal ceremonies of Eskimo or South Sea Island tribes. The passage into womanhood stresses the lethal and fleshly aspects of adult female sexuality. The 'mad cat', the 'bad animal' (as John Reed calls Jane),[4] who is shut up and punished will reappear later in the novel as the totally animalistic, maddened, and brutalised Bertha Mason; *her* secret chamber is simply another red-room at the top of another house.

The obsession with the 'animal' appetites and manifestations of the body, and the extreme revulsion from female sexuality are also articulated through one of the submerged literary allusions in the text to *Gulliver's Travels*. This book has been one of Jane's favourites, but after her experience in the red-room it becomes an ominous and portentous fable; Gulliver seems no longer a canny adventurer, but 'a most desolate wanderer in most dread and dangerous regions',[5] a pilgrim in the adult world like herself. Like Gulliver, Jane moves from the nursery world of Lilliput to an encounter with the threatening and Brobdingnagian Reverend Brocklehurst ('What a face he had, now that it was almost on a level with mine! what a great nose! and what a mouth! and what large, prominent teeth!'),[6] and an increasing Calvinist awareness of the 'vile body' that leads to the climactic encounter with Bertha, the female Yahoo in her foul den.

A strain of intense female sexual fantasy and eroticism runs through the first four chapters of the novel and contributes to their extraordinary and thrilling immediacy. The scene in the red-room unmistakably echoes the flagellation ceremonies of Victorian pornography. As in whipping scenes in *The Pearl* and other underground Victorian erotica, the *mise-en-scène* is a remote chamber with a voluptuous decor, and the struggling victim is carried by female servants. Jane is threatened with a bondage made more titillating because the bonds are to be a maid's garters: '"If you don't sit still, you must be tied down," said Bessie. "Miss Abbot, lend me your garters; she would break mine directly." Miss Abbot turned to divest a stout leg of the necessary ligature. This preparation for bonds, and the additional ignomiy it inferred, took a little of the excitement out of me.' This threatened chastisement of the flesh, although not actually carried out in the red-room scene, is a motif that links Jane with Helen Burns, who submissively accepts a flogging at Lowood School from a teacher named Miss Scatcherd. Jane herself, we learn later, has been flogged on the 'neck' in Mrs Reed's bedroom.[7]

Whipping girls to subdue the unruly flesh and the rebellious spirit was a routine punishment for the Victorians, as well as a potent sexual fantasy; as late as the 1870s the *Englishwoman's Domestic Magazine* conducted an enthusiastic correspondence column on the correct way to carry out the procedure. It is interesting here to note that sexual discipline is administered to women by other women, as agents for men. Bessie (Jane's favourite servant) and Miss Abbot, acting on behalf of Mrs Reed, who in turn is avenging her son, lock Jane up; at Lowood the kindly Miss Temple starves the girls because 'she has to answer to Mr Brocklehurst for all she does';[8] at Thornfield Grace Poole is hired by Rochester as Bertha's jailor. Thus the feminine heroine grows up in a world without female solidarity, where women in fact police each other on behalf of patriarchal tyranny. There is sporadic sisterhood and kindness between the women in this world, and Jane finds it ultimately at Marsh End with Diana and Mary Rivers; but on the whole these women are helpless to aid each other, even if they want to.

Lowood School, where Jane is sent by her aunt, is the penitentiary for which the red-room was the tribunal. Like Lowick, Casaubon's home in *Middlemarch*, Lowood represents sexual diminishment and repression. In this pseudo-convent, Jane undergoes a prolonged sensual discipline. Here the girls are systematically 'starved' (in Yorkshire dialect the word means 'frozen' as well as 'hungry'), and deprived of all sensory gratification. Clad in stiff brown dresses, 'which gave an air of oddity even to the prettiest', and shorn of their hair, the last sign of their femininity, the girls of Lowood are instructed in the chastity they will need for their future lives as poor teachers and governesses. Brocklehurst proclaims that his mission 'is to mortify in these girls the lusts of the flesh'.[9]

As an institution, Lowood disciplines its inmates by attempting to destroy their individuality at the same time that it punishes and starves their sexuality. Distinctions between the little girls and the 'great girls', the pre-adolescents and the young women, are obliterated by the uniform all are forced to wear. The purpose of Brocklehurst in starving the 'vile bodies' is to create the intensely spiritualised creature the Victorians idealised as the Angel in the

House. Virtually sexless, this creature, as Alexander Welsh provocatively suggests in *The City of Dickens*, is in fact the Angel of Death, who has mystical powers of intercession in the supernatural order, and whose separation from the body is the projection of the Victorian terror of the physical reminders of birth and mortality.[10] The Angel of Lowood is Helen Burns, the perfect victim and the representation of the feminine spirit in its most disembodied form. Helen is a tribute to the Lowood system: pious, intellectual, indifferent to her material surroundings, resigned to the abuse of her body, and, inevitably, consumptive. She is one extreme aspect of Jane's personality, for Jane too is tempted by the world of the spirit and the intellect, and has a strong streak of masochism. Helen is the woman who would make a perfect bride for St John Rivers; she is his female counterpart. But although Helen, 'with the aspect of an angel', inspires Jane to transcend the body and its passions, Jane, rebellious on her 'pedestal of infamy' in the classroom, resists the force of spiritual institutionalisation, as she will later resist the physical institutionalisation of marriage with Rochester.[11] Ultimately, it is Helen's death that provides the climax of the Lowood experience. She dies in Jane's arms, and Jane achieves a kind of victory: the harsh regime of Lowood is modified, its torments palliated. Like Bertha Mason, Helen is sacrificed to make way for Jane's fuller freedom.

The 'animal' aspects of womanhood, which have been severely repressed during Jane's sojourn at Lowood, reassert themselves when, at eighteen, she goes as governess to Thornfield Hall. Bertha Mason, who is confined to, and who *is*, the 'third story' of Thornfield, is the incarnation of the flesh, of female sexuality in its most irredeemably bestial and terrifying form. Brontë's treatment of the myth of the Mad Wife is brilliantly comprehensive and reverberative, and rich with historical, medical, and sociological implications, as well as with psychological force.

Bertha's origins in folk history and literature are interesting in themselves. There are numerous literary precedents in the Gothic novel, particularly Mrs Radcliffe's *Sicilian Romance*, for mysterious captives; the situation, in fact, is repeated to the point of appearing archetypal. Other explanations for Bertha depend upon real case histories that Brontë had encountered. Mrs Gaskell mentions one in her *Life of Charlotte Brontë*; Q. D. Leavis refers to another, a Yorkshire legend about North Lees Hall Farm, where a mad wife had allegedly been incarcerated. Indeed, there were several Yorkshire houses with legends of imprisoned madwomen: Wycollar Hall, near Colne, and Norton Conyers, which had a chamber called 'the madwoman's room'.[12] The legends themselves express a cultural attitude toward female passion as a potentially dangerous force that must be punished and confined. In the novel, Bertha is described as 'the foul German spectre – the vampyre', 'a demon', 'a hag', 'an Indian Messalina', and 'a witch'. Each of these is a traditional figure of female deviance with its own history in folklore. The vampire, who sucked men's blood (as Bertha does when she stabs her brother), and the witch, who visited men by night and rode them to exhaustion, were the products of elemental fears of women. H. R. Hays suggests that in England the 'basic charge against the witch as a night demon and seducer springs clearly from the experiences of a repressed and celibate male clergy', that is, from erotic dreams accompanied by nocturnal emissions.[13]

Brontë herself, alluding to the latest developments in Victorian psychiatric theory, attributed Bertha's behaviour to 'moral madness'.[14] Opposed to the eighteenth-century belief that insanity meant deranged reason, the concept of 'moral insanity', introduced by James Cowles Pritchard in 1835, held madness to be 'a morbid perversion of the natural feelings, affections, inclinations, temper, habits, moral dispositions, and natural impulses, without any remarkable disorder or defect of the intellect, or knowing and reasoning faculties, and particularly without any insane illusion or hallucination.'[15] Women were thought to be more susceptible than men to such disorders and could even inherit them. Sexual appetite was considered one of the chief symptoms of moral insanity in women; it was subject to severe sanctions and was regarded as abnormal or pathological. Dr William Acton, author of the standard textbook on *The Functions and Disorders of the Reproductive Organs* (1857) admitted that he had occasionally seen cases in the divorce courts of 'women who have sexual desires so strong that they surpass those of men'. Acton also acknowledged 'the existence of sexual excitement terminating even in nymphomania, a form of insanity which those accustomed to visit lunatic asylums must be fully conversant with; but, with these sad exceptions, there can be no doubt that sexual feeling in the female is in the majority of cases in abeyance.'[16]

The periodicity of Bertha's attacks suggests a connection to the menstrual cycle, which many Victorian physicians understood as a system for the control of female sexuality. Bertha has 'lucid intervals of days – sometimes weeks', and her attack on Jane comes when the moon is 'blood-red and half-overcast'.[17] 'In God's infinite wisdom', a London physician wrote in 1844, 'might not this monthly discharge be ordained for the purpose of controlling woman's violent sexual passions ... by unloading the uterine vessels ... so as to prevent the promiscuous intercourse which would prove destructive to the purest ... interests of civil life?'[18] As Carroll Smith-Rosenberg points out, the image of the 'maniacal and destructive woman' closely parallels that of the sexually powerful woman: 'Menstruation, nineteenth century physicians worried, could drive some women temporarily insane; menstruating women might go berserk, destroying furniture, attacking family and strangers alike. ... Those "unfortunate women" subject to such excessive menstrual influence,' one doctor suggested, 'should for their own good and that of society be incarcerated for the length of their menstrual years.'[19]

In precise contrast to the angelic Helen, Bertha is big, as big as Rochester, corpulent, florid, and violent. When Jane sees her in the chamber on the third story, she is almost subhuman:

> In the deep shade, at the farther end of the room, a figure ran backwards and forwards. What it was, whether beast or human being, one could not, at first sight tell; it grovelled, seemingly on all fours; it snatched and growled like some strange wild animal; but it was covered with clothing, and a quantity of dark, grizzled hair, wild as a mane, hid its head and face.[20]

Like Gulliver observing the Yahoos, Jane is pushed almost to the brink of breakdown by her recognition of aspects of herself in this 'clothed hyena'. Much of Bertha's dehumanisation, Rochester's account makes clear, is the result of her confinement, not its cause. After ten years of imprisonment, Bertha has become a caged beast. Given the lunacy laws in England, incidentally, Rochester has kept the dowry for which he married her, but cannot file for divorce even in the ecclesiastical courts. Rochester's complicity in the destruction of his wife's spirit is indicated in Jane's recognition of the third story's resemblance to a corridor in 'Bluebeard's castle', in Rochester's accounts of his sexual exploitation of Bertha, Céline, Giacinta, and Clara, and in Jane's uneasy awareness that his smile 'was such as a sultan might bestow on a slave'.[21]

Madness is explicitly associated with female sexual passion, with the body, with the fiery emotions Jane admits to feeling for

Rochester. In trying to persuade her to become his mistress, Rochester argues that Jane is a special case: 'If you were mad', he asks, 'do you think I should hate you?' 'I do indeed, sir', Jane replies; and she is surely correct.[22] Thus it becomes inevitable that Bertha's death, the purging of the lusts of the flesh, must precede any successful union between Rochester and Jane. When they finally marry, they have become equals, not only because Rochester, in losing his hand and his sight, has learned how it feels to be helpless and how to accept help, but also because Jane, in destroying the dark passion of her own psyche, has become truly her 'own mistress'.[23]

From Elaine Showalter, *A Literature of Their Own: British Women Novelists from Brontë to Lessing* (London, 1978), pp. 112–22.

NOTES

[In the ground-breaking study from which this essay comes, Elaine Showalter offers an account of 'the female literary tradition in the English novel from the generation of the Brontës to the present day' (p. 11). Building on the work of such earlier feminist literary historians as Patricia Meyer Spacks (*The Female Imagination* [New York, 1975]) and Ellen Moers (*Literary Women* [London, 1977]), she seeks to demonstrate 'the ways in which the self-awareness of the woman writer has translated itself into a literary form in a specific place and time-span, how this self-awareness has changed and developed, and where it might lead' (p. 12). Showalter's title is taken from *The Subjection of Women* (1869), in which John Stuart Mill suggests that 'if women lived in a different country from men, and had never read any of their writings, they would have a literature of their own'. Her view is that women have indeed, in a sense, lived in a different country from men – a distinctive 'subculture within the framework of a larger society', and that consequently they *have* developed a literary tradition 'of their own'. In the chapter from which this extract comes, she argues that Brontë's work, along with that of George Eliot, belongs to the first, 'feminine', phase of this tradition: that in which women writers sought to create fictional heroines 'who could combine strength and intelligence with feminine tenderness, tact, and domestic expertise' (p. 100). If George Eliot's Maggie Tulliver in *The Mill on the Floss* is, in this period, 'the heroine of renunciation', Jane Eyre, she suggests, is 'the heroine of fulfilment': one who achieves 'as full and healthy a womanhood' as the feminine novelist could conceive. Ed.]

1. Ch. 3, p. 56. Page references are to the Penguin edition, edited by Queenie Leavis (Harmonsdworth, 1966).

2. Ch. 1, p. 42.

3. Ch. 2, p. 45.

4. Ch. 1, p. 41; ch. 2, p. 44.

5. Ch. 3, p. 53.

6. Ch. 4, p. 64.

7. Ch. 2, p. 44. For a discussion of Victorian flagellation literature see Steven Marcus, 'A Child is Being Beaten', in *The Other Victorians* (New York, 1966). Marcus is dealing with male sexual fantasies, however. In their edition of *Jane Eyre*, Jane Jack and Margaret Smith note that the word 'neck' 'used sometimes to be used with a wider significance than now, for a woman's breast or (as here) shoulders. There is an element of the Victorian euphemism about it' (*Jane Eyre* [Oxford, 1969], p. 586, n. 61). For a recent discussion of Victorian corporal punishment of girls, see Mary S. Hartman, 'Child-Abuse and Self-Abuse: Two Victorian Cases', *History of Childhood Quarterly* (Fall 1974), 240–1.

8. Ch. 5, p. 82.

9. Ch. 5, p. 79; ch. 7, p. 96.

10. Alexander Welsh, *The City of Dickens* (London, 1971), pp. 155–60, 222–5. Welsh suggests that Jane herself has Angelic qualities, but the novel emphasises her unwillingness to accept the role; when Brocklehurst tells her about the child who emulates the angels by learning psalms, Jane replies, 'Psalms are not interesting' (ch. 4, p. 65). As a young woman, she tells Rochester emphatically, 'I am not an angel … and I will not be one till I die: I will be myself' (ch. 24, p. 288).

11. Ch. 7, p. 99.

12. Introduction to *Jane Eyre*, p. 9. H. F. Chorley, reviewing *Jane Eyre* in the *Athenaeum* in 1847, also knew of a possible source. See Miriam Allott (ed.), *The Brontës: The Critical Heritage* (London, 1974), p. 72.

13. H. R. Hays, *The Dangerous Sex: the Myth of Feminine Evil* (New York, 1965), p. 42.

14. Letter to W. S. Smith, 4 January 1848, in Clement Shorter, *The Brontës: Life and Letters*, I (London, 1908), p. 383.

15. Eric T. Carlson and Norman Dain, 'The Meaning of Moral Insanity', *Bulletin of the History of Medicine*, 36 (1962), 131. See also 'Moral Insanity', in Vieda Skultans, *Madness and Morals: Ideas on Insanity in the Nineteenth Century* (London, 1975), pp. 180–200.

16. Quoted in Marcus, *The Other Victorians*, p. 31.

17. Ch. 27, p. 336; ch. 25, p. 304.

18. George Robert Rowe, *On Some Most Important Disorders of Women* (London, 1844), pp. 27–8, quoted in Carroll Smith-Rosenberg, 'Puberty to Menopause: The Cycle of Femininity in Nineteenth-Century America', *Feminist Studies* 1 (1973), p. 25.

19. Edward Tilt, *The Change of Life* (New York, 1882), p. 13, quoted in Smith-Rosenberg, 'Puberty to Menopause', p. 25. See also Skultans, *Madness and Morals*, pp. 223–40.

20. Ch. 26, p. 321.

21. Ch. 11, p. 138; ch. 24, p. 297.

22. Ch. 27, pp. 328–9.

23. Ch. 37, p. 459.

4

Jane Eyre Class-ified

JINA POLITI

> There was no possibility of taking a walk that day. We had been
> wandering, indeed, in the leafless shrubbery an hour in the morning;
> but since dinner ... the cold winter wind had brought with it clouds
> so sombre, and a rain so penetrating, that further outdoor exercise
> was now out of the question.[1]

Nothing in this first paragraph with which *Jane Eyre* begins betrays
the violent rending apart of this apparently innocent 'we' into an 'I'
sequestered firmly from 'them'. Unsuspecting, the reader passes
over it (as over so many inclusive 'we's') little expecting or wishing
to be undeceived of its cohesiveness. Yet, Charlotte Brontë, in the
first chapters of the novel, sets out to shatter the comforts of the
first-person plural and with it the myth of a common humanity.
Her narrative, like the girl-child, will situate itself in opposition to
the 'warped system of things' plucking 'the mask from the face of
the Pharisee' – though the world, says the writer in her Preface,
'may not like to see these ideas dissevered, for it has been accustomed to blend them'.

This activity of ideology ceaselessly blending its contradictions
into a smooth, unfissured uniformity, the narrative purposes to
expose even at the risk of incurring the reader's hatred. For the
world, we read further in the Preface, 'may hate him who dares to
scrutinise and expose, to raise the gilding and show base metal
under it, to penetrate the sepulchre and reveal carnal relics'. Yet,
contrary to conscious intentions, the narrative together with the
girl-child will grow from revolted marginality to quiescent socialisation, reblending the contradictions which it initially exposed, thus

securing its survival through the convention of a 'happy ending'. Revolution will bend to capitulation and the text will celebrate the very ideology which it set out to expose. For it is only in the first five chapters that Jane's voice is heard. Once incarcerated in the Charity Institution the underhand process of speaking her will begin. Significantly, it is only in the first five chapters that the reader has to work with two distinctive discourses – little Jane's and the mature narrator's. As the narrative progresses, the two discourses blend into one.

The opening scene in which Jane is kept at a distance from the family tableau composed by Mrs Reed and her obnoxious children, is an instancing in fiction of the social relations which characterised Victorian society. Jane, as girl and dependent orphan, lives her position of subordination, yet this position is fraught with ambiguity. For, like the *petit-bourgeois*, Jane cannot be placed in the slot of the working class, neither can she be considered part of her aunt's class since she is propertyless and a dependant. Jane exists in marginality, and the space of this marginality is that of the unaccommodated *petit-bourgeois* – embarrassing in relation to the class above. Mrs Reed, while preserving the social distance, is intent on ideological appropriation. In pressing the point that Jane cannot be considered one of 'them' until she 'acquire a more sociable and childlike disposition, a more attractive and sprightly manner – something lighter, franker, more natural as it were' before being admitted to the privileges 'intended only for contented, happy little children' (p. 39). Mrs Reed is simply voicing the ideological representation constituting the bourgeois 'natural' for little girls. Jane must squeeze into this stereotype before she can be granted permission to join the first-person plural. Little Jane, however, knows already that Pygmalion is a social myth and that emulation is not a passport to the class above. Quite shrewdly, she will, therefore, refuse all along to emit false class signals, until the estate which she inherits automatically gives her the right to assume the stereotypes.

Rejection occurs from below as well as from above: 'No; you are less than a servant, for you do nothing for your keep', says the maid Abbot (p. 44). The social contradiction in which Jane is caught, the 'between classes', is articulated by the child when the doctor presents her with a choice. In the child's mind, the alternative to her insufferable condition in the Reed household is even more insufferable: joining the working class means deprivation of the bourgeois, material comforts and of the possibility for social advancement. These, the child is not prepared to exchange for kindness and love:

> No; I should not like to belong to poor people ... to learn to speak like them, to adopt their manners, to be uneducated, to grow up like one of the poor women I saw sometimes nursing their children or washing their clothes at the cottage doors of the village of Gateshead: no, I was not heroic enough to purchase liberty at the price of caste.
>
> (pp. 56–7)

Little Jane, then, is determined to become *a different kind of woman* from the ones she observed at the cottage doors, and it is only when she is safe from such a fate, as Mrs Rochester, that she can gloss over her class feelings with the hypocritical comment 'I was not heroic enough to purchase liberty at the price of caste'. It is not without significance that this comment is expressed through the language of exchange by the mature narrator. And yet Charlotte Brontë did intend Jane as 'heroic', and most interpretations of the novel seem to conform with her ideological stance rather than with the text's economics.[2]

However, before coming to this mundane knowledge which commits Jane to a complicity with the upper class, she has to experience the ecstasy and the horror of revolution. Revolution is precipitated in *Jane Eyre* through the realisation that the ruling class decides what limits to impose on speech. Transgressing these limits, breaking loose from the controls, means to pass from the natural to the un-natural, from sanity to insanity, from ego identity to mass anonymity, from female to male discourse: 'Unless you can speak pleasantly', orders Mrs Reed, 'remain silent' (p. 39). It is not accidental that after being ordered to silence Jane is placed by the writer in the window-seat womb and in the company of books. Reading does not open for the child the gates of dreamland, but prepares her to be born out of the window-seat and into revolution. This meta-fictional implication concerning the subversive potential of books reflects back on the text's conscious intentions: Bewick's *History of the British Birds* becomes for Jane a tract on flight and freedom; Goldsmith's *History of Rome* a manual on insurrection. 'I had', says the child, 'drawn parallels in silence' (p. 43). What about *Jane Eyre* and the parallels open to its readers? In the *Quarterly Review* for December 1848, Elizabeth Rigby hastened to voice the parallels in the hope of forestalling their effects:

There is that pervading tone of ungodly discontent which is at once the most prominent and the most subtle evil which the law and the pulpit, which all civilised society in fact has at the present day to contend with. We do not hesitate to say that the tone of mind and thought which has overthrown authority and violated every code human and divine abroad, and fostered Chartism and rebellion at home, is the same which has also written *Jane Eyre*.[3]

What Elizabeth Rigby failed to see was that that other tone of mind and thought which strengthened authority, preserved by wile and force every code human and divine and brutally suppressed chartism and rebellion at home, was also insidiously writing itself into *Jane Eyre*, effectively silencing *the other*. Jane Eyre, when she assumes the status of governess, conspires with Mr Rochester to stifle little Adèle's speech.

Significantly, the novel's beginning is constituted by the moment of revolt realised in the confrontation between the girl-child and the bully boy. The social relation of domination/subordination is signified again through the impositions applied by the master class upon speech: '"What do you want?" I asked with awkward diffidence, "Say, 'What do you want Master Reed'"', was the answer' (p. 41). This term 'Master' will undergo significant transformations in the course of the narrative. It will not disappear as the revolutionary moment promises, nor will it continue to be pronounced with the tones consequent on the suppression of the insurrection which indicate that the need for revolt and the desire for liberation are still alive in the consciousness of the speaker. The term 'Master' will be preserved and the tone of its pronouncement will gradually change to the register of sexual, feminine sweetness and submissiveness. The political ideology behind the transformations of this term will be that people, i.e., races, nations, classes and women are happy in inequality and have no reason to revolt against the domination/subordination structure of their social existence so long as they are free to *choose* their masters and so long as this freedom of choice hides its exploitative purposes behind the humanitarian guise. In the case of John Reed versus little Jane the structure is brutally undisguised, as it is when the Charity Institution is under the Brocklehurst Mastership. In these circumstances, though the conditions of existence become unbearable, the state of rebellion remains a constant possibility. When, however, exploitation forgets its true practices in the philanthropic, missionary zeal, and the Institution is put under a benevolent Governorship, the inmates, imprisoned in gratitude for the symbolic capital so liberally bestowed upon them, fail to see not only that the structure of their social existence has in no way altered, but also that they have been deprived of the incentive to revolution which could alter it. Thus, later on, the text will conceal the complicity of the Church with Imperialism and will present St John as the disinterested missionary whose only purpose in life is to help the uncivilised Indians choose for themselves the true and only Master. The fact that Jane cowers before his frigid, ardent determination only means that she is meant for the 'second' type of christian life which is accomplished in holy marriage, whereas St John belongs to the first type, that of a higher calling which dictates a form of conduct that escapes the understanding of ordinary mortals. His 'difference' is only a mark of his transcendent calling, the path to christian heroism achieved only through the annihilation of the individual self.

In the last chapter of the novel, the term 'Master' which initially exposed the social contradictions, functions so as to deny their existence. '"My dear Master"', exclaims Jane, '"I have found you out – I am come back to you"' (p. 459). It is this adjective 'dear' which magically transforms the domination/subordination social experience. It is also the moment in the novel of holy matrimony between a landed gentleman and a lady restored to her estate – a moment which initiates her into the dominant role of *mistress*.

It is not only Jane, however, who accepts with glee to forever live out the roles designed for her at the Charity Institution. Mr Rochester himself now acknowledges a Master, a higher Master who causes the transformations effected in the temper and not in the structure of social relations, as well as in the mechanics of the plot. This Master is no other than Divine Providence. It is not without significance that the novel begins with rebellion and ends with St John's communication of obedience and prostration: 'My Master', writes St John to the civilised world, 'has forewarned me. Daily He announces more distinctly, "Surely I come quickly!" and hourly I more eagerly respond, "Amen; even so, come, Lord Jesus!".'

This ideology which represents the master/servant as locked not in mortal combat but in the bonds of love is the one which is writing itself into *Jane Eyre* and, generally, in the text of Victorian fiction. It is the ideology which began to be produced in England after the French Revolution and upon which, as I shall argue later, the text's nationalistic code is grounded. Jane Eyre's interiority is a reflection of England's exteriority. The scene mentioned above between the two children encapsulates the sexual, social and political contradictions of the Victorian Era. For it is not only the subordination arising out of the sacred rights of property which transcend gender difference and finally determine the master/or mistress/servant relation which finds expression in this scene. It is also the physical, psychological and legal subordination of female to male:

> 'What were you doing behind the curtain?' he asked.
> 'I was reading.'
> 'Show the book.'
> I returned to the window and fetched it thence.
> 'You have no business to take our books; you are a dependant, mamma says; you have no money; your father left you none. ... Now I'll teach you to rummage my bookshelves: for they *are* mine; all the house belongs to me, or will do in a few years.'
>
> (p. 42)

Notice the subtle transformation of 'our' books to 'my'. John Reed, from spokesman of his class's property rights, ends as a spokesman of his male rights; 'mamma' will herself be dispossessed of her house 'in a few years'. It is not without significance that in the sentence 'for they *are* mine' Charlotte Brontë italicises the verb thus making the bully boy's tone of voice come alive.

Jane's submissiveness is shown in her lack of courage to transgress the limits imposed on speech: 'Accustomed to John Reed's abuse, I never had an idea of replying to it: my care was how to endure the blow which would certainly follow the insult' (p. 42). Passive defence is transformed into aggressive attack when in the revolutionary moment the voice transgresses the warning signs and trespasses into the realms of forbidden discourse:

> My terror had passed its climax; other feelings succeeded. 'Wicked and cruel boy!' I said. 'You are a murderer – you are a slave-driver – you are like the Roman emperors!' I had read Goldsmith's *History of Rome*, and had ... drawn parallels in silence, which I never thought thus to have declared aloud.
>
> (p. 43)

Declaring *aloud* becomes, then, a precondition for the liberation of physical violence and force. Once Jane pronounces her condition she finds the strength to stand up to the older boy and to physically subdue him. Jane's consequent arrest and imprisonment in the red-room constitutes the significant moment during which the subject splits into an 'I' and its narrator – the moment when acting-in-the-world assumes such vertiginous momentum and speech such un-dreamed-of freedoms that the rationalising, domesticating voice of narration has to step in. Hegemonic literature always comes to the rescue of history and transfixes it into its a-temporal modes. When the narrative voice says: 'I resisted all the way: a new thing for me' it is reporting an objective state of affairs. When, however, it ex-plains: 'the fact is, I was a trifle beside myself; or rather *out* of myself, as the French would say' (p. 44), it undertakes the ideolo-gical reconstruction of that which the revolutionary moment demol-ished. Mrs Rochester reimposes the 'no trespassing signs, the limits demarcating the in/out'.

It is important that the word 'French' appears at this point in the narrative and in connexion with the state of being *out* of one's self. Charlotte Brontë italicises the foreign *out*. Here, the text is not simply signifying Mrs Rochester's linguistic achievements and her progress from being 'a mad cat', 'a noxious thing' as a child to being an accomplished, refined lady-writer of her memoirs. It is pri-marily signifying nineteenth-century English beliefs concerning the state of revolution. Revolution was that aberrant state in which an individual, a class or a nation went 'beside' itself – *hors de soi même* – a condition indelibly linked in the English mind with the frenzy and irrationality of the French Revolution.

It is from this moment onwards that the narrative will begin to construct its ideological, nationalistic discourse on the opposition French/English, an opposition which in turn will subsume contra-dictory representations of femininity symbolising a natural and an un-natural political behaviour which at a deeper level signifies the native hostility and fear of anything *foreign*. Mr Rochester's Creole wife is driven insane by her sexual promiscuity and is incarcerated, unwisely, in the attic; unwisely because no matter what the re-straints, one should not nurture a snake in one's bosom. It is on the Continent that Mr Rochester falls into the nets of Duessa – a French woman in whose person are concentrated whoredom, de-ception, wile and the immorality of the stage. Her fickle, feminine, bastard child Adèle will in turn be incarcerated in a sane, English educational institution where, Mrs Rochester informs us, 'as she grew up, a sound English education corrected in a great measure her French defects; and when she left school, I found her a pleasing

and obliging companion – docile, good-tempered, and well principled' (p. 475). Fidessa dwells in, or is England.

The ideology upon which the nationalistic code is constructed is
that which equates revolution with unabashed, female sexuality as
represented by the 'French actress' – in short, with degeneration,
prostitution, atheism and insanity. On *this* side of the Channel,
where Mr Rochester brings little Adèle 'out of the slime and mud of
Paris to grow up clean in the wholesome soil of an English country
garden' (p. 176), philanthropy, a natural propensity in the English
character for the higher pleasures of the hedonistic calculus, for
monogamous bliss and industrious habits, made the mimicry of
spectral revolution an unnecessary gesture. Adèle is mindless of
limits, she is prone to 'prattle' and other 'freedoms' 'which betrayed
in her a superficiality of character inherited probably from her
mother, hardly congenial to an English mind' (p. 176). Thus, to be
out of one's self, that is, to dare cross over into the space of rebelliousness, was something 'biologically' inconsistent with the
'English mind'.

I should like now to examine the moment in the mirror and its
ideological implications with respect to the state of rebellion and
sexual discourse:

> Returning, I had to cross before the looking glass; my fascinated
> glance involuntarily explored the depth it revealed. All looked colder
> and darker in the visionary hollow than in reality: and the strange
> little figure there gazing at me with a white face and arms specking
> the gloom, and glittering eyes of fear moving where all else was still,
> had the effect of a real spirit: I thought it like one of the tiny phan-
> toms, half fairy, half imp, Bessie's evening stories represented as
> coming out of lone, ferny dells in moors, and appearing before the
> eyes of belated travellers.
>
> (p. 46)

This moment, when the subject splits into its double, is a precondition for autobiographical narratives. In the present instance, the
figural materialisation of this precondition announces also the
novel's structural rift into two distinct narrative modes – the realist,
where rebellion materialises, and the fantasy, where the erotic fable
and its sexual-ideological discourse are organised.

Jane, it will be remembered, appears in the dusk 'half fairy, half
imp' before the eyes of the belated traveller Mr Rochester, the wandering *Gytrash* come home to Fidessa to turn into penitent christian.

This 'fairy' language which Mr Rochester half-ironically introduces as a mode of communication with Jane will determine their sexual roles and discourse:

> 'No wonder you have rather the look of another world. I marvelled where you had got that sort of face. When you came on me in Hay Lane last night, I thought unaccountably of fairy tales, and had half a mind to demand whether you had bewitched my horse: I am not sure yet.'
>
> (p. 153)

Revolted Jane is absent from the mirror. The reflection upon which she is gazing is not a coherency, it is a vision deprived of subjectivity, an *it* de-sexualised and fully de-socialised. It is the shriek of revolt made remote and insubstantial in the hollow of the mirror, rendered totally impotent and ineffectual by being fantasised and imprisoned in the 'fairy' discourse. De-materialised, Jane's revolted image is relegated to the realm of the un-natural, the uncanny, the un-real, the fantastic. Thus, the rebel girl, confronted in the social mirror with the aberrant representation of revolt, realises the practical necessity of disconnecting herself from her bodily image. As of this moment, the 'other' Jane becomes an anagram of her surname, she becomes *eery*. Realist discourse in which rebelliousness materialised passes through the mirror, in whose hollow Jane Eery will henceforth live herself and Mr Rochester in the fairy-tale mode. The *hors de soi même*, the rebellious discourse, will finally be exorcised together with the bodily image by coming to lodge safely in Mr Rochester's sexual repartee. Mr Rochester will never tire of calling Jane his 'witch', his 'imp', his 'fairy', his 'fiend', terms which in another tone of voice are also used by him to designate his mad wife.

This verbal metamorphosis seems to excite Mr Rochester's sexual imagination. Social revolution may have been distasteful to upper-class Victorians, but the French, fiendish female was supremely seductive. Of course, Mr Rochester would never have engaged in this type of verbal sex-play with a lady of his class. Class difference with Jane, though, provides an extra dose of sexual arousal as it reproduces more strongly the domination/subordination relation. By designating Jane with epithets which belong to the image in the mirror, Mr Rochester defines her as a whore in language. Behind her nun-like exterior, Mr Rochester projects the child which in the words of the maid Abbot 'always had it in her' and must, therefore, be 'tied down'. The 'mad cat', which is whorish revolution, is then tied down and exorcised through the distancing medium of language and the structure of duplicity comes to mark the text's sexual discourse. Jane's paintings, which Mr Rochester so deeply admires, function as signs of the confinement of female sexuality and its consequent fears: the first encodes male aggressiveness, rape, death through loss of the invaluable, virginal ring; the second establishes the representation of woman-as-mother since the body is represented from the waist up, the lower part being lost in vapours; the third, which bears the inscription 'the shape which shape has none', repeats the paradox of the bodiless body in the mirror.

It is after confronting her image in the mirror that Jane begins to acquiesce in the limits imposed on speech. Henceforth, she will never find herself again in the state of being *out* of herself, 'as if my tongue pronounced words without my will consenting to their utterance: something spoke out of me over which I had no control' (p. 60). Before leaving Gateshead Hall Jane has learnt her lesson: 'I was going to say something about what passed between me and Mrs Reed; but on second thoughts I considered it better to remain silent on that head' (p. 71). As long as the body is exiled into the fairy discourse which composes their sexual repartee Jane does not feel threatened. But the moment in which Mr Rochester feels like putting 'words' into practice, Jane is called to assert her 'Englishness':

> He rose and came towards me, and I saw his face all kindled, and his full falcon-eye flashing, and tenderness and passion in every lineament. I quailed momentarily – then I rallied. Soft scene, daring demonstration, I would not have; and I stood in peril of both; a weapon of defence must be prepared – I whetted my tongue.
>
> (p. 301)

Speech as instrument of liberation and revolt is here put to the service of Victorian morals: 'With this needle of repartee I'll keep you from the edge of the gulf too and, moreover, maintain by its pungent aid that distance between you and myself most conducive to our real mutual advantage.' This 'pungent', 'needle repartee' perfectly describes the transference of sexuality from the body to speech.

As was previously mentioned, *Jane Eyre* is marked by a contradiction in form. The first ten chapters of the novel organise the writing on the conventions of realism, but once Jane is out of the

Charity Institution and into the world the writing incarcerates her in an a-temporal fantasy mode. Social determination, which provided the scaffold upon which character and action were elaborated and which formed the basis of the explanatory model operating in the narrator's discourse, suddenly becomes that of figural enunciation. The realist mode is dropped, as if the writer feared the contentual direction of her narrative. After the tenth chapter what the writing is striving to do is to silence, efface, inscribe *over* its narrative past. The 'between narrative modes' is perhaps a reflection of the 'between classes' in which Jane is caught. In his 'Class, Power and Charlotte Brontë' Terry Eagleton points to this contradiction as marking all of Charlotte Brontë's heroines. He writes.

> Her protagonists are an extraordinary contradictory amalgam of smouldering rebelliousness and prim conventionalism, gushing. Romantic fantasy and canny hard-headedness, quivering sensitivity and blunt rationality. It is, in fact, a contradiction closely related to their roles as governesses or private tutors. The governess is a servant, trapped within a rigid social function which demands industriousness, subservience and self-sacrifice; but she is also an 'upper' servant, and so (unlike, supposedly, other servants) furnished with an imaginative awareness and cultivated sensibility which are precisely her stock-in-trade as a teacher. She lives at that ambiguous point in the social structure at which two worlds – an interior one of emotional hungering, and an external one of harshly mechanical necessity – meet and collide.[4]

Jane is assigned her role of governess in the repressive, Charity Institution. Again, it is by impositions on speech and by exemplary discourses that her transformation into an upright, industrious, prim governess is effected. Between the *Scylla* of duty and kindness as represented by Miss Temple, who had always something 'of refined propriety in her language, which precluded deviation into the ardent, the excited, the eager', and the *Charybdis* of religious ecstasy as represented by Helen Burns whose 'soul sat on her lips and language flowed ... a swelling spring of pure, full, fervid eloquence' (pp. 104–5), the petit-bourgeois orphan learns that restraints endow her with a symbolic capital which, though it does not raise her like real capital to the freedoms and frivolities of the upper class, yet serves to distinguish her from the crass sexuality of the working class. Caliban is metamorphosed into Ariel and this is nowhere stated so clearly as in Mr Rochester's mixed metaphor:

Whatever I do with its cage, I cannot get at it – the savage, beautiful creature! If I tear, if I rend the slight prison, my outrage will only let the captive loose. Conqueror I might be of the house; but the inmate would escape to heaven before I could call myself possessor of its clay dwelling place. And it is you, spirit – with will and energy, and virtue and purity – that I want: not alone your brittle frame.

(p. 345)

Mr Brocklehurst's mission, which was 'to mortify in these girls the lusts of the flesh, to teach them to clothe themselves with shamefacedness and sobriety, not with braided hair and costly apparel' (p. 96), fully succeeded with Jane Eyre. In refusing the costly materials which Mr Rochester wishes to offer her as his future bride, Jane does not assert her independence from the oriental representation of woman as object. She merely confirms Mr Brocklehurst's de-sexualising ideology which splits the female image according to class into that of quaker sobriety and that which to the mind of the socially subordinate female (but not to the mind of the socially dominant female) is made to appear as signifying frivolous sensuality. *Jane Eyre* constructs a new female stereotype: the highly principled, unattractive woman, the anti-woman to the French coquette. Her role is to protect the English male from falling into 'French' ways, and thus, indirectly, she becomes the pillar of the nation. Jane, from being governess to a child, becomes governess to a man and governess to the nation. This type of female perfectly suited the imperialistic, militaristic temper of the period.

Jane's social status as governess, however, is a trick of the plot. For though the writer's conscious intentions were aimed at celebrating the ethics of work, showing how it was through her work that Jane won her liberation from class and male subordination, the plot suddenly gets diverted away from the Gospel of work. Bourgeois ideology can only be proved valid in fiction if it is shown to function through a transcendent system of rewards. Jane runs away from Rochester only to return to her paternal origins; to work briefly as school mistress to the peasantry; to inherit a significant property which will relieve her from the obligation of salaried work and will reveal to her the joys of domestic management. In short, Jane runs away so that the workings of Divine Providence may bring about her rise in social status and save her marriage to Mr Rochester from becoming a social offence. Once married, Jane Eyre can step into a light blue dress and spend her entire day talking idly with her husband – 'we talk, I believe, all day long' (p. 476) – while income from investment and rents pours in.

The rift in the narrative structure necessitates the operation of two contradictory types of plot. As was previously mentioned, in the first chapters the plot is grounded on grim, social determination. No 'miraculous' accidents occur to change little Jane's lot. In the fantasy mode, however, as in Comedy, plot is grounded in the accidental, the miraculous, chance, that which the text itself names 'Divine Providence'. Thus, Jane is rewarded by being made to join the leisure class, or rather, by being made to re-discover her original position in that class.

Charlotte Brontë, as is evident in the Preface and in certain passages where she consciously voices her ideology, set out to liberate woman from the representations in which patriarchal Victorian ideology held her. She also set out to vindicate the socially underprivileged woman. Yet *Jane Eyre* comes to celebrate the very *ethos* upon which bourgeois capitalism and its patriarchal ideology rest. What the novel originally sets out to de-mask, it then artfully conceals. Although the plot explicitly refuses at first to organise its future on the comic convention of 'foundling re-instated' it forgets its promises and reconstitutes Jane as a subject of Comedy. In suppressing social causation and in admitting the workings of Providence, it also denies its authorship by making God complicit in the writing of the novel.

In the world of *Jane Eyre* 'improper' discourse has no place. Revolution, sexuality, insanity, belong 'abroad'. These Mr Rochester locks in the attic, and places Grace Poole, the working-class woman, to guard them! Drink, which like books offers the possiblity of liberation, allows the spectre to emerge to burn down mansions and to tear the hypocritical marriage veils. But the novel's movement is not towards liberation. It is towards a tidying, a consolidating of class positions.

From *Literature and History*, 8:1 (1982), 56–66.

NOTES

[Jina Politi's essay appeared in a journal founded in 1975 'to meet a need for self-examination within history and literary studies and for dialogue between them' (*Literature and History*, 1 [1975], 1). *Literature and*

History quickly came to be distinguished by its commitment to socialist politics and to materialist criticism: it played a significant part in the politicisation of English studies in British universities and polytechnics in the 1970s and 80s. Most of the contributors to this journal have shared a sense of the literary text as neither timelessly true nor politically neutral but as shaped by the concerns of its particular time and place, and as reflecting or engaging with the assumptions and interests of particular social groups. In this essay, Jina Politi argues that, for all its ostensible 'rebelliousness', *Jane Eyre* is ultimately complicitous with the ideological interests of the early Victorian ruling class. In its Marxist perspective, and its sense that *Jane Eyre* is an ideologically divided text, her reading has some affinities with that of Terry Eagleton, whose *Myths of Power: a Marxist Study of the Brontës* (London, 1975) sees the tension between rebellion and conformity in the novel as 'a fictionally transformed version of the tensions and alliances between the two social classes which dominated the Brontës' world: the industrial bourgeoisie, and the landed gentry or aristocracy' (p. 4). But unlike Eagleton's, Politi's 'class-ification' of *Jane Eyre* is complicated by an awareness of gender, and by a concern with the ways in which the assumptions of class and of patriarchy are intertwined in the text. Ed.]

1. Charlotte Brontë, *Jane Eyre*, ed. Q. D. Leavis (Harmondsworth, 1979), p. 39. All further references are to this edition, and appear in brackets in the text.

2. For an illuminating discussion on the text's economics see Nancy Pell, 'Resistance, Rebellion and Marriage: The Economics of *Jane Eyre*', *Nineteenth-Century Fiction*, 31:4 (March 1977), 397–420.

3. Elizabeth Rigby, '*Vanity Fair, Jane Eyre*, and the Governesses' Benevolent Institution Report for 1847', *Quarterly Review*, 84 (1848–9), 173–4.

4. Terry Eagleton, *Critical Quarterly*, 14:3 (Autumn 1972), 226.

5

Colonialism and the Figurative Strategy of *Jane Eyre*

SUSAN MEYER

In her childhood and adolescence in the late 1820s and the 1830s, Charlotte Brontë wrote hundreds of pages of fiction set in an imaginary British colony in Africa. Her stories demonstrate some knowledge of African history and of the recent history of British colonialism in Africa: she makes reference to the Ashanti Wars of the 1820s, uses the names of some actual Ashanti leaders, and locates her colony in a spot on the west coast of Africa which the British were considering colonising. Other aspects of Brontë's juvenile stories suggest her knowledge of events in the British West Indian colonies as well. Specific tortures used by West Indian planters on rebellious slaves appear in Brontë's early fiction, enacted on both black and white characters, and her most important black character, Quashia Quamina, who leads periodic revolutions against her white colonists, bears the surname of Quamina, the black slave who led the Demerara uprising of 1823 in British Guiana – as well as a name derived from the racist epithet 'Quashee'.[1]

Colonialism is also present – and used figuratively – in each of Brontë's major novels. The heroines of *Shirley* (1849) and *Villette* (1853) are both compared to people of non-white races experiencing the force of European imperialism. Louis Moore and M. Paul, the men whom the heroines love, either leave or threaten to leave

Europe for the colonies, and in each case the man's dominating relationship with a colonial people is represented as a substitute for his relationship with the rebellious heroine. In order to determine if Shirley loves him, Louis Moore tells her that he intends to go to North America and live with the Indians, where, he immediately suggests, he will take one of the 'sordid savages' as his wife.[2] Similarly, at the end of *Villette*, M. Paul departs for the French West Indian colony of Guadeloupe, to look after an estate there, instead of marrying Lucy. Such an estate would indeed have needed supervision in the early 1850s, as the French slaves had just been emancipated in 1848. Brontë suggests the tumultuous state of the colony by the ending she gives the novel: M. Paul may be killed off by one of the tropical storms that Brontë, like writers as diverse as Monk Lewis and Harriet Martineau, associates with the rage and the revenge of the black West Indians.[3] If M. Paul is a white colonist, Lucy is like a native resisting control: Brontë has Lucy think of her own creative impulse as a storm god, 'a dark Baal'. These metaphors make the novel's potentially tragic ending more ambiguous: it may not be entirely a tragedy if M. Paul is indeed killed by a storm and does not return from dominating West Indian blacks to marry the Lucy he calls 'sauvage'.[4]

The metaphorical use of race relations to represent conflictual gender relations is even more overt in Brontë's *The Professor* (1846). The novel begins as an unreceived letter, whose intended recipient has disappeared into 'a government appointment in one of the colonies'.[5] William Crimsworth's own subsequent experiences among the young women of a Belgian boarding school are represented as a parallel act of colonisation. Crimsworth discreetly compares his Belgian-Catholic girl students to blacks whom he must forcibly keep under control. He likens one Caroline, for example, to a runaway West Indian slave when he describes her curling, 'somewhat coarse hair', 'rolling black eyes', and lips 'as full as those of a hot-blooded Maroon' (p. 86).[6] Even the atypical half-Swiss, half-English Frances Henri whom Crimsworth marries shows a potential rebelliousness against male domination that the novel figures using the imagery of race. Frances tells Crimsworth, with 'a strange kind of spirit', that if her husband were a drunkard or a tyrant, marriage would be slavery, and that 'against slavery all right thinkers revolt' (p. 255). The metaphor is even more explicit when Frances tells Hunsden, who is matching wits with her in an argument about Switzerland, that if he marries a Swiss wife and then maligns her native country, his wife will arise one night and smother him 'even as your own Shakespeare's Othello smothered Desdemona' (p. 242). This imaginary wife's rebellion against women's subordination and against her gender role – she behaves like an angry man – precipitates her figurative blackness.

Even in the two existing chapters of Brontë's final and unfinished novel *Emma* (1853), race seems to be about to play an important figurative role: the heroine's suddenly apparent blackness suggests her social disenfranchisement due to her gender, age, and social class. The two chapters are set in a boarding school and focus on a little girl, known as Matilda Fitzgibbon, who appears at first to be an heiress, but whose father disappears after leaving her at the school and cannot be located to pay her fees at the end of the first term. Matilda Fitzgibbon is revealed, at the end of the second chapter, to be of a race, or at least a physical appearance, that renders her susceptible to the following insult: "'If we were only in the good old times", said Mr Ellin "where we ought to be – you might just send Miss Matilda out to the Plantations in Virginia – sell her for what she's worth and pay yourself –.'"[7] This revelation has been prepared for by several previous passages. Matilda, the narrator has informed us, has a physical appearance that makes her inadequate as a wealthy 'shew-pupil', a physiognomy that repels the headmistress and causes her a 'gradually increasing peculiarity of feeling' (pp. 309, 312), and 'such a face as fortunately had not its parallel on the premises' (p. 313). Brontë has also given Matilda the name 'Fitz/gibbon', one that suggests racist epithets when it is read in the context of the nineteenth-century scientific commonplace that blacks were low on the scale of being, closer to apes than to white Europeans: Matilda's last name is a patronymic that brands her the offspring of a monkey. Yet in a sense Matilda becomes black only at the moment in the novel in which she loses her social standing. Only then do any of those around her make any explicit references to her race or skin colouring, and only then does the reader become aware of what it is that is 'repulsive' in her 'physiognomy'. When Matilda becomes isolated, orphaned, unrooted, and poor – and more vulnerable and sympathetic – she is transformed by the narrative into a black child.

Brontë uses these references to relations between Europeans and races subjected to the might of European imperialism – in these instances, primarily native Americans and African slaves in the West Indies and the United States, although elsewhere in her fiction other peoples serve a similar metaphorical function – to represent various configurations of power in British society: female subordination in sexual relationships, female insurrection and rage against male domination, and the oppressive class position of the female without family ties and a middle-class income. She does so with a mixture of both sympathy for the oppressed and a conventional assertion of white racial supremacy: Matilda's apparently dark face is represented as repulsive, yet the situation that provokes Mr Ellin's harsh racism also evokes the reader's sympathy for Matilda. Lucy Snowe's strength of character is one of her most admirable traits – and yet to represent it Brontë invokes the Eurocentric idea of colonised savages. The figurative use of race relations in Brontë's major fiction reveals a conflict between sympathy for the oppressed and a hostile sense of racial supremacy, one that becomes most apparent in *Jane Eyre* (1847).

I

In the opening chapters of *Jane Eyre*, race is a controlling metaphor – the young Jane is compared to a slave both at Gateshead, as she resists John Reed's tyranny, and at Lowood where she argues the need to resist unjust domination and angrily states that she would refuse to be publicly 'flogged', only later to find herself subjected to another form of public humiliation like 'a slave or victim'.[8] Although in a few of these references Brontë represses the recent and immediate history of British slaveholding by alluding in the same passages to a safely remote history of Roman acts of enslavement ('You are like a murderer – you are like a slave-driver – you are like the Roman emperors!' (p. 8) Jane cries out to John Reed in the opening chapter) the history of Britain's slaveholding, only nine years past at the time the novel was published, is strongly evoked by such references. Indeed the novel will later hint at unflattering links between the British and the Roman empires. As the novel continues, the metaphor of slavery takes on such a central status that, although the novel remains situated in the domestic space, Brontë imports a character from the territory of the colonies (that territory also of her childhood writings) to give the metaphor a vivid presence. This realisation of the metaphor through the creation of a character brings Brontë into a more inescapable confrontation with the history of British race relations. And Brontë's metaphorical use of race has a certain fidelity to the history of British imperialism.

Brontë alludes to non-white races in the novel – primarily African slaves and Indians, though also Persians, Turks, and native Americans – in passages where she is evoking the idea of unjust oppression. But Brontë makes class and gender oppression the overt significance of these other races, displacing the historical reasons why non-white people might suggest the idea of oppression, at some level of consciousness, to nineteenth-century British readers. What begins then as an implicit critique of British domination and an identification with the oppressed collapses into merely an appropriation of the imagery of slavery, as the West Indian slave becomes the novel's archetypal image of the oppressed 'dark races'. Nonetheless, the novel's closure fails, in interesting ways, to screen out entirely the history of British imperialist oppression.

This complex metaphorical use of race explains much of the difficulty of understanding the politics of *Jane Eyre*. In an important reading of the significance of colonialism in this novel, Gayatri Spivak argues that 'the unquestioned ideology of imperialist axiomatics' informs Brontë's narrative and enables the individualistic social progress of the character Jane that has been celebrated by 'US mainstream feminists'. For her, Bertha, a 'white Jamaican Creole', is a 'native "subject"', indeterminately placed between human and animal and consequently excluded from the individualistic humanity that the novel's feminism claims for Jane.[9] While I agree with Spivak's broad critique of an individualistic strain of feminism, where I find her reading problematic is in its analysis of the workings of imperialist ideology and its relation to feminism, both in general and in *Jane Eyre*.

Spivak describes Bertha as at once a white woman and (as a native-born Jamaican white) a 'native', that is as what she terms, with little definition, a 'native "subject"'.[10] She is thus able to designate Bertha as either native or white in order to criticise both Brontë's *Jane Eyre* and Jean Rhys's *Wide Sargasso Sea* as manifestations of exclusive feminist individualism. *Jane Eyre*, she argues, gives the white Jane individuality at the expense of the 'native' Bertha; *Wide Sargasso Sea*, on the other hand, retells the story of *Jane Eyre* from Bertha's perspective and thus merely 'rewrites a canonical English text within the European novelistic tradition in the interest of the white Creole rather than the native' (p. 253). Bertha is either native or not native to suit Spivak's critique. Thus it is by sleight of hand that Spivak shows feminism to be inevitably complicitous with imperialism.

My own proposition is that the interconnection between the ideology of male domination and the ideology of racial domination, manifested in the comparisons between white women and people of non-white races in many texts in this period of European imperialist expansion, in fact resulted in a very different relation between imperialist ideology and the developing resistance of nineteenth-century British women to the gender hierarchy. *Jane Eyre* was written in an ideological context in which white women were frequently compared to people of non-white races, especially blacks, in order to emphasise the inferiority of both to white men. But as Brontë constructs the trope in *Jane Eyre*, the yoking between the two terms of the metaphor turns not on shared inferiority but on shared oppression. Although this figurative strategy does not preclude racism, it inevitably produces the suggestion that people of these 'other' races are also oppressed. While for the most part the novel suppresses the damning history of racial oppression and slavery, its ending betrays an anxiety that imperialism and oppression of other races constitute a stain upon English history and that the novel's own appropriation of non-white races for figurative ends bears a disturbing resemblance to that history. Thus although the ending of the novel does essentially permit the racial hierarchies of European imperialism to fall back into place, *Jane Eyre* is characterised not by Spivak's 'unquestioned ideology' of imperialism, but by an ideology of imperialism that is questioned – and then reaffirmed – in interesting and illuminating ways.

An interpretation of the significance of the British empire in *Jane Eyre* must begin by making sense of Bertha Mason Rochester, the mad, drunken West Indian wife whom Rochester keeps locked up on the third floor of his ancestral mansion. Bertha functions in the novel as the central locus of Brontë's anxieties about the presence of oppression in England, anxieties that motivate the plot and drive it to its conclusion. The conclusion of the novel then settles these anxieties, partly by eliminating the character who seems to embody them. Yet Bertha only comes into the novel after about a third of its action has already taken place. As she emerges in the novel, anxieties that have been located elsewhere, notably in the character of Jane herself, become absorbed and centralised in the figure of Bertha, thus preparing the way for her final annihilation.

I read Bertha's odd ambiguity of race – an ambiguity that is constructed by the text itself, rather than one that needs to be mapped onto it – as directly related to her function as a representative of dangers that threaten the world of the novel. She is the heiress to a West Indian fortune, the daughter of a father who is a West Indian planter and merchant, and the sister of the yellow-skinned yet socially white Mr Mason. She is also a woman whom the younger son of an aristocratic British family would consider marrying, and so she is clearly imagined as white – or as passing for white – in the novel's retrospective narrative. Critics of the novel, including Spivak, who describes her as a white Creole, have consistently assumed that Bertha is a white woman, basing the assumption on this part of the narrative, although Bertha has often been described as a 'swarthy' or 'dark' white woman.[11] But when she actually emerges as a character in the action of the novel, the narrative associates Bertha with blacks, particularly with the black Jamaican anti-slavery rebels, the Maroons. In the form in which she becomes visible in the novel, Bertha has *become* black as she is constructed by the narrative, much as Matilda Fitzgibbon becomes black in *Emma*.

Even in Rochester's account of the time before their marriage, when Bertha Mason was 'a fine woman, ... tall, dark, and majestic', there are hints, as there are in the early descriptions of Matilda Fitzgibbon, of the ambiguity of her race. Immediately after Rochester describes Bertha as 'tall, dark, and majestic' he continues 'her family wished to secure me, because I was of a good race' (p. 389). In the context of a colony where blacks outnumbered whites by twelve to one, where it was a routine and accepted island practice for white planters to force female slaves to become their mistresses, and where whites on the island were uneasily aware of the large population of mulattoes (many of whom had been emancipated), Rochester's phrase accrues a significance beyond its immediate reference to lineage, to his old family name.[12] Spoken in the context of a colony in which race relations were growing increasingly explosive and were becoming a constant preoccupation, Rochester's phrase cannot avoid evoking other meanings of the word 'race', and thus suggesting that Bertha herself may not be of as 'good' a race as he. Bertha is the daughter, as Richard Mason oddly, and, it would seem, unnecessarily declares in his official attestation to her marriage with Rochester, 'of Jonas Mason, merchant, and of Antoinetta his wife, a Creole' (p. 366).

The ambiguity of Bertha's race is marked by this designation of her mother as a Creole. The word 'creole' was used in the nineteenth century to refer to both blacks and whites born in the West Indies, a usage that caused some confusion: as the India-born

British barrister and historian John Malcolm Forbes Ludlow put it in 1862, 'There are creole whites, creole negroes, creole horses, &c.; and creole whites are, of all persons, the most anxious to be deemed of pure white blood'.[13] When Rochester exclaims of Bertha, 'She came of a mad family: – idiots and maniacs through three generations! Her mother, the Creole, was both a mad woman and a drunkard!' he locates both madness and drunkenness in his wife's maternal line, which is again emphatically and ambiguously labelled 'Creole' (p. 369). By doing so, he associates that line with two of the most common stereotypes associated with blacks in the nineteenth century.[14]

As Bertha emerges as a character in the novel, her blackness is made more explicit, despite Rochester's wish to convince Jane, and perhaps temporarily himself, that 'the swelled black face' and 'exaggerated stature' of the woman she has seen are 'figments of imagination, results of nightmare' (p. 360). But when Jane sees Bertha's face reflected in her mirror, and describes that face to Rochester, the *topoi* of racial 'otherness' are very evident. Jane tells Rochester that the face was

> 'Fearful and ghastly to me – oh sir, I never saw a face like it! It was a discoloured face – it was a savage face. I wish I could forget the roll of the red eyes and the fearful blackened inflation of the lineaments!'
> 'Ghosts are usually pale, Jane.'
> 'This, sir, was purple: the lips were swelled and dark; the brows furrowed; the black eye-brows wildly raised over the bloodshot eyes.'
>
> (p. 358)

The emphasis on Bertha's colouring in this passage – she is emphatically not 'pale' but 'discoloured', 'purple', 'blackened' – along with the references to rolling eyes and to full 'swelled', 'dark' lips, all insistently and conventionally mark Bertha as black. Jane's use of the word 'savage' underlines the implication of her description of Bertha's features, and the redness that she sees in Bertha's rolling eyes suggests the drunkenness that, following the nineteenth-century convention, Brontë has associated with Africans since her childhood. When Bertha's 'lurid visage flame[s] over' Jane (p. 359) as she lies in bed, causing her to lose consciousness, the ambiguously dark blood Bertha has inherited from her maternal line becomes fully evident. The scene recalls the passage from Brontë's Roe Head Journal in which the revolutionary African leader Quashia, victorious in an uprising against the white British colonists and triumphantly occupying the palace built by the colonists, revels drunkenly, in symbolic violation, on the 'silken couch' of the white queen. Like the rebellious Quashia, leading an uprising against the white colonists, the Jamaican Bertha-become-black is the fiction's incarnation of the desire for revenge on the part of colonised peoples, and Brontë's language suggests that such a desire for revenge is not unwarranted. The association of Bertha with fire recalls Jane's earlier question to herself:

> What crime was this, that lived incarnate in this sequestered mansion, and could neither be expelled nor subdued by the owner? – What mystery, that broke out, now in fire and now in blood, at the deadest hours of the night?
>
> (p. 264)

The language of this passage strongly evokes descriptions of slave uprisings in the British West Indies, where slaves used fires both to destroy property and to signal to each other that an uprising was taking place. White colonists of course responded to slave insurrections with great anxiety, like that expressed by one writer for *Blackwood's* in October 1823, in response to the news of the Demerara slave uprising:

> Give them [the abolitionists] an opportunity of making a few grand flowery speeches about liberty, and they will read, without one shudder, the narrative of a whole colony bathed in blood and fire, over their chocolate the next morning.[15]

Brontë began writing *Jane Eyre* in 1846, eight years after the full emancipation of the British West Indian slaves in 1838. At the time Brontë was writing the novel, emancipation and the recent British participation in human slavery were certainly in the national consciousness: having set their own slaves free, the British immediately began to put pressure on other countries, their economic competitors, to do likewise. The main events of the novel definitely occur prior to emancipation. Q. D. Leavis has shown that it may not be possible to pinpoint the closing moment of the novel further than within a range of twenty-seven years, between 1819 and 1846.[16] If we assume, when Jane says at the end of her autobiography, 'I have now been married ten years' (p. 576), that the date is at the latest 1846, when Brontë began writing the novel, then Jane's marriage with Rochester takes place no later than 1836. In the year before their marriage Rochester tells Jane that he has kept Bertha locked for ten years in his third-story room: 'She has now for ten years made [it] a wild beast's den – a goblin's cell' [p. 394]). At the latest, then, Rochester first locked Bertha in that room in 1825, and since he lived with her first for four years, they would have been married in 1821. Brontë doubtless meant to leave the precise date of the novel ambiguous – she marks the year of Rochester's and Bertha's wedding with a dash in Richard Mason's attestation to their marriage – but it is clear that even at the latest possible dates for the events of the novel, they occur well before emancipation, which was declared in 1834 but only complete in 1838. As I have suggested above, Brontë may have meant for the events of the novel to occur in the 1820s and 30s, during the years in which, due to the economic decline of the British sugar colonies in the West Indies, planters imposed increasing hardship on the slaves and increasingly feared their revolt. When Bertha escapes from her ten years' imprisonment to attempt periodically to stab and burn her oppressors alive, and, as Rochester says, to hang her 'black and scarlet visage over the nest of my dove' (p. 395), she is symbolically enacting precisely the sort of revolt feared by the British colonists in Jamaica.

But why would Brontë write a novel permeated with the imagery of slavery, and suggesting the possibility of a slave uprising, in 1846, after the emancipation of the British (though not the US or French) slaves had already taken place? Indeed in 1846 it was evident that the British West Indian colonies were failing rapidly, and the focus of British colonial attention was shifting to India. Perhaps the eight years since emancipation provided enough historical distance for Brontë to make a serious and public, although implicit, critique of British slavery and British imperialism in the West Indies. Although that critique is suppressed, in some passages in the novel, by more overt references to other historical instances of slavery, and although the novel uses slavery for figurative purposes, nonetheless it in places does engage with the history of British slavery in the West Indies as a reality independent of its figurative uses. The story of Bertha, however finally unsympathetic to her as a human being, nonetheless does make an indictment of British imperialism in the West Indies and the stained wealth that came from its oppressive rule. When Jane wonders 'what crime ... live[s] incarnate' in Rochester's luxurious mansion that can 'neither be expelled nor subdued by the owner' (p. 264) the novel suggests that the black-visaged Bertha, imprisoned out of sight in a luxurious British mansion, does indeed 'incarnate' a historical crime. Rochester himself describes Thornfield as a 'tent of Achan' (p. 383), alluding to Joshua 7, in which Achan takes spoils wrongfully from another people and buries it under his tent, thus bringing down a curse upon all the children of Israel. The third floor of the mansion, where Bertha is imprisoned, Jane thinks, is 'a shrine of memory' to which 'furniture once appropriated to the lower apartments had from time to time been removed ... as fashions changed' (p. 127). The symbolically resonant language Brontë uses as Jane tours the house suggests that Thornfield, and particularly its third floor, to which Bertha has been removed, stands as a material embodiment of the history of the English ruling class as represented by the Rochesters, whom Mrs Fairfax, acting simultaneously as family historian and guide to the house – that is, guide to the 'house of Rochester' in both senses – acknowledges to have been 'rather a violent than a quiet race in their time' (p. 128). The atmosphere of the third floor of this house is heavy in the novel with the repressed history of crimes committed by a violent race, crimes that have been removed from sight as fashions changed. Jane's response to this place dense with history – she is intrigued but 'by no means covet[s] a night's repose on one of those wide and heavy beds' (p. 137) – suggests her awareness of the oppressive atmosphere of the history of the British empire, and her uneasiness lest she, by lying in the bed of the Rochesters, should get caught up in it.

II

Brontë's description of the room where Bertha has been locked up for ten years – without a window, with only one lamp hung from a symbolic chain – also reveals her awareness that the black-visaged Bertha, like Quashia Quamina, has ample reason to be taking revenge on a 'violent race'. In *Jane Eyre* Brontë subtly suggests that the history locked up in the English 'shrine of memory' is one of 'crime incarnate' in Bertha. But the slavery evoked by Bertha's colouring and imprisonment, and the slave uprisings suggested by her nocturnal violence, have a more deliberate figurative function in the novel. Bertha's most deliberate narrative function is to exist as a representative of the 'dark races' in the empire, and particularly of African slaves, to give them a human presence that lends a vividness to Brontë's metaphorical use of race.

As in her juvenilia and less prominently in her other major novels, Brontë uses black slavery in *Jane Eyre* as a metaphor for economic oppression. Several critics who analyse the novel's class politics determine that the novel is ultimately conservative in this respect. Terry Eagleton reads Brontë's novels as 'myths' that work toward balancing individualistic bourgeois values and conservative aristocratic values. He argues that her novels, including *Jane Eyre*, do this in part through conservative endings in which the protagonists 'negotiate passionate self-fulfilment on terms which preserve the social and moral conventions intact' by taking positions within the social system that has oppressed them earlier in the novel.[17] Some subsequent critics, notably Jina Politi and Kathryn Sutherland, concur with Eagleton's assessment of the novel's class politics, while expanding the critique to include the trajectory of the novel's gender politics. As Politi puts it, while Brontë 'set[s] out to vindicate the socially underprivileged woman', the novel, through its anxiety about revolution, which is coded as French and immoral, 'comes to celebrate the very *ethos* upon which bourgeois capitalism and its patriarchal ideology rest'.[18]

Both Carol Ohmann and Igor Webb see a more radical thrust in the gender and class politics of *Jane Eyre*.[19] Ohmann argues that Brontë is concerned with gender and class 'deprivation', and that, caught between her conservatism and her radicalism, she only offers a solution on an individual level. But, Ohmann argues, 'in the very rendering of Jane Eyre's longing for fulfilment, Brontë conveys a moral imperative with broadly social implications' although the novel does not follow these out.[20] Webb sees Jane as the carrier of a 'revolutionary individualism' through whom the novel struggles against inequality of gender and class. He too sees the novel as able to achieve revolutionary equality only on an individual level: 'the full transformation of society seems daunting, and the novel retreats into its overgrown paradise. This paradise serves at once as a criticism of that other, public world and as an announcement of the deep, dispiriting gulf between active self-fulfilment and social possibility.'[21]

With Ohmann and Webb, I see a more revolutionary impulse in *Jane Eyre* than do Eagleton, Politi, and Sutherland. Yet I find Brontë's struggle in *Jane Eyre* against inequality of class both broader and more limited than Ohmann and Webb do. Indeed, the critique of a realist novel for offering only an individual solution to an oppressive social system (a critique also made by Spivak) is itself problematic. Without slipping into the genre of utopian narrative, a realist novel, focusing, in the nature of the genre, on a limited number of characters, could hardly *enact* a social solution on a broader level than the individual. Yet such generic constraints do not necessarily render the critique of the novel as a perniciously individualistic genre an apt one. The relatively 'individual' solutions to social problems necessarily enacted by a novel can have the larger suggestiveness of those enacted by a parable, or by that most populist of prose genres, the folk tale. The generalisable nature of Jane's problems, the language in which *Jane Eyre*'s solution to social problems is worked out, and particularly the allusions to the French Revolution, suggest that Jane's individual story is that of a representative lower-middle-class woman, and that the story of her success emblematises a solution to larger social problems.

That individual story does argue the need for a broader redistribution of wealth, just as it argues the need for greater gender equality. At the same time, however, the novel specifically limits the recipients of this newly equalised wealth to one group, the lower middle class. The novel's position on economic redistribution and on gender politics is worked out through its central racial metaphor.

Throughout the novel, the marginality and disempowerment Jane experiences due to her class and gender positioning are represented through a metaphorical linking between Jane and several of the nineteenth century's so-called 'dark races'. In the novel's opening scene, she sits in her window seat, exiled from the drawing room, 'cross-legged, like a Turk' (p. 4). She cries out in rage against Mrs Reed 'in a savage, high voice' (p. 40), and when she tells Helen that she believes in striking back against injustice, she is told that 'heathens and savage tribes hold that doctrine, but Christians and civilised nations disown it' (p. 65). That Helen's principle of civilised passivity in the face of oppression is an echo of the self-serving rhetoric of the powerful and is not at a deep level endorsed by the novel is evident in the repetition of her language a few pages later, when the sanctimonious Mr Brocklehurst compares Jane to a Hindu, proclaiming that 'this girl, this child, the native of a Christian land' is 'worse than many a little heathen who says its prayers to Brahma and kneels before Juggernaut' (pp. 76–7). In Jane's adulthood, Rochester sees in her passions that 'may rage furiously, like true heathens, as they are' (p. 252), although held in check by her reason, and he finds in her resolute, wild spirit a 'savage, beautiful creature' (p. 405). When Jane confronts the angry, passionate Rochester, after the revelation of his previous marriage, she feels, in her attempt to assert control, 'as the Indian, perhaps, feels when he slips over the rapid in his canoe' (p. 386).

The novel compares the rebellious Jane, without much different-iation between them, to an entire array of 'dark races' experiencing the force of European imperialism in the nineteenth century – Turks, Hindus, native Americans, and the generic heathen and savage. Although Brontë's ambivalence is certainly evident in the recurring use of the words 'heathen' and 'savage', the novel nonetheless repeatedly affirms Jane's passionate rebellion against her social marginality. The most frequent recurrence of the racial metaphor in the novel is the sometimes covert, sometimes overt comparison of Jane to an African slave. The novel uses the idea of the enslaved Africans (eventually made spectacularly present through Bertha) as its most dramatic rendition of the concept of racial domination, and thus most frequently uses the slave to repre-sent class and gender inequality in England.

As in her early African tales, Brontë does not use slavery as a metaphor for the lot of the working class but for that of the lower-middle class. Both Jane and the narrator invoke the metaphor not in response to the work Jane has to perform but in response to the attitude she has to endure from her class superiors. When as a child Jane first bursts out at John Reed, she cries, 'You are like a mur-derer – you are like a slave-driver' and the adult Jane explains to the reader, 'I had drawn parallels in silence, which I never thought thus to have declared aloud' (p. 8). The adult narrator accepts the parallel, and in fact makes the child's simile into a more emphatic metaphor when she continues, 'I was conscious that a moment's mutiny had already rendered me liable to strange penalties, and like any other rebel slave, I felt resolved, in my desperation, to go all lengths' (p. 9). Although the use of the word 'like' in this sentence almost disguises the trope as a simile, in fact the formulation 'like *any other*' definitively designates Jane a slave and then describes her as behaving like others in the same position. Later, when Jane has been placed by Brocklehurst on the stool, she thinks of herself as 'a slave or victim'. The novel itself draws a parallel between slavery and Jane's social position as a child through Bertha. Jane's sudden explosion of fury against her treatment at Gateshead occurs in her tenth year there: Mrs Reed complains to the adult Jane, 'To this day I feel it impossible to understand: how for nine years you could be patient and quiescent under any treatment, and in the tenth break out all fire and violence' (p. 300). Jane brings herself to 'mutiny' and becomes a 'rebel slave' in her tenth year, like Bertha who after ten years in her third floor room 'br[eaks] out, now in fire and now in blood' (p. 264).

The imagery of social class as slavery recurs in Jane's adulthood. Rochester refers to her labour as 'governessing slavery' (p. 340), but Jane's work at Thornfield becomes like slavery to her only when Rochester arrives with his ruling-class friends and she comes into contact with the dehumanising regard of her class superiors. Before this, those around Jane treat her as a social equal. Mrs Fairfax helps Jane remove her bonnet and shawl when she first arrives, and Adèle is too young and also of too dubious an origin to treat her governess with superiority. Brontë explicitly constructs the atmosphere between the three of them – though significantly *not* between the three of them and the servants – as a utopian retreat from a world where inequalities of class are constantly present. Mrs Fairfax distinctly marks the exclusion of the working class from this classless utopia when she tells Jane, just after expressing her delight that Jane has come to be her companion: 'You know in winter time, one feels dreary quite alone, in the best quarters. I say alone – Leah is a nice girl to be sure, and John and his wife are very decent people; but then you see they are only servants, and one can't converse with them on terms of equality: one must keep them at a due distance, for fear of losing one's authority' (p. 116). Some awareness of the costs even of having a class lower than one's own, a problem with which the novel is in general very little concerned, comes through in this passage. For the most part, however, *Jane Eyre* pays scant attention to the working class. Instead it draws parallels between slavery and Jane's social position as one of the disempowered lower middle class.

For Jane, the feeling of class slavery occurs most poignantly in the context of her awareness of the economic inequality between her and Rochester. She comments after their engagement that receiving his valuable gifts makes her feel like a degraded slave. Indeed, it is at this point that Jane writes to her uncle in Madeira, thus setting off the chain of events that will prevent her subjection to such financial slavery, first by impeding her wedding to Rochester, and then, when she finally does marry him, by bringing her the inherited wealth that enables her to meet him on more equal financial terms.

The crucial passage in which Jane sees Bertha's black face behind a wedding veil, in her own mirror, and then watches Bertha tear the veil in half, epitomises the other form of slavery that Bertha both incarnates for Jane and then enables her to avoid. Feminist critics have frequently commented on this passage, interpreting Bertha as either the surrogate or the double who expresses Jane's rage against the restraints of gender. Sandra Gilbert and Susan Gubar particularly elaborate on this pattern in the novel, describing Bertha as Jane's 'dark double', the untamed, animal-like embodiment of Jane's flaming rage.[22] It is important to see this darkness in the context of the racial dynamics of nineteenth-century Britain: by invoking racially loaded terms – 'blackened', 'purple', 'savage' – to describe the Jamaican Bertha, Brontë is using the emotional force of the idea of slavery and explosive race relations in the wake of British emancipation to represent the tensions of the gender hierarchy in England.

The imagery of slavery is both pervasive in the context of gender inequality in the novel and closely tied to the recent history of the British empire. When Rochester tells Jane, as he narrates the story of his life, 'hiring a mistress is the next worst thing to buying a slave: both are often by nature, and always by position, inferior; and to live familiarly with inferiors is degrading' (pp. 397–8), his words take on a startling resonance in the context of the story he has just told. Rochester acquired a West Indian fortune by marrying a Jamaican wife and subsequently lived in Jamaica for four years. A wealthy white man living in Jamaica before emancipation would undoubtedly have had slaves to wait upon him, and his Jamaican fortune would have been the product of slave labour, so when Rochester discusses what it is like to buy and live with slaves he knows what he is talking about. When he compares his relationships with women to keeping slaves, then, the parallel is given a shocking vividness by his own history as a slave master. But it is in the character of Rochester's wife, somewhat surprisingly, not one of his mistresses, that the metaphor of slavery is most vividly realised. Rochester draws this parallel just after the reader, with Jane, has seen his wife's 'black and scarlet' face emerging from her prison, an event that makes clear that a wife of Rochester, perhaps even more than a mistress, is in the position of being his 'slave'. When Jane, who has just been pondering over assuming the name 'Mrs Rochester', looks in the mirror and sees a black face behind a wedding veil, we realise that becoming even a wife to a man like

Rochester, with his history in the colonies and his dominating character, is dangerous.

III

Jane Eyre associates non-white races with the idea of oppression by drawing parallels between people of the 'dark races', black slaves in particular, and those oppressed by the hierarchies of social class and gender in Britain. So far the narrative function of the dark-featured Bertha and of the novel's allusions to the British empire has a certain fidelity to history. The novel's various allusions to peoples of non-white races are not, however, free from racism. The use of the slave as a figure focuses attention not so much on the oppression of blacks as on the domestic situation within England. By using the slave as the ultimate point on the scale of racial oppression, the novel also to some extent collapses all the other 'dark races' to which it alludes into the figure of the slave, in a way not unlike the anatomist Robert Knox's conflation of all the 'dark races' into the figure of the Negro: 'Mr Gibbon speaks of the obvious physical inferiority of the Negro: he means, no doubt, the dark races generally, for the remark applies to all'.[23] Nonetheless, Brontë's metaphor at least implicitly acknowledges the oppressive situation of the peoples experiencing the force of the British empire. Oddly, however, the allusions to dark skin and to empire also arise in precisely the opposite context in the novel, one most strikingly represented in the descriptions of Blanche Ingram.

The haughty Blanche, with her 'dark and imperious' eye, who treats Jane as hardly human, appears in the novel in part to illustrate the painful injustice of class inequality (p. 231). Yet when Mrs Fairfax describes Blanche to Jane, she emphasises her darkness. 'She was dressed in pure white', Mrs Fairfax relates, and she had an 'olive complexion, dark and clear', hair 'raven-black ... and in front the longest, the glossiest curls I ever saw' (p. 199). When Jane first sees Blanche, she too emphasises her darkness – 'Miss Ingram was dark as a Spaniard' Jane notes – adding that Blanche has a 'low brow', a skull conformation that, like dark skin, was a mark of racial inferiority according to the nineteenth-century science of race differences (p. 216). Rochester later describes Bertha as a woman 'in the style of Blanche Ingram' (p. 389), and he also directly compares Blanche to African women: he might be speaking of Bertha when he describes

Blanche to Jane as 'a real strapper ... big, brown, and buxom; with hair just such as the ladies of Carthage must have had' (p. 275).

These references to Blanche's darkness, and to her similarities to non-British people with dark skin, only make sense in the context of the odd phrase, 'dark and imperious'. The use of the word 'imperious' to describe Blanche's ruling-class sense of superiority recalls the contact between the British and the 'dark races' of the British empire. In that contact, it was not the dark-skinned people who were imperious, or in the position of imperialist power, but the British themselves. By associating the qualities of darkness and imperiousness, Brontë suggests that imperialism brings out both these undesirable qualities in the imperialist, that the British aristocracy in particular has been sullied, darkened, and made imperious and oppressive by the workings of empire. The arrogance arising from the wielding of despotic force, as well as a contaminating contact with the 'dark races', has sullied the British and in particular made the aristocracy unpleasantly imperious, the novel suggests.[24] Blanche Ingram dresses in white, is given by her mother the pet name 'my lily-flower' (p. 223), and her given name itself denotes her whiteness. But by mockingly juxtaposing this aristocratic Englishwoman's dark colouring, and her dark imperiousness, with her sense of herself as the lily-white flower of English womanhood, Brontë suggests that the class structure at home has been contaminated by imperialism abroad.

More mocking hints about the similarity between the British ruling class and non-white races occur in the descriptions of the Reeds. John Reed reviles his mother for 'her dark skin, similar to his own' (p. 13), and later grows into a young man whom some call handsome, the former nursemaid Bessie says uneasily, dissenting and pointing out that he has 'such thick lips' (p. 122).[25] Mrs Reed's already dark face in her last illness becomes 'disfigured and discoloured' (p. 304) – and thus like Bertha's 'discoloured face' (p. 358). Mrs Reed also has the 'prognathous' skull, that is, one with a low measurement on the graduated scale of facial angles, typified by a protruding jaw and a low forehead, which nineteenth-century science considered characteristic of the lower races. This upper-class Englishwoman has 'a somewhat large face, the under-jaw being much developed and very solid; her brow was low, her chin large and prominent' (p. 38).[26]

Brontë also criticises the aristocratic Lady Ingram by subtly comparing her both to Bertha and to the non-white races. Lady Ingram, who derides governesses in front of Jane, and who within Jane's hearing pronounces that she sees in Jane's physiognomy 'all the faults of her class' (p. 221) has features 'inflated and darkened' with pride (p. 215), just as Bertha has a 'blackened inflation of the lineaments' (p. 358). Lady Ingram has 'Roman features', and a haughty sense of superiority derived from her position in the British empire. She wears, Jane says, 'a shawl turban of some gold-wrought Indian fabric [which] invested her (I suppose she thought) with a truly imperial dignity' (p. 215). The novel draws unflattering parallels between the British empire, evoked by Lady Ingram's Indian shawl, and the Roman empire, whose emperors, the young Jane has implied, in comparing John Reed to them, are murderers and slave drivers. By associating the British empire with the Roman empire Brontë hints uneasily at a possibly parallel future: with these tainted, aristocratic representatives and with slaves of its own, the British empire may be headed for its own decline and fall. The despotism of the British upper classes, Brontë's mocking hints about their similarity to the non-white races imply, is one effect of the British involvement in empire.

By making these sly, intermittent allusions to non-white races when describing the British aristocracy, Brontë gives the 'dark races' the metaphorical role of representing the presence of oppression in the novel. This elaboration of the metaphor relies on a sense of history considerably more Anglocentric than that which underlies the metaphorical yoking of white women and people of non-white races as mutually disempowered. Because it assigns these two contradictory associations to the non-white races, using them to represent both the oppressed and the oppressor, the novel follows this logic: oppression in any of its manifestations is foreign to the English, thus the non-white races signify oppression within England, either subjection to or participation in the unjust distribution of power.

This is the most equivocal move in the novel's figurative strategy. It can be seen, for instance, in the use of the word 'caste' in the novel. When Jane, as a governess, reprimands herself sternly, as she feels herself falling in love with Rochester, 'He is not of your order: keep to your caste' (p. 202), and when she says that, as a child, she feared to leave the Reeds to go to the Eyre relatives she has heard termed a 'beggarly set', noting 'I was not heroic enough to purchase liberty at the price of caste' (p. 24), Brontë names what is unjust and humanly divisive in the English class system in such a way as to suggest that such injustices are not intrinsically English at all, that they belong by their nature instead to other races.[27] The novel's anti-imperialist politics, such examples suggest, are more self-interested than benevolent. The opposition to imperialism arises not primarily out of concern for the well-being of the people directly damaged by British imperialism – the African slaves in the West Indian colonies, the Indians whose economy was being destroyed under British rule – but out of concern for the British who were, as the novel's figurative structure represents it, being contaminated by their contact with the unjust social systems indigenous to the people with dark skin.

The novel also associates the oppression of women with the social practices of peoples other than the English. The allusions that do so arise primarily during the part of the novel describing Rochester and Jane's betrothal, as it is at this point that Rochester most directly asserts, and threatens in the future to assert, the power of his position in the gender hierarchy. In these passages, Brontë suggests that it is a characteristic of men of dark-skinned races to dominate women, as she repeatedly evokes imagery of Indian wives forced to die in 'suttee', and of women imprisoned in Turkish harems. The word 'slave' occurs in these passages, but Brontë here veers away from making a direct parallel with the British enslavement of Africans by associating Rochester's dominating masculine power over Jane with that not of a British but of an Eastern slave master. This part of the novel is rich in images of Turkish and Persian despots, sultans who reward their favourite slaves with jewels. The history of British participation in slavery arises at one point in this part of the novel – Rochester echoes the abolitionists' slogan when he tells Jane that she is too restrained with 'a man and a brother' (p. 170) – but the novel persistently displaces the blame for slavery onto the 'dark races' themselves, only alluding directly to slavery as practised by dark-skinned people. At one point, for example, the novel uses strong and shocking imagery of slavery to describe the position of wives, but despite references to such aspects of British slavery as slave markets, fetters, and mutiny, the scenario Brontë invokes is not of British imperialist domination but of the despotic, oppressive customs of non-whites. Rochester has just compared himself to 'the Grand Turk', declaring that he prefers his 'one little English girl' to the Turk's 'whole seraglio' (p. 339). Jane immediately picks up on this 'eastern allusion' because she has been thinking that his treatment of her, now that she is to be his wife, has become like a sultan's treatment of a favourite slave. She responds:

> 'I'll not stand you an inch in the stead of a seraglio. ... If you have a fancy for anything in that line, away with you, sir, to the bazaars of Stamboul without delay; and lay out in extensive slave-purchases some of that spare cash you seem so at a loss to spend satisfactorily here.'
>
> 'And what will you do, Janet, while I am bargaining for so many tons of flesh and such an assortment of black eyes?'
>
> 'I'll be preparing myself to go out as a missionary to preach liberty to them that are enslaved – your harem inmates amongst the rest. I'll get admitted there, and I'll stir up mutiny; and you, three-tailed bashaw as you are, sir, shall in a trice find yourself fettered amongst our hands: nor will I, for one, consent to cut your bonds till you have signed a charter, the most liberal that despot ever yet conferred.'
>
> (p. 339)

Jane evidently has a sense of greater similitude with 'enslaved' Turkish women than Rochester has anticipated. After all, she sits 'cross-legged, like a Turk' in the novel's opening chapter, and has compared herself to a 'revolted slave'. As the passage begins she at first seems to be distancing herself from 'them that are enslaved': she proclaims that she will not stand Rochester in 'the stead of a seraglio', and she initially positions herself as a missionary to the enslaved women. But the continuity between the imagery in this passage and that elsewhere in the novel suggests that Jane knows how to help other women out of slavery because she has been a slave herself and because she now fears becoming one again. As the passage continues, it increasingly positions Jane *with* the owned, commodified Turkish women. She tells Rochester that he will find himself fettered 'amongst *our* hands' and says that she 'for one' will not free him until he has signed a charter, presumably freeing *all* women from his despotic superiority.

But if Jane is likened to enslaved Turkish women in this passage, Rochester, in his gender-authorised despotism, is also like a person of the 'dark races', here the Turkish 'three-tailed bashaw'. By associating Rochester's position at the top of the oppressive gender hierarchy, like Jane's position at the bottom, with the 'dark races', and with their practice of what it denominates 'slavery', the novel marks all aspects of oppression 'other' – non-British, non-white, and the result of a besmirching contact with other peoples. In so doing it represses the history of British imperialist domination, and, in particular, British enslavement of Africans. Even when Rochester directly asserts his power over Jane, speaking of 'attach[ing her] to a chain' (p. 341), the novel compares him to a sultan, rather than to a white-skinned British slave master. All aspects of oppression, through this twist in the novel's figurative strategy, become something the British are in danger of being sullied by, something foreign and 'other' to them.

IV

In opposition to this danger – the danger of the contagious inequality characteristic of other races – Brontë poses an alternative directly out of middle-class domestic ideology: keeping a clean house at home in England.[28] Part of what the novel solves in its conclusion is the problem of contamination from abroad. Rochester's mutilation keeps him at home, and thus within the space of the values the novel codes as English and domestic: in response to Jane's anxious questions, the innkeeper tells her, 'Aye – aye – he's in England; he can't get out of England, I fancy – he's a fixture now' (p. 548). Clean and unclean, healthy and unhealthy environments form a central symbolic structure in the novel, and what is clean is represented as intrinsically English. In *Shirley*, Caroline's illness is anticipated by a passage about the arrival of 'the yellow taint of pestilence, covering white Western isles with the poisoned exhalations of the East, dimming the lattices of English homes with the breath of Indian plague' (*Shirley*, p. 421). Similarly, in *Jane Eyre* Brontë associates unhealthy, plague-ridden, contagious environments with other peoples and with the unjust distribution of power – a phenomenon, the novel suggests, that is itself a 'poisoned exhalation of the East', not native to 'white Western isles'.

When Rochester decides to leave Jamaica, where he has participated in slavery and taken a dark wife whom he will treat as a slave, the novel poses the opposition between oppressive Jamaica and pure England in terms of atmosphere. As Rochester recounts it:

> It was a fiery West-Indian night; one of the description that frequently precede the hurricanes of those climates: being unable to sleep in bed, I got up and opened the window. The air was like sulphur steams – I could find no refreshment anywhere. Mosquitoes came buzzing in and hummed sullenly round the room ... the moon was setting in the waves, broad and red, like a hot cannon-ball – she

threw her last bloody glance over a world quivering with the ferment
of tempest. I was physically influenced by the atmosphere. ... I meant
to shoot myself. ...

A wind fresh from Europe blew over the ocean and rushed through
the open casement: the storm broke, streamed, thundered, blazed,
and the air grew pure. I then framed and fixed a resolution.

(pp. 392–3)

Under the influence of 'the sweet wind from Europe' Rochester resolves to return to England, to 'be clean in [his] own sight' (p. 392)
by leaving this place which is, Brontë's imagery suggests, the locus
of colonial oppression.

In a very similar passage Jane associates freedom and oppression
with healthy and unhealthy environments. After she has fled
Thornfield and settled at Morton she reprimands herself for repin-
ing: which is better, Jane asks herself (p. 459), 'to be a slave in a
fool's paradise at Marseilles – fevered with delusive bliss one hour –
suffocating with the bitterest tears of remorse and shame the next –
or to be a village-schoolmistress, free and honest, in a breezy moun-
tain nook in the healthy heart of England?' Jane here imagines the
gender and class slavery she would endure as Rochester's mistress
as a feverish, suffocating, southern atmosphere, while the alternative is the free, healthy, and rigorous atmosphere of England.[29]

The damp pestilential fog of Lowood charity-school is one of the
novel's most drastically unhealthy environments; the atmosphere at
this orphan institution where Jane thinks of herself as 'a slave or
victim' is the direct result of cruel economic inequities. After so
many students die of the typhus fever fostered by the unhealthy environment, 'several wealthy and benevolent individuals in the
county' transform it into a less oppressive institution by the act of
cleaning: a new building is erected in a healthier location, and
'brackish, fetid water' (p. 98) is no longer used in preparation of the
children's food.

Creating a clean, healthy, middle-class environment stands as the
novel's symbolic alternative to an involvement in unjust oppression.
As Rochester is engaging in his most manipulative attempt to assure
himself of Jane's love, by bringing home an apparent rival, he also
orders that his house be cleaned. A great fuss is made over cleaning
the house Jane had innocently thought to be 'beautifully clean and
well-arranged' already (p. 205). 'Such scrubbing', Jane says, 'such
brushing, such washing of paint and beating of carpets, such taking
down and putting up of pictures, such polishing of mirrors and

lustres, such lighting of fires in bed-rooms, such airing of sheets and feather-beds on hearths, I never beheld, either before or since' (p. 205). Yet despite all the cleaning, the presence remains in Thornfield that makes Rochester call it 'a great plague-house' (p. 175). What Rochester needs to have cleaned out of his house as he is trying to attain Jane's love is the black-faced wife in his attic, that wife whose 'breath (faugh!) [once] mixed with the air [he] breathed' (p. 392), and who represents his sullying, inegalitarian colonial past. All that he can do with the 'plague' in his house is to hire someone to clean her away into a remote locked room. As a re- minder of that plague, Grace Poole periodically emerges, amidst all the cleaning, from the third story, 'damping' Jane's cheerfulness and causing her 'dark' conjectures, in order, as both the most expert cleaner and as evidence of the great stain in the house, to give advice to the other servants: 'just to say a word, perhaps ... about the proper way to polish a grate, or clean a marble mantlepiece, or take stains from papered walls' (p. 206).

The other great cleaning activity in the novel occurs as Jane decides to 'clean down' Moor House, and it marks a more success- ful attempt at washing away injustice than the one at Thornfield. Jane cleans the house to celebrate the egalitarian distribution of her newly acquired legacy, which will enable her to live there happily with her new-found family. Brontë writes of Jane's egalitarian divi- sion of her fortune using the rhetoric of a revolution against in- equalities of class, although this revolution symbolically represents a redistribution of wealth in favour of only a limited group of people, the lower middle class. When St John tells Jane that he, Diana, and Mary will be her brother and sisters without this sacrifice of her 'just rights', she responds, with a tone of passionate conviction Brontë obviously endorses (p. 494):

> Brother? Yes; at the distance of a thousand leagues! Sisters? Yes; slaving amongst strangers! I, wealthy – gorged with gold I never earned and do not merit! You, pennyless! Famous equality and fraternisation! Close union! Intimate attachment!

This sort of redistribution of wealth, Brontë suggests, giving Jane the language of the French revolution – 'Liberté! Egalité! Fraternité!' – will right the wrongs of the lower middle class, and clean from it the dark mark of oppression. Its women will no longer have to 'slave' among strangers like people of other races; its men will no longer have to venture into the distant, dangerous environment of other races in the colonies. In celebrating the equal distribution of wealth, the novel also offers an implicit rebuke to the upper class, for had Rochester's father been willing to divide his estate equally between his sons, Rochester, the younger brother, would never have become sullied by the contaminating environment of the West Indian colonies. With Jane, from the perspective of the middle class, Brontë redefines the claims of brotherhood, as her plot redistributes wealth: truly acknowledged fraternity, the novel suggests, requires distributing wealth equally, not, with an injustice that emanates from the upper class, letting a middle-class brother or sister remain a penniless 'slave'.

But to only a limited group among those who might ask, 'Am I not a man and a brother?' does the novel answer, 'Yes'. The plot of *Jane Eyre* works toward a redistribution of power and wealth, equalisation and an end to oppression just as Jane herself does, but its utopia remains partial; its 'revolution' improves only the lot of the middle class, closing out both the working class and those from whom the figure of slavery has been appropriated in the first place. As Jane phrases her 'revolution', it is one that specifically depends on erasing the mark of the 'dark races'.

To signify her utopian end to economic injustice, Jane creates a clean, healthy environment, free of plague: her aim, she tells St John, is 'to *clean down* (do you comprehend the full force of the expression?) to *clean down* Moor-House from chamber to cellar' (p. 498). Jane works literally to set her own house in order, creating a clean, healthy, egalitarian, middle-class, domestic environment as the alternative to inequality and injustice. This environment is not, however, to the taste of St John, who wants to force Jane into an inegalitarian marriage and to take her to the unhealthy atmosphere of British India (both of which she says would kill her) to help him preach to dark-skinned people his rather different values of hierarchical subordination. Jane recognises this difference in mentality and their incompatibility when St John does not appreciate her house cleaning, her cleaning of the 'plague' of inequality out of the domestic space of England. 'This parlour is not his sphere', she realises, 'the Himalayan ridge, or Caffre bush, even the plague-cursed Guinea Coast swamp, would suit him better' (p. 502).

St John's association with 'plague-cursed' colonial environments rather than with England, cleanliness, and home reveals his preference, within the novel's symbolic framework, for domination rather than equality, that is, for values precisely at odds with those affirmed by both Jane and the novel itself. There has been virtual consensus, among those who touch on the issue of imperialism in the novel, that St John is the voice of the novel's own imperialist ideology.[30] But to read him in this way is to elide all the ways in which the novel calls this character into question. And the novel's critique of St John is hard to overlook: Jane insistently describes him as stony, dominating, and heartless. In an article on the novel's ending, Carolyn Williams attends in detail to the novel's intertextual last words, in which Jane quotes St John quoting the last words of the Bible, the section of the novel most repeatedly cited by other critics as evidence of Brontë's endorsement of St John's imperialist missionary activity. In her reading of these last paragraphs, Williams argues convincingly that the novel protests against the 'coercive mediation' represented by St John, who claims to speak for Nature and for God, 'a protest that is at once Protestant ... and feminist in its force'.[31] The novel represents St John as presumptuously assuming the voice of God in relation to Jane. Williams focuses on St John's mediating relation to Jane, and only briefly mentions his relation to the Indians whom he sails off to civilise, but the implicit parallels drawn by the novel between Jane and the Indians suggest that St John intends to take on an equally dubious mediating role in relation to the Hindus, learning their language the better to assume the voice of God toward them as well. The novel's critique of St John's dubious mediations is thus also intrinsically a critique of his missionary imperialism: his desire to 'hew down' others' 'prejudices of creed' (p. 578).

Indeed, from the moment St John is first physically described, he is associated with an icy racial superiority implicitly condemned by the novel, as Jane is its first target. St John himself has the Grecian physiognomy considered by nineteenth-century racial taxonomy the highest exemplar of racial type. Charles White's influential account of racial gradation, for example, describes the racial hierarchy using facial angles, as follows: 'The facial line of a monkey makes an angle of 42 [degrees], with the horizontal line; that of an orangoutang, 58; that of a negro, 70; of a Chinese, 75; of an European, 80 or 90. The Roman painters preferred the angle of 95; the Grecian antique, 100.'[32] But St John's description in the novel is less than appealing. As Jane notes, 'it is seldom, indeed, an English face comes so near the antique models as did his' (p. 440). St John is (chillingly) more like a statue or a painting representing a racial archetype than he is like a human being. When St John reveals his disinclination toward domesticity, Jane describes his forehead as 'still and pale as a white stone' (p. 501); he has 'blue, pictorial-looking eyes' (p. 440). And when Jane first looks at him she finds him as easy to examine as if he had been 'a statue instead of a man' (p. 440). She continues:

> He was young – perhaps from twenty-eight to thirty – tall, slender; his face riveted the eye: it was like a Greek face, very pure in outline; quite a straight, classic nose; quite an Athenian mouth and chin. ... His eyes were large and blue, with brown lashes; his high forehead, colourless as ivory, was partially streaked over by careless locks of fair hair.
>   This is a gentle delineation, is it not, reader? Yet he whom it describes scarcely impressed one with the idea of a gentle, a yielding, an impressible, or even of a placid nature. Quiescent as he now sat, there was something about his nostril, his mouth, his brow, which, to my perceptions, indicated elements within either restless, or hard, or eager.
>
>   (p. 440)

From his position at the apex of the white race, St John offers as his first commentary on Jane a declaration of her physical inferiority. Against his sister's protestation to the contrary, and within Jane's hearing, he declares Jane to be 'plain': 'the grace and harmony of beauty are quite wanting in those features' (p. 433). As Jane puts it, after her first description of him, 'he might well be a little shocked at the irregularity of my lineaments, his own being so harmonious' (p. 440). Later Jane experiences St John's insistent tutelage, precisely the sort he intends to exercise on the Hindus, as an impossible demand for her physical transformation, for her ascent on the racial scale: 'He wanted to train me to an elevation I could never reach: it racked me hourly to aspire to the standard he uplifted. The thing was as impossible as to mould my irregular features to his correct and classic pattern, to give to my changeable green eyes the sea blue tint and solemn lustre of his own' (p. 509).

Recent critics have claimed that while Brontë condemns the way in which St John treats Jane, she approves of his intentions with regard to the Indians, that the parallel we see between the two was one she herself could not have seen.[33] Yet in passages like those I quote above in which she invokes (and challenges) the idea of a racial scale in which all should aspire to attain St John's forehead of white stone, it is Brontë herself who draws the parallel between Jane's position in relation to St John and that of the Indians whom he sails off to civilise with the derogatory gaze of his 'sea blue' eyes. Indeed, at one point St John himself draws a parallel between Jane and the natives of India. In doing so, St John resembles the other self-righteous minister to whom Jane has been like a Hindu: the Reverend Brocklehurst. When St John tells Jane that should she refuse to come to India with him she may be 'numbered with those who have denied the faith and are worse than infidels!' (p. 522), he echoes Brocklehurst's declaration that the child Jane, although 'the native of a Christian land', is 'worse than many a little heathen who says its prayers to Brahma and kneels before Juggernaut' (pp. 76–7). The echo hints that St John's fervent quest to convert the infidels is as misguided, and as destructive, as Brocklehurst's charitable missions.

In the final pages of the novel, Brontë again compares Jane to the natives of India. When Jane taunts Rochester after they reunite at Ferndean, by evoking his suspicions that she may be in love with St John, whose fair 'Grecian profile' she has just described for him, she perceives that jealousy has stung him. That sting is good for him, she comments, adding, 'I would not, therefore, immediately charm the snake' (p. 565). This final description of Jane as a snake charmer, in an image again associating her, although in an indubitably orientalist fashion, with the natives of India, once more suggests that the novel by no means unambiguously endorses St John's Indian mission.

It is crucial as well that Jane refuses to accompany St John to India as a missionary. Instead of deciding that it is her vocation to enter St John's environment of plague, dark-skinned people, and hierarchical oppression, Jane experiences an alternative call to return to a house which, being larger than Moor House and more stained by inequality and injustice, it will be considerably more difficult to 'clean down' – Rochester's Thornfield. But of course when she gets there she finds that this home Rochester once described as a plague-house has already been cleaned down. Brontë's plot participates in the same activity as Jane – cleaning, purifying, trying to create a domestic, English world free of oppression. The plot works precisely in the terms of Jane's French-inflected rhetoric of revolution. It redistributes wealth and the power of gender, and it does so both through the agency of Bertha, and then by cleaning her, as the staining woman of the 'dark races' who has represented oppression, out of the world of the novel.

In the ending of the novel, Brontë has created the world she can imagine free of the forms of oppression against which the novel most passionately protests, inequalities of gender and economic injustice toward the lower middle class. The energies that made the novel's contemporary readers anxious lie in its utopian closure: the ending, as the echo of the French revolutionary slogan suggests, symbolically enacts Brontë's conception of a social revolution on behalf of women and the lower middle class. The mutilation of Rochester and the loss of his property in Thornfield redistributes power between him and the newly propertied Jane. Jane tells her former master emphatically that she is now both independent and rich: 'I am', she says, 'my own mistress' (p. 556). And in the last chapter Jane explicitly describes their marriage as egalitarian, unlike most: 'I hold myself supremely blest – blest beyond what language can express; because I am my husband's life as fully as he is mine' (p. 576).

The ending of the novel severely punishes Rochester both for his figurative enslavement of women and for his acquisition of colonial wealth. The blinding of Rochester recalls a passage from David Hume's essay 'Of Love and Marriage' in which Hume recounts an anecdote told of the Scythian women, who, tired of their subordination in marriage, conspired to surprise the men 'in drink, or asleep; bound them all fast in chains; and having called a solemn council of the whole sex, ... debated what expedient should be used to improve the present advantage, and prevent their falling again into slavery'.[34] Despite their former enslavement, the women do not relish the idea of killing the men, and

> it was, therefore, agreed to put out the eyes of the whole male sex, and thereby resign in all future time the vanity which they could draw from their beauty, in order to secure their authority. We must no longer pretend to dress and show, said they; but then we shall be free from slavery. We shall hear no more tender sighs; but in return we shall hear no more imperious commands.[35]

For Jane, who has never had beauty, and for whom the obligation of elaborate dress, the obligation to make herself into a showy visual object for Rochester, has itself made her feel like a slave, the blinding of Rochester is liberating: it takes from him any power of male visual evaluation of her. As the servant Mary says at the end of the sightless Rochester, and his feelings for Jane, 'i' his een she's fair beautiful, onybody may see that' (p. 575). Fulfilling Rochester's own allusion to the accursed wealth wrongfully stolen by Achan, Brontë's ending enacts also a purifying destruction of Rochester's ill-gotten colonial wealth, like that of Achan who is 'stoned with stones and burned with fire' (Joshua 7:25) for bringing the 'accursed thing' into the camp of Israel. Rochester, unlike Achan, survives, but his 'tent of Achan', the luxurious, oppressive plague-house to which he has brought an ill-gotten colonial fortune, is destroyed as his misbegotten wealth is symbolically exorcised from the novel.

But the symbolic revolution against both inequalities of gender and the economic injustices suffered by the middle class, and even the purifying away of the ill-gotten wealth of empire, are made possible in the novel by another sort of oppression and suppression. This symbolic revolution is initiated by the dark woman who has been imported from the colonies to signify both the oppressed and the oppressor. Bertha institutes the great act of cleaning in the novel, which burns away Rochester's oppressive colonial wealth and diminishes the power of his gender, but then she herself is cleaned away, burned and as it were purified from the novel. Brontë creates a character of the non-white races to use as the vividly embodied signifier of oppression in the novel, and then has this sign, by the explosive instability of the situation it embodies, destroy itself.

Jane Eyre ends with the purified, more egalitarian world created by this figurative sacrifice of the 'dark races', Brontë's complex modification of available metaphors. But the novel does not end as peacefully as we might expect after this act of annihilation. The ending of the novel betrays Brontë's uneasiness about her own figurative tactics, about the way in which her metaphorical use of race involves erasing the humanity of those of other races. This uneasiness becomes evident in the way the spectre of the racial 'other' remains to haunt the ending of the novel, refusing to be fully erased, although evaporated into the form of the 'dank and insalubrious' mist that hovers over Ferndean, where Jane and Rochester settle after the cleaning down of Thornfield (pp. 550–1). The dank and unhealthy atmosphere of Ferndean is reminiscent of other oppressive, unhealthy environments in the novel and of Grace Poole's periodical emergences from the attic, 'damping' Jane's spirits. It disrupts the utopian qualities of the ending, indicating that the world of the novel is still not fully purified from the unhealthy atmosphere of unjust hierarchy. And the unjust inequality that the insalubrious atmosphere signifies, now that it no longer refers to class or gender oppression, must be the original form of oppression that the novel has tried so hard to displace and repress: the oppression of various non-white races by the British.

The atmosphere of Ferndean recalls the fact that, even if Rochester's tainted colonial wealth has been burned away by the ending of the novel, as the Achan allusion strongly suggests, the very wealth Jane is able to bring him, enabling her to meet him on more equal terms, and the very wealth she distributes with such a scrupulously egalitarian and 'revolutionary' spirit, has a colonial source. It comes from her uncle in Madeira, who is an agent for a Jamaican wine manufacturer, Bertha's brother. The location of Jane's uncle John in Madeira, off Morocco, on the West African coast, where Richard Mason stops on his way home from England, also indirectly suggests, through Mason's itinerary, the triangular route of the British slave traders, and suggests that John Eyre's wealth is implicated in the slave trade. The resonant details of the scene in which Brontë has Jane acquire her fortune mark Jane's financial and literary implication in colonialism as well. St John announces Jane's accession to fortune by pulling the letter out of a 'morocco pocket-book' (p. 483), and he is able to identify Jane as the heiress because she has written her name, on a white sheet of paper, in 'Indian ink' (p. 486).

In this way the novel implicates the act of writing itself in colonialism. The pigment in which Jane has absently traced her name, like the leather of St John's wallet, has a colonial provenance, as the names of both reveal.[36] The words Jane writes in Indian ink are both her own name and the novel's title. Specifically writing 'Jane Eyre', the passage suggests, creating one's own triumphant identity as a woman no longer oppressed by class or gender inequalities at home in England – or writing *Jane Eyre*, the fiction of a redistribution of wealth and of power between men and women – depends on a colonial ink. Whether advertently or not, Brontë acknowledges that dependence in the conclusion of *Jane Eyre*. Like imperialist trade itself, bringing home the spoils of other countries to become commodities in England, such as Indian ink, the use of the racial 'other' as a metaphor for class and gender struggles in England commodifies the dark-skinned people of the British empire as they exist in historical actuality and transforms them into East or West Indian ink, ink with which to write a novel about ending injustices within England.

The eruption of the words 'Indian ink' into the novel at this telling moment hints at Brontë's uneasiness about the East Indian ventures to which England was turning in 1848, as well as about the West Indian colonies that were by then clearly becoming unprofitable after the abolition of slavery. St John, who is given the last words in the novel, writes them from India as he is dying. He is killed off by the insalubrious atmosphere of domination in British India, where he undoubtedly has made the Indians feel, as he did Jane, the inferiority of their non-Grecian features. With the same retributive poetic justice Rochester is nearly killed when his West Indian 'plague-house' collapses on him. Brontë's anxiety about British imperialism is everywhere apparent in the ending of *Jane Eyre*. The novel is finally unable to rest easily in its figurative strategy and its Anglocentric anti-imperialist politics: its opposition to colonial contact, which it portrays as contaminating and self-destructive for the English people, and its advocacy of a middle-class English domesticity freed from some of the most blatant forms of gender and class inequality. *Jane Eyre* is thus a fascinating example of the associations – and dissociations – between a resistance to the ideology of male domination and a resistance to the ideology of imperialist domination.

The critique of imperialism that the novel promises to make through its metaphorical yoking of forms of oppression finally collapses into a mere uneasiness about the effects of empire on domestic social relations in England. That disquietude is the only remnant of Brontë's potentially radical revision of ideas about the similitude of white women and colonised peoples, and it is the only incomplete element in the ideological closure of the novel. The insalubrious mist that suggests British contact in the empire with other races, diffused throughout the ending of the novel, betrays Brontë's lingering anxiety about British imperialism and about her own literary treatment of other races, about the way in which, through her figurative tactics, she has tried to make the world of her novel 'clean'.

From Susan L. Meyer, *Imperialism at Home: Race in Victorian Women's Fiction* (Ithaca, NY, 1996), pp. 60–95.

NOTES

[This essay, which originally appeared in a slightly different form in *Victorian Studies*, 33:2 (Winter 1990), 247–68, reflects an increasing concern in Victorian studies not merely with issues of class and gender but also with issues of race. In her seminal essay 'Three women's texts and a critique of imperialism' (*Critical Inquiry*, 12 [1985], 243–61) Gayatri Chakravorty Spivak attacked the appropriation of *Jane Eyre* as 'a cult text of feminism', arguing that Jane's individualist triumph, made possible by Bertha Rochester's death, is paradigmatic of a feminist methodology which requires 'a self-immolating colonial subject for the glorification of the social mission of the coloniser'. Here, Meyer explores the figurative use of race in *Jane Eyre* less polemically and more extensively, suggesting that the novel's deployment of colonialist discourse is altogether more contradictory than Spivak allows. What she finds in *Jane Eyre* is not an unquestioned ideology of imperialism, but one which is 'questioned – and then reaffirmed – in interesting and illuminating ways'. Since Meyer's essay first appeared, there has been a burgeoning of interest in the question of race in *Jane Eyre*: the reader is referred to the section on *Further Reading* for a brief account of some of the most interesting critical handlings of this theme. References in this essay are to the Clarendon edition of *Jane Eyre*, ed. Jane Jack and Margaret Smith (Oxford, 1969). Ed.]

1. See Susan Meyer, '"Black" Rage and White Women: Ideological Self-Formation in Charlotte Brontë's African Tales', *South Central Review*, 8:4 (1991), 28–40 and Christine Alexander, *The Early Writings of Charlotte Brontë* (Oxford, 1983), p. 30. Alexander points out that the Brontë children located their colony in Fernando Po, which a writer for *Blackwood's Magazine* had been advocating as an apt spot for British colonisation.

2. Charlotte Brontë, *Shirley*, ed. Herbert Rosengarten and Margaret Smith (Oxford, 1981), p. 613.

3. In 'The Isle of Devils', a thinly disguised verse-narrative about race relations in the British West Indies, Monk Lewis creates a horrible monster, 'black as the storm', who rapes a beautiful white virgin after her ship is wrecked near his island during a tempest. See Matthew Lewis, 'The Isle of Devils' (1815) in *Journal of a West Indian Proprietor* (London, 1834), pp. 261–89. In Harriet Martineau's far more progressive and self-aware anti-slavery novel, *Demerara*, a West Indian hurricane enacts the rage the slaves themselves cannot: the slaves in her novel exult at the ravages the storm commits on their master's property, cry out with 'horrid yells' as they watch their overseer drowning, and seem 'like imps of the storm' (Harriet Martineau, *Demerara*, in *Illustrations of Political Economy* [London, 1834], II, pp. 109–12). Brontë herself uses similar imagery in her juvenile Roe Head Journal when a wild storm evokes in her the vision of Africans in revolution against British colonists.

4. Charlotte Brontë, *Villette*, ed. Herbert Rosengarten and Margaret Smith (Oxford, 1984), p. 456. For a discussion of the abolition of slavery in the French West Indian colonies, see F. R. Aguier, S. C. Gordon, D. G. Hall and M. Reckord, *The Making of the West Indies*

(London, 1960), pp. 200–1; J. H. Parry and P. M. Sherlock, *A Short History of the West Indies* (New York, 1957), p. 219. Parry and Sherlock note that 'the events of 1848–49, which marked the end of slavery, foreshadowed also the end of white political supremacy ... in Martinique and Guadeloupe'.

5. Charlotte Brontë, *The Professor*, ed. Margaret Smith and Herbert Rosengarten (Oxford, 1987), p. 14. Subsequent references are included in the text.

6. Every slave plantation colony in the West Indies had its 'maroons', roaming communities of runaway slaves who had banded together and survived in the uncultivated areas of the colony. The Jamaican maroons were particularly successful and particularly threatening to the British colonists. See Michael Craton, *Testing the Chains: Resistance to Slavery in the British West Indies* (Ithaca, NY, 1982), especially pp. 61–7.

7. Charlotte Brontë, 'Emma', appended to *The Professor*, ed. Smith and Rosengarten, pp. 322–3. Subsequent references are included in the text. Ellin's 'joke' becomes even less amusing when we recall that the schoolmistress would have been prevented from selling Matilda as a slave not because black slavery no longer existed in Virginia – slavery in the United States lasted through the end of the Civil War in 1865 – but simply because England had abolished the slave trade in 1808. See Michael Craton, *Sinews of Empire: A Short History of British Slavery* (New York, 1974), pp. 239–84 for an account of the abolition and emancipation movements in England.

8. Charlotte Brontë, *Jane Eyre*, ed. Jane Jack and Margaret Smith (Oxford, 1969), pp. 63, 78. Subsequent references are included in the text.

9. Gayatri Chakravorty Spivak, 'Three women's texts and a critique of imperialism', *Critical Inquiry*, 12 (1985), 243–61. Two previous critics have made brief allusions to the significance of race in *Jane Eyre*. R. J. Dingley notes in his 'Rochester as Slave: An Allusion in *Jane Eyre*' that Rochester uses the phrase 'a man and a brother' in speaking to Jane (*Notes and Queries*, 31 [1984], p. 66). Dingley interprets the phrase as Rochester's impulsively premature declaration that the intensity of his passion makes him Jane's 'slave'. Patricia Beer frames the chapter on Charlotte Brontë in her *Reader, I Married Him: A Study of the Women Characters of Jane Austen, Charlotte Brontë, Elizabeth Gaskell and George Eliot* (New York, 1974), pp. 84–126, by suggesting that the novel draws an analogy between women and slaves and noting that Brontë, unlike Jane Austen, made 'serious ... comment' on this form of the 'slave trade' (p. 84), but she goes no further in exploring the analogy. Since the first publication of this essay as 'Colonialism and the Figurative Strategy of *Jane Eyre*' in

Victorian Studies, 33:2 (1990), 247–68, three subsequent critics have taken up the treatment of race relations in the novel. See Jenny Sharpe, *Allegories of Empire: the Figure of Woman in the Colonial Text* (Minneapolis, 1993), pp. 27–56; Elsie Michie, 'From Simianised Irish to Oriental Despots: Heathcliff, Rochester and Racial Difference', *Novel*, 25:2 (1992), 125–40; Suvendrini Perera, *Reaches of Empire: the English Novel from Edgeworth to Dickens* (New York, 1991), pp. 79–102.

10. Here Spivak may be alluding to Homi Bhabha's notion of a unified 'colonial subject' that encompasses both the coloniser and colonised (Homi K. Bhabha, 'The Other Question. ... The Stereotype and Colonial Discourse', *Screen*, 24:19). Abdul R. JanMohamed ably takes issue with this notion in 'The Economy of Manichean Allegory: the Function of Racial Difference in Colonialist Literature', *Critical Inquiry*, 12 (1985), 59–87.

11. See, for example, Adrienne Rich's reference to Bertha's 'dark sensual beauty' in 'Jane Eyre: the Temptations of a Motherless Woman' (1973), reprinted in her *On Lies, Secrets and Silence: Selected Prose 1966–1978* (New York, 1979), or Sandra Gilbert and Susan Gubar's description of Bertha as 'a Creole – swarthy, "livid", etc.', in *The Madwoman in the Attic: the Woman Writer and the Nineteenth-Century Literary Imagination* (New Haven, CT, 1979), p. 680n.

12. See Winthrop Jordan, *The White Man's Burden: Historical Origins of Racism in the United States* (New York, 1974), pp. 70–3 and Craton, *Sinews of Empire*, pp. 176, 181–6, 223–6 for the practice of and attitudes toward interracial sex and manumission in the English colonies.

13. John Malcolm Forbes Ludlow, *A Sketch of the History of the United States* (Cambridge, 1862), p. 316. This passage is quoted in *The Oxford English Dictionary*, 2nd edn (Oxford, 1989), IV, p. 7.

14. For the association of the racial 'other' with madness, see Sander Gilman, *Difference and Pathology: Stereotypes of Sexuality, Race, and Madness* (Ithaca, NY, 1985), especially ch. 5. A more lengthy discussion of the ambiguity of the word 'Creole' appears in Christopher Miller, *Blank Darkness: Africanist Discourses in French* (Chicago, 1985), pp. 93–107.

15. 'The West Indian Controversy', *Blackwood's Edinburgh Magazine*, 14 (1823), p. 442.

16. Q. D. Leavis, in Q. D. Leavis (ed.), *Jane Eyre* (New York, 1984), pp. 487–9.

17. Terry Eagleton, *Myths of Power: a Marxist Study of the Brontës* (New York, 1975), pp. 4, 16.

18. Jina Politi, '*Jane Eyre* Class-ified', *Literature and History*, 8 (1) (1982), 66. [Reprinted in this volume – see p. 78. Ed.] See also Kathryn Sutherland, '*Jane Eyre*'s Literary History: the Case for *Mansfield Park*', *English Literary History*, 59 (1992), 409–40.

19. Carol Ohmann, 'Historical Reality and "Divine Appointment" in Charlotte Brontë's Fiction', *Signs*, 2 (1977), 757–78; Igor Webb, *From Custom to Capital: the English Novel and the Industrial Revolution* (Ithaca, NY, 1981), pp. 70–86.

20. Ohmann, 'Historical Reality', 762.

21. Webb, *From Custom to Capital*, p. 86.

22. See Patricia Meyer Spacks, *The Female Imagination* (New York, 1972), pp. 64–5; Rich, 'Temptations', pp. 97–9; Gilbert and Gubar, *Madwoman in the Attic*, pp. 336–71.

23. Robert Knox, *The Races of Men: A Fragment* (Philadelphia, 1850), p. 151.

24. For a treatment of the European fear of 'going native' in the colonies, which includes a discussion of Kurtz in Conrad's *The Heart of Darkness*, see Patrick Brantlinger, 'Victorians and Africans: the Genealogy of the Myth of the Dark Continent', *Critical Inquiry*, 12 (1985), 166–203.

25. I would like to thank Katherine Snyder for referring me to this passage.

26. See Charles White, *An Account of the Regular Gradation in Man and in Different Animals and Vegetables* (London, 1799), p. 51n. Or compare the well-known essay by the American physician Samuel Cartwright, 'Natural History of the Prognathous Species of Mankind', in which he cites Cuvier to explain, succinctly, that the word 'prognathous' 'is a technical term derived from *pro*, before, and *gnathos*, the jaws, indicating that the muzzle or mouth is anterior to the brain. The lower animals, according to Cuvier, are distinguished from the European and Mongol man by the mouth and face projecting further forward in the profile than the brain. ... The typical negroes of adult age, when tried by this rule, are proved to belong to a different species from the man of Europe or Asia ... their mouth and jaws projecting beyond the forehead contain the anterior lobes of the brain. Moreover, their faces are proportionally larger than their crania' (*New York Day-Book*, 10 November 1857; reprinted in Eric L. McKitrick [ed.], *Slavery Defended: the Views of the Old South* [Englewood Cliffs, NJ, 1963], pp. 139–40).

27. At the novel's end, St John goes to India to 'hew down like a giant the prejudices of creed and caste that encumber it', although the novel has made clear that such energy is better spent attempting to obliterate this sort of prejudice in England.

28. See Leonore Davidoff's analysis of the relationship between the upper middle-class Victorian writer A. J. Munby and his servant Hannah Cullwick in 'Class and Gender in Victorian England', in *Sex and Class in Women's History*, ed. Judith L. Newton, Mary P. Ryan and Judith R. Walkowitz (Boston, 1983), pp. 17–71, and Peter Stallybrass and Allon White, 'The City: The Sewer, the Gaze and the Contaminating Touch' in *The Politics and Poetics of Transgression* (Ithaca, NY, 1986), pp. 125–48, for two discussions of the nineteenth-century bourgeoisie's equation of dirt and pollution with 'the lower orders'.

29. Patricia Beer also notes that 'the fresh air and the open countryside remain [for Jane] symbols of personal freedom and independence' which she opposes to the thought of suffocation as Rochester's 'slave' (Beer, *Reader, I Married Him*, p. 126).

30. Francis G. Hutchins writes in *The Illusion of Permanence: British Imperialism in India* (Princeton, NJ, 1967), p. 32, that while Jane rejected St John's 'tyranny for herself', she (and, he implies, Brontë with her) 'warmly rejoiced to see it exercised in India where she felt its sternness would be beneficial'. Politi similarly contends that 'the text will conceal the complicity of the Church with Imperialism and will present St John as the disinterested missionary' (Politi, '*Jane Eyre* Class-ified', 59). [See this volume, p. 82. Ed.] Spivak also sees 'the unquestioned idiom of imperialist presuppositions' in the novel's concluding description of St John (Spivak, 'Three women's texts', 249). Parama Roy, in 'Unaccommodated Woman and the Poetics of Property in *Jane Eyre*', *Studies in English Literature*, 29 (1989), 721, finds 'a reflexive endorsement of patriarchalism in the chapters on St John and his vocation to convert the heathen', and claims that Brontë has 'the most unambiguous respect for the missionary's job' (723). Michie claims that the novel represents missionary work as 'pure' (Michie, 'From Simianised Irish to Oriental Despots', 138), and Sharpe argues that 'the grand narrative' of the colonial 'civilising mission', voiced by St John, legitimates and creates a space for Jane's creation of her autobiographical self (Sharpe, *Allegories of Empire*, p. 38). David Bromwich, responding to Spivak, differs from the prevailing reading not by questioning the valuation of Rivers as the voice of the novel's ideology, but by claiming, without textual elaboration, that 'the novel identifies Rivers as belonging to an evangelical sect that fought hard for the abolition of slavery: his parentage, though at a distance, includes men like Zachary Macaulay. If described as imperialist, it ought to be described carefully' (David Bromwich, *A Choice of Inheritance* [Cambridge, MA, 1989]), p. 267.

31. Carolyn Williams, 'Closing the Book: the Intertextual End of *Jane Eyre*', in *Victorian Connections*, ed. Jerome McGann (Charlottesville, VA, 1989), pp. 80–1. [Reprinted in this volume – see p. 227. Ed.]

32. White, *Account of the Regular Gradation in Man*, p. 51n.

33. See, for example, Roy, 'Unaccommodated Woman', 723.

34. David Hume, 'Of Love and Marriage', in *Essays: Moral, Political and Literary*, ed. Eugene F. Miller (Indianapolis, 1985), p. 559.

35. Ibid, p. 559.

36. According to the *OED*, Indian ink, also and more accurately known as China ink, is 'a black pigment made in China and Japan, sold in sticks; understood to consist of lampblack made into a paste with a solution of gum and dried'.

6

Jane Eyre

PENNY BOUMELHA

GINGER-NUTS

Counselling the young Jane Eyre in the avoidance of going to Hell, the Reverend Mr Brocklehurst tells her an anecdote:

> 'I have a little boy, younger than you, who knows six Psalms by heart; and when you ask him which he would rather have, a ginger-bread-nut to eat, or a verse of a Psalm to learn, he says: "Oh! the verse of a Psalm! Angels sing Psalms;" says he, "I wish to be a little angel here below;" he then gets two nuts in recompense for his infant piety.'[1]

This story passes without comment, other than Jane's infant impiety that '"Psalms are not interesting"', and it is hard to know who, if anyone, is being ironised here: Mr Brocklehurst, with his stupendous obliviousness to manipulation, seems the most obvious candidate. But this fable of deferred gratification rehearses in little, and with the same puzzling apparent lack of self-consciousness, the path that Jane herself will follow in the course of her narrative, a course which leads her quite flagrantly into the best of both worlds, into material wealth and spiritual capital, into the satisfaction of appetite and the self-satisfaction of sacrifice. Jane, of course, has somewhat clearer notions of the proper sphere for angels than the pious infant, and indeed than Rochester, who appears to think they are interchangeable with witches and fairies, and are to be had in the house as mistresses, if not wives: '"I am no angel", she tells him, "and I will not be one till I die"' (p. 262). Nevertheless, Providence, like Mr Brocklehurst, rewards her choice of principle over pleasure with plenty of gingerbread, lavishly gilded. What has troubled many readings of the novel has been precisely this coincidence of the narrating and narrated Janes, the sense that no textual space is left for consideration of the way in which the oppressed and rebellious child turns into the lady, the victim of the Red-Room into the keeper of the keys in the patriarchal household. One longstanding answer to the problem has been to refer it back to Brontë herself, to deplore a lapse into 'wish-fulfilment' which can, as often as not, be in its turn attributed to the author's marital and sexual status at the time of composition: 'the invention of a thirty-year old virgin' as one commentator succinctly, if offensively, puts it.[2] Alternatively, some have attributed some level of disguised motivation to the character herself, taking the 'providence' of the narrative less as divine intervention than as foresight, prudent and timely care for the future: so, Eagleton finds 'a good deal of dexterous calculation' in Jane's pursuit of Mr Rochester's money.[3]

The problem of the unremarked ideological shift in the novel becomes acute, of course, in feminist readings, and there has developed something of a dichotomy. On the one hand, more narrowly class- and race-blind interpretations have celebrated here a feminist version of what Hermione Lee calls an 'epic of self-determination':[4] the painful acquisition of identity ('"I am Jane Eyre"' [p. 439]), of independence ('"I am independent, sir, as well as rich: I am my own mistress"' [p. 440]), and of a marriage of equals ('I am my husband's life as fully as he is mine' [p. 456]). This reading, focusing on the realist level of the narrative – a persecuted orphan, a rebellious girl, a woman finding satisfaction in education and work, a female narrator finding the language to tell her own story – in the process also takes on, in Gayatri Spivak's words, 'the mesmerising focus of the "subject-constitution" of the female individualist'[5] that has so often been the tale feminist criticism tells itself. On the other hand, if the focus is adjusted to take in those marginalised but constitutive textual discourses of class and race, another story emerges: 'no social revolutionary', argues Lee R. Edwards, 'Jane is rather a displaced spiritual aristocrat'; Politi analyses how 'the narrative together with the girl-child will grow from revolted marginality to quiescent socialisation, reblending the contradictions which it initially exposed, thus securing its survival through the convention of a "happy ending"'; and Weissman concludes that 'the end of the book reveals the first half for what it is – not the rage of the Romantic radical who wants justice, but the rage of the outsider who just wants to get in.'[6]

Most tellingly, perhaps, our attention is then drawn to those other women whose stories are occluded by Jane's: for example, to Bessie, female servant whose tales and ballads are Jane's alternative education, in orphanhood, in class position, and in narrating; to Grace Poole, working-class woman who guards the secrets of female delinquency and 'giant propensities' (p. 310) in the heart of the 'gentleman's manor-house' (p. 100); and, above all, to Bertha Mason Rochester.[7] Bertha: not only madwoman in the attic,[8] after all, but also skeleton in the closet, the 'dark' secret, the maddening burden of imperialism concealed in the heart of every English gentleman's house of the time. Dark, but not black: while the word 'creole' marks a double displacement of origins, Bertha is fixed as white by her status as daughter of settler planters. Maddening, but not maddened: the intrinsic, racial/familial nature of Bertha's 'moral madness'[9] serves to exculpate Rochester, and with him the English gentry class, from so much as complicity in her plight.

Jane Eyre, like many another Victorian novel, turns upon questions of inheritance, but here in an unusually multiple and self-mirroring form. Every main character in the novel is involved in a series of inheritances diverted and denied, and each of these is restored by the end of the book. Most importantly for my purposes here, all of them derive from Jamaica and from Bertha's blood relations, that same blood that is 'tainted' with madness and vice. Here, you might say, lies the source of the ginger for Jane's ginger-nuts. Through Uncle Eyre's connection with the planter family, the Masons, this inheritance links Jane into the financial chain that ultimately binds together the military (Diana's naval husband), the clergy (Mary's clergyman husband) and the cultural imperialism of St John Rivers, who will use his share of the inheritance to 'labour for his race' (p. 457) in India. Most obviously, Jamaica is the source of Rochester's wealth; his father's adherence to the rules of primogeniture having denied the second son an inheritance, he is led into a marital exchange by which he acquires thirty thousand pounds and an indissoluble tie to 'tainted' blood, and the Mason family the advantages of connection with his 'good race' (p. 309). This is the story which cannot be fully spoken in the novel: it erupts, nonetheless, in Bertha's wordless laugh and 'eccentric murmurs' (p. 111) and in the document, riven with blanks, that testifies to the unbreakable tie between Rochester and what is secret, shameful and suppressed (p. 293).

There are, I think, ten explicit references to slavery in *Jane Eyre*. They allude to slavery in Ancient Rome and in the seraglio, to the slaveries of paid work as a governess and of dependence as a mistress. None of them refers to the slave trade upon which the fortunes of all in the novel are based. Quakers, of course, had been among the first and most prominent opponents of English slavery, but Jane's own Quakerishness, so often commented upon, leads her only as far as a stern opposition to distant or metaphorical forms of enslavement.[10] This brings us close to one of the central problems of the novel, and in turn of certain kinds of feminist readings of it: the apparently blithe predication of the liberty and happiness of a few upon the confinement and suffering of the many. There is a single glimpse of this, in a different sort of context, during the episode of the typhus epidemic at Lowood, when Jane first begins to explore those 'prospects' in the wider world to which the novel so often adverts: she remarks here, as she will remark nowhere else, that 'for this unwonted liberty and pleasure, there was a cause' (p. 77). And that cause is, precisely, that other girls cannot go where she is freed to go.

In saying this, I do not wish for a moment to deny that *Jane Eyre* can bring all the pleasures of a paradigmatic 'woman's novel'. It is a canonical novel in a 'high' genre, the *Bildungsroman*, composed of the intermingling and collision of a number of 'low' or para-literary forms, many of them associated with women as readers or writers: the Gothic novel, the ballad, the folk-tale, the fairy-tale, romantic fiction, the governess novel, children's fiction, spiritual autobiography, have all been detected within it, and some of them discussed in detail.[11] The point is that contemporary feminist criticism must not, surely, reproduce the silences and occlusions of nineteenth-century English culture in allowing the white, middle-class woman to stand as its own 'paradigmatic woman'. Of course, generations of female readers have thrilled to Jane's double success story, to the vindication of her principles and the high romance of her return to Rochester, though a not uncommon sneaking dissatisfaction with the last chapters betrays, I think, an awareness of its mystification, through the notorious literalised pun that is Rochester's telepathic summons, of the 'vocation' of the woman. I do not think it is necessary to take an accusatory attitude towards Brontë (and it is clearly futile to take such a stance towards Jane) in order to analyse what is happening in *Jane Eyre*: it is possible to trace in the trajectory, in the very form of the novel, a complex configuration of the determinations of class, kin, gender and – what is nowhere spoken but is omnipresent – race that interacts and conflicts to turn Jane Eyre the '"mad cat"' (p. 12) and 'revolted slave' (p. 14) of the opening into the Mrs Rochester of the close. The difficulty is to honour what can be honoured of its female heroism without suppressing a recognition of the social formation to which, along with her twenty thousand pounds, Jane is heir.

MOTHERS AND FATHERS

It has been suggested that there is a matriarchal story within *Jane Eyre*, of Jane's turning to and learning from mother figures.[12] There is the shadow of such a narrative in the novel, but it is, I think, a defeatist one in which Jane tests the limits of a mother-centred world and is turned back to the patriarchal determinations of kinship and inheritance. In any case, it is important to note at the outset that Jane begins less as a conscientious objector to the patriarchal organisation of society than as an outcast from it. Her earliest awareness of injustice results, not particularly from generalised or abstract principle, but rather from the sense of being denied what is rightfully hers – and ultimately, of course, she will be shown to be justified in this. This sense becomes apparent even on the opening page, when the initial first-person plural – 'we had been wandering ... in the leafless shrubbery' (p. 7) – splits as Jane is marked as, grammatically even, not one of us. The pain of this split for her is recorded in a sentence where syntactical inversion serves to assert simultaneously her self-awareness and the unnaturalness of the event: 'Me, she had dispensed from joining the group' (p. 7). This exclusion from the family grouping – one repeated and finally overcome in the recurrence of that particular family configuration (mother, brother, two sisters) in the novel – brings with it, as it must, an exile from class: '"You are a dependant, mama says; you have no money; your father left you none; you ought to beg, and not to live here with gentlemen's children like us"' (p. 11). John Reed, too, is proved right: Jane does come to beg, and only when she finds an inheritance is she able to live on terms of equality with 'gentlemen's children'. Bessie confirms that Jane's class position is less a descent than a state of suspension: '"You are less than a servant, for you do nothing for your keep"' (p. 12). And patriarchy is at once built into this double rejection: '"Now, I'll teach you to rummage my bookshelves: for they *are* mine; all the house belongs to me, or will do in a few years"' (p. 11). All, then – family, class, inheritance – hinges upon patrilineage. That culture, too, has a double role in the house of the master, that books have power to *hurt* as well as to enlarge horizons, is also apparent when the very book she has found 'profoundly interesting' (p. 9), however mysterious, is flung at her head and cuts it open. So Jane is triply disinherited in the first chapter of the novel, while obliged to live within the structures of inheritance, and hence that very poignant moment when she feels 'an inexpressible relief, a soothing conviction of protection and security, when I knew there was a stranger in the room' (p. 19).

The later Jane, the narrator, offers a retrospective justification of the behaviour of the Reeds by suggesting that neither the kinship of likeness ('I was like nobody there' [p. 15]) nor the kinship of the family ('They were not bound to regard with affection ... a heterogeneous thing' [p. 15]) obliges them to any more humane treatment. The novel will continue to explore this double meaning of kinship – being like, being related – until their triumphal reinstatement at the ending, with the finding of the Rivers family and her marriage with Rochester. Here, though, Jane's initial weapon and revenge against persecution comes in the first of those instances when 'something' not herself speaks through her; here, she all but ventriloquises the voice of Uncle Reed: 'something spoke out of me over which I had no control' (p. 27). Her question, so terrible as to strike her aunt dumb, is '"What would Uncle Reed say to you if he were alive?"' (p. 27), and it asserts not (or not only) a generalised moral reproach, but the power of the family and of the father within it. Elaine Showalter has remarked on the fact that *Jane Eyre* is virtually peopled with female surrogates for absent powerful males[13] – Mrs Reed, Miss Temple, Mrs Fairfax, Grace Poole – but it is remarkable that only Jane, here briefly among them, takes on the unique power of invoking (not, of course, uttering) the very words of this absentee landlord of patriarchal ideology.

So, then, Mrs Reed the archetypal 'bad mother' figure is rebuked by means of the authority of the father figure, and this sets the pattern for a series of neglectful, powerless or inadequate surrogate mothers in the novel. Miss Temple, for example, who 'had stood me in the stead of mother' (p. 85), now marries and leaves the community of women that is Lowood, and Jane's comments on the event leave no doubt that she regards this as in some part a defection: she 'was lost to me' and 'with her was gone every settled feeling, every association that had made Lowood in some degree a home to me' (pp. 84–5). Mrs Fairfax, at first sight such a grand-motherly figure with her 'widow's cap, black silk gown and snowy muslin apron ... occupied in knitting' (p. 96), soon proves to be 'no great dame, but a dependant like my self' (p. 101) and thus as dis-qualified from power as Jane. As mother, in any case, Mrs Fairfax proves of no assistance: she sees, and attempts to communicate, that Jane is in great danger, but can do nothing about it. After the revelation of Bertha's continuing existence and wifely status, it is in following the advice of the moon-mother in her 'trance-like dream' (p. 324) that Jane is brought to her lowest point in the novel (though, arguably, by the intervention of providence, also to family and fortune). The moon's advice – '"My daughter, flee temptation"' (p. 324) – is one of a number of transposed Biblical and religious references in the novel that interact with its anti-clericalism to ad-umbrate a possible female-centred religion;[14] it seems almost an answer to that part of the Lord's Prayer – addressed as it is to our *Father* – in which Christians ask 'Lead us not into temptation'.

But when Jane leaves Thornfield, fleeing temptation at the behest of the mother, she becomes absolutely destitute, without family or money or possessions of any sort. According to Gilbert and Gubar, the moment on the heath is emblematic of 'the essential homeless-ness – the nameless, placeless and contingent status – of women in a patriarchal society';[15] we surely do not need to accept this idea of 'essential contingency', though, to see how Jane here functions as the very type of the woman falling (or forced) outside all those structures – family, marriage, class, work – by which a patriarchal ordering of society is structured and replicates itself. It is at this point that Jane, with no point of anchorage in the patriarchal society which is the only society available to her, makes her sole ref-erence to 'the universal mother, Nature: I will suck her breast and ask repose' (p. 327). This 'universal mother' proves, however, to be without nourishment. Mothers and daughters stand in somewhat fraught relations in the novel, and not least because daughters can always, through that lawful sexuality of the marriage bed which is itself imaged in Bertha as monstrous,[16] become mothers – Jane's child-dreams, in which the child proves a burden and the mother an unsafe refuge, pick up the threatening instability of the relationship. Jane Eyre, and *Jane Eyre*, derive a double power from the *appetitive* representation of the woman – those famous images of hunger are the vehicle not only of a general deprivation, after all, but also of instinctual appetite – and from the possibility of the woman's refusal to satisfy it; Jane refuses to eat as often as she eats in the novel.[17] But here, on the heath, instinctual appetite is shown to demand satisfaction within the social world and the breast of the 'universal mother' nourishes only within the asocial world of the natural. Lizards and bees, perhaps, find what they need, 'But I was a human being, and had a human being's wants: I must not linger where there was nothing to supply them' (p. 329). The mothering moon of myth and the mothering earth of nature cannot fulfil the most minimal needs of the woman as fully social being, and this fantasied matriarchal world has no power within the world of social organisation that is necessary for survival.[18]

But a return to such a society is not easy for a woman 'without a resource: without a friend: without a coin' (pp. 330–1), and Jane's question of survival – '"And what do the women do?"' (p. 331) – has no easy or satisfactory answer: '"I know n't," was the answer. "Some does one thing, and some another. Poor folk mun get on as they can"' (p. 331). What the women do, it seems, is reinforce and enforce the power of those patriarchal structures Jane seems at this point to evade. Her attempts, at this moment of fullest deprivation and exile, to effect a re-entry into social structures are made through appeal to women. And all of them – the baker, the woman who does not want a servant, and finally Hannah – rebuff her; the most that is on offer is a mess of rejected pigswill. Refused entry, Jane finally collapses at the very door of a houseful of women: 'Alas, this isolation – this banishment from my kind!' (p. 340). Only the returning St John, like some sanctified John Reed, has the power to admit the beggar into the house of gentlemen's children, and his first act is to acknowledge, but also to take control over, that unsatisfied appetite that has structured her narrative thus far: '"Not too much at first – restrain her … she has had enough!" And he withdrew the cup of milk and the plate of bread' (p. 341).

Thereafter begins Jane's full incorporation into patriarchal society; and with it, as Jina Politi has noted, begins the novel's definitive shift away from the social determinations of realist narration and into the plot concatenations of accident, coincidence, miracle.[19] In short, thereafter begins the fullest sense of the providential narrative, the story dispensed and directed by Our Father, in which the woman who comes to know her place (her origin, her family, her marriage) inherits the earth. And, as if to reinforce this point, the providential theme means that what Jane receives is what was always meant for her; the money she acquires is no mysterious gratuity, but an inheritance that ties her fully into family, home and class by its assertion of kin. With this confirmation of kindred as relationship behind her, Jane is empowered to make the choice of kinship as likeness in her marriage; and her choice of the gentleman Rochester serves in its turn to confirm the status of 'lady' which was clearly always in some sense hers. Bessie has expressed this clearly earlier in the novel: "'Oh you are quite a lady, Miss Jane! I knew you would be"' (p. 93), and Jane later authorises it unequivocally: 'Bessie Leaven had said I was quite a lady; and she spoke truth; I was a lady' (p. 159).

For while Jane has sometimes been economically and socially dependent, her perceptions of her own class status have been unwavering; she has from the first rejected the possibility of "'belong[ing] to poor people"' (p. 24), even to the point of asserting allegiances of class over those of blood. Patronage is the tone which belongs to her dealings with all those who fall beneath her perception of herself in terms of class or English-ness; 'docile' is her highest term of approbation for such characters, as for her Yorkshire pupils and the reconstructed, 'de-Frenchified' Adèle. She is surprised to find of her 'heavy-looking, gaping rustics' that 'there was a difference amongst them as amongst the educated' (p. 370); and her greatest intimate among the servants she deals with is called Leaven, as if to note her role in what is otherwise, for Jane, the lump of the working class. Even at her moment of greatest deprivation, this class feeling is clearly in evidence. As Jane stands, penniless and half-starved, outside the window of the Rivers home, she sees a clean and modestly furnished room, and 'an elderly woman, somewhat rough-looking, but scrupulously clean, like all about her' (p. 336). Her comment upon the scene assimilates Hannah the servant into the furniture: 'I noticed these *objects* cursorily only' (p. 336; my italics). On the other hand, Diana and Mary, 'young, graceful women – ladies in every point' form 'a group of more interest' (p. 336). Jane's sense of the relationship between the three women turns entirely upon the sense – shared with some others (less infallible readers than Jane) in the novel – that class is written legibly upon the body: 'they could not be the daughters of the elderly person at the table; for she looked like a rustic, and they were all delicacy and cultivation' (p. 335). Jane, 'outcast, vagrant, and disowned by the wide world' (p. 342) though she is at this point, nevertheless retains a sense of class affiliation that has nothing to do with economics;[20] her reproof to Hannah is that she has '"made it a species of reproach that I had no 'brass' and no house"' (p. 347), but Hannah's error has been, not a lack of charitable response, but rather '"supposing me a beggar. I am no beggar ... in your sense of the word"' (p. 345). This correction is underwritten and authorised by her assertion that she is '"very ... book-learned"' (p. 345). Jane, then, is not what she seems, no beggar even when she is undeniably begging, and that is because she is *naturally* a lady.

The idea of a natural status is closely tied to the idea of a natural character which figures prominently in the novel, reinforced by the use of physiognomy and phrenology to describe and delimit the characters; these pseudo-sciences offer a reading of character that, for the skilled reader, is immediate and unchangeable, though it is possible to fail to fulfil the potential they imply.[21] So it is that Rochester is 'naturally a man of better tendencies, higher principles, and purer tastes than such as circumstances had developed' (p. 148), and so is 'naturally and inevitably loved' by Jane (p. 254). Bertha's '"pigmy intellect"' and '"giant propensities"' result from '"a nature the most gross, impure, depraved I ever saw"' (p. 311); and mistresses are "often by nature, and always by position, inferior"' (p. 316). What is odd about Jane's relation to all of this is that being 'natural' is something that does not come naturally to her; it is something which she must grow into. Mrs Reed cannot love her or accept her into the family until she acquires '"a more ... child-like disposition ... something lighter, franker, more natural, as it were"' (p. 7), for instance, and Rochester hopes that '"in time ... you will learn to be natural with me"' (p. 140). So, neither the early rebellious Jane nor the middle-period subdued Jane is 'natural', or rather they are not seen as such. And, although this has obviously to do with repressions and restrictions, it also suggests that neither the propertyless dependant nor the paid employee is the 'real', the 'natural' Jane. That character emerges only after the discovery of the inheritance, and she is Jane the natural lady whose rebellion gives way to complicity and whose wish for paid work and wide horizons is overtaken by the sense that '"domestic endearments and household joys"' are '"the best things the world has"' (p. 395).

The languages of class and of political conflict come, in the course of the novel, to be eroticised into a language of affinity and mutual dependence. Just as 'master' changes as the narrative progresses from representing a brutal assertion of power and privilege (John Reed's insistence on being called '"*Master* Reed"' [p. 9]) to the mark of an intimate and voluntary submission ('"my dear Master ... I am come back to you"' [p. 439]), so too the child Jane who opposes her doctrine of revolt to Helen's defence of Charles I (p. 57) becomes the woman who fantasises erotic flirtation in terms of sultans and slaves, '"aristocratic tastes"' and '"plebeian brides"' (p. 283). This fantasy of a cross-class marriage is supplanted by Jane's apparent transformation from '"plebeian bride"' to her '"own mistress"' (p. 440), confirming in terms of class the rightness of the marrying couple. Politi has argued that 'Jane runs away so that the workings of Divine Providence may bring about her rise in social status and save her marriage to Mr Rochester from becoming a social offence.'[22] My point is that Jane's 'rise in social status' comes in fact as a confirmation of what is already there rather than a transformation. Nature and providence are invoked to underwrite and reinstate the social institutions of class; marriage to Mr Rochester, then, is the culmination of Jane's installation in the social space Divine Providence and natural character have alike designed for her, and in this way she comes, in the fullest range of senses, to know her place.

'INCIDENT, LIFE, FIRE, FEELING' (p. 110)

In what I have said so far, as in those comments on the novel from Edwards, Politi and Weissman quoted at the beginning of the chapter (and these can be taken to represent a number of other, similar views), it is evident that what is problematic is primarily the ending of the novel, or rather, perhaps, the question of the relation of ending to beginning. The plot trajectory that takes Jane from exile to keeper of the keys, from *déclassée* to lady, from outcast of family structure to restorer and vessel of patrilineage ('the boy had inherited his own eyes' [p. 457]), from defence of the necessity and dignity of work to mystique of the woman's calling: that is what cuts so dramatically and undeniably across those obviously appealing 'heroic' readings of the vindication and achievements of Jane.[23] It is possible, however, to look at the ending as only one among a series of narrative moments, as Beaty has argued:

> The ending enforces a conservative, conformist, providential reading but it cannot erase the *experience* of the reading, which has involved the projection of alternative configurations over long stretches of the plot and subsumed innumerable details.[24]

That is to say, the sequence of the plot need not abolish the range of narrative possibilities intimated in the course of the text: we need not establish our own unitary and providential narrative of reading to set beside Jane's.

There is, of course, another story to tell in the novel and that is the story that allows her to write her woman's autobiography, not as 'Mrs Edward Rochester' but as Jane Eyre. The fortune which brings about Jane's inheritance of her woman's place also (by alerting her uncle to her intentions) disrupts that tale of '"the same theme – courtship; and ... the same catastrophe – marriage"' (p. 201); what brings her a family also bestows upon her 'an independency' (p. 271). The mechanisms by which Jane progressively gains entry to all that has been denied her, or by which providence and Charlotte Brontë bring about her satisfying revenge on all those who have injured or thwarted her, are in a sense explorations – however tentative, however fantasied – of the kinds and limits of power available to the middle-class white woman in the particular society the novel represents. Jane's *Bildungsroman*, in a way that is probably more characteristic of a hero's than a heroine's text, shows us *what* she learns, shows her at work in the world, shows her, above all, arriving at a choice, albeit a restricted one, of possible vocations at the end. In the course of the novel Jane has three jobs, five homes, three families of a sort, two proposals of marriage. If her travel is restricted, at least she nearly goes to the South of France, nearly goes to Madeira, nearly goes to India. She learns French, German and Hindustani. She lives alone, receives male visitors in her bedroom in the middle of the night and hears confidences of financial treachery and sexual profligacy. She saves a life, proposes marriage and gives away thousands of pounds. She longs for broader horizons, pleads for a wider range of activities for women, gives an impassioned defence of the right to feeling of those who are '"poor, obscure, plain, and little"' (p. 255). She suffers, fights back, stands by her principles, vanquishes her enemies, and ends up 'supremely blest' (p. 456). That Jane's 'calling' turns out finally to be the voice of Rochester and a quiet wedding should not obscure the extraordinarily wide range of narrative possibilities the novel offers its central female character.

Jane Eyre seems, too, to offer a world of physical restriction against which she chafes, continually searching for prospects through windows. And yet, set against this air of enclosure and restraint there is the intense and startling physicality of the novel: its evocation of mental and emotional torment through freezing frosts and blazing fires, the 'disseverment of bone and vein' (p. 325), floods and shipwrecks, starvation and punishment. Dreams and omens, natural symbols and mystic calls – in short the whole panoply of the supernatural – are enlisted in the service of what remain, after all, entirely human and secular appetites.[25] Jane's inner life, whatever her modest demeanour, seems to rage across heaven and earth in a kind of cosmic psychodrama. And all of this, of course, in Charlotte Brontë's 'fortissimo' style.[26]

This singleness of focus extends even to making most of the characters projections or fragments of Jane Eyre, J. E., 'je', the narrating 'I'. They seem to be called up – as it were materialised – by Jane's needs and experiments, as Karen Chase has demonstrated;[27] so, when Mrs Reed demands '"perfect submission and stillness"' (p. 18) as the condition of liberation, Helen embodies these qualities and their limitations as tactics of survival; Jane pleads for '"a new servitude"' (p. 86) and Mr Rochester literally falls at her feet; she longs for 'incident, life, fire, feeling' (p. 110) and Bertha's mirthless laugh offers a sardonic commentary on what these may mean; and when Jane seeks to become 'ice and rock' (p. 304) and to live by religious principle, St John Rivers appears with his dangerously tempting offer of the undelighting rigours of a missionary position. That Jane, 'witch' as Rochester frequently calls her, has brought these characters into being is clear partly in the often abrupt and mysterious manner of their appearance – Rochester's dim arrival through the dusk, St John's disembodied voice ('"All men must die"' [p. 340]) in response to her resignation to the will of God.

And it is notable that almost all who come into contact with Jane are burned, singed, seared: Helen burns with consumption, Bertha – the 'Angria' version of Mrs Rochester – leaps into the flames she has kindled on what she believes to be her rival's bed, St John Rivers 'hides a fever in his vitals' (p. 361), Rochester is seared in eye and hand before he can have her. It is as if the passion of the unsatisfied Jane will consume what threatens or denies her, just as the inflammatory passion of the actress Vashti, in *Villette*, will make the theatre burst into flames. But Jane is saved from spontaneous combustion; as St Paul and *Jane Eyre* in their different ways affirm, it is better to marry than to burn, and the 'socialisation of the psyche', in Pell's phrase,[28] ultimately reduces Jane's cosmic passions to the less terrifying dimensions of the dank and insalubrious Ferndean.

This story of passion, ambition and power continually restates and challenges that contradiction between feminine and heroic character ideals, self-abnegation and self-assertion, so common in Victorian novels centring upon a growing woman.[29] There is, unquestionably, a heroic narrative of consciousness in *Jane Eyre* in which self-assertion threatens an expansion that will absorb the whole world, but this fantasied female power is continually tethered and troubled by the realist narrative of social determination and patriarchal imbrication. It is the tension between the two – sometimes seen as an opposition between Gothic and realist elements, or Romantic and realist, or fairy-tale and novel – that gives this novel its peculiar intensity and force, acting out as it does at the very level of form the mutual dependencies and incompatibilities of desire and restraint.

From Penny Boumelha, *Charlotte Brontë* (Hemel Hempstead, 1990), pp. 58–77.

NOTES

[The book from which this essay is taken is one of a series on Key Women Writers, whose purpose was to offer a feminist re-examination of the work of women writers with established places in the mainstream of literary tradition. Penny Boumelha draws on Marxist and psychoanalytic, as well as on feminist theory, in her discussion of *Jane Eyre*. And in doing so, she does not merely offer a reading of the novel: she engages, also, with some major questions in contemporary feminist criticism – the problems raised by 'the identification of heroic individuals as bearers of feminist anger or argument' (Introduction, p. 8), the importance for feminism of issues of class and race, the ways in which a work shaped by another historical moment may speak to present political concerns. In her Introduction (not reprinted here) Boumelha considers the interaction in Brontë's fiction of the 'heroine's plot' of romance and the 'hero's plot' of vocation, and the ways in which that interaction destabilises the ostensible resolution of Jane's tale. 'In Jane Eyre's sequestered marriage to a sightless husband' there is, she argues, 'a core of utopian desire, of critique of the very plots that make closure possible' (p. 37). In the essay reprinted here Boumelha offers a more extensive reading, focusing on those features of the novel which seem to pose unresolved problems for a developing feminist criticism, and pointing, suggestively, toward a view of *Jane Eyre* which, whilst acknowledging its ideological boundedness, 'honours' its capacity still to trouble and to stir. Textual references are to the World's Classics edition of *Jane Eyre*, ed. Margaret Smith (Oxford, 1980; reprinted 1987). Ed.]

1. *Jane Eyre*, p. 33.

2. Joseph Prescott, '*Jane Eyre*: A Romantic Exemplum With a Difference', in *Twelve Original Essays on Great English Novels*, ed. Charles Shapiro (Detroit, 1960), p. 91.

3. Terry Eagleton, *Myths of Power: a Marxist Study of the Brontës* (London, 1975), p. 18.

4. Hermione Lee, 'Emblems and Enigmas in *Jane Eyre*', *English*, 30 (Autumn 1981), 223.

5. Gayatri Chakravorty Spivak, 'Three Women's Texts and a Critique of Imperialism', *Critical Inquiry*, 12 (1985), 243–61, 245; reprinted in '*Race*', *Writing, and Difference*, ed. Henry Louis Gates, Jr (Chicago, 1986), pp. 262–80. For a critique of Spivak's argument, see Laura E. Donaldson, 'The Miranda Complex: Colonialism and the Question of Feminist Reading', *Diacritics*, 18 (1988), 65–77.

6. Respectively Lee R. Edwards, *Psyche as Hero: Female Heroism and Fictional Form* (Middletown, CT, 1984), p. 76; Jina Politi, '*Jane Eyre* Class-ified', *Literature and History*, 8 (1982), 56 [reprinted in this volume – see p. 78. Ed.]; Judith Weissman, *Half Savage and Hardy and Free: Women and Rural Radicalism in the Nineteenth-century Novel* (Middletown, CT, 1987), p. 84.

7. See, respectively, Peter J. Bellis, 'In the Window-Seat: Vision and Power in *Jane Eyre*', *English Literary History*, 54 (1987), 639–52; Politi, '*Jane Eyre* Class-ified'; Spivak, 'Three Women's Texts'. Jean Rhys, *Wide Sargasso Sea* (London, 1966), is of course a kind of 'restoration' of Bertha's story.

8. I am using the phrase, of course, to invoke the issues raised in the important feminist discussion of the novel in Sandra M. Gilbert and Susan Gubar, *The Madwoman in the Attic: The Woman Writer and the Nineteenth-Century Literary Imagination* (New Haven, CT, 1979).

9. Cf. Philip W. Martin, *Mad Women in Romantic Writing* (Brighton, 1987), pp. 124–39. James Cowles Pritchard's theory of 'moral madness', on which Brontë based the pathology of Bertha Rochester, is discussed in Peter Grudin, 'Jane and the Other Mrs Rochester: Excess and Restraint in *Jane Eyre*', *Novel*, 10 (1977), 145–57.

10. The only other 'Quakerish' character in the novel is Grace Poole (p. 157), and this forms part of an interesting set of connections between the two characters.

11. Among the most useful of the genre-based accounts of the novel are the following: a stimulating, if unsympathetic and gender-blind, account of *Jane Eyre* as *Bildungsroman* in Franco Moretti, *The Way of the World: the 'Bildungsroman' in European Culture* (London,

1987); on Gothic elements, Robert B. Heilman, 'Charlotte Brontë's "New" Gothic', in *From Jane Austen to Joseph Conrad: Essays Collected in Memory of James T. Hillhouse*, ed. Robert C. Rathburn and Martin Steinmann, Jr (Minneapolis, 1958), pp. 118–32, reprinted in *The Brontës: A Collection of Critical Essays*, ed. Ian Gregor (Englewood Cliffs, NJ, 1970), pp. 96–109, and Marxist-Feminist Literature Collective, 'Women's Writing: *Jane Eyre, Shirley, Villette, Aurora Leigh*', in *1848: the Sociology of Literature*, ed. Francis Barker et al. (Colchester, 1978), pp. 185–206); on folk- and fairy-tale, Paula Sullivan, 'Fairy Tale Elements in *Jane Eyre*', *Journal of Popular Culture*, 12 (1978), 61–74; on the governess novel, Harriet Björk, *The Language of Truth: Charlotte Brontë, the Woman Question and the Novel* (Lund Studies in English, 1974), and Inga-Stina Ewbank, *Their Proper Sphere: A Study of the Brontë Sisters as Early Victorian Female Novelists* (London, 1966); on allegory and emblem-books, Lee, 'Emblems and Enigmas'.

12. Most famously, in Adrienne Rich, 'Jane Eyre: the Temptations of a Motherless Woman', *MS*, 2 (October, 1973), reprinted in her *On Lies, Secrets and Silence: Selected Prose 1966–1978* (New York, 1979), pp. 89–106.

13. Elaine Showalter, *A Literature of Their Own: British Women Novelists from Brontë to Lessing* (Princeton, NJ, 1977), pp. 112–24. [Reprinted in this volume – see pp. 68–77. Ed.]

14. I am thinking here of such matters as Jane's appropriation of the words of Christ on p. 20 and of Biblical quotation, e.g. on p. 453.

15. *The Madwoman in the Attic*, p. 364. We might see in Jane's flight from Thornfield to the heath a version of that 'female plot' outlined by Sandra M. Gilbert, 'Life's Empty Pack: Notes Toward a Literary Daughteronomy', *Critical Inquiry*, 11 (1985), 355–84: the woman who 'flees from culture (her father's palace) to nature (the great wood), trying to transform herself into a creature of nature … rather than aquiesce in the extreme demands culture is making upon her' (p. 377). Gilbert suggests, however, that this flight is commonly motivated by the need 'to escape paternal desire'.

16. Cf. Sullivan, 'Fairy Tale Elements', p. 68.

17. Helena Michie, *The Flesh Made Word: Female Figures and Women's Bodies* (New York, 1987), pp. 12–29, traces the depiction of women's hunger and its relation to sexuality in Victorian writing. Her claim that, like other nineteenth-century heroines, Jane is 'never actually seen eating' (p. 15) is surely inaccurate, however.

18. Cf. Margaret Homans, *Bearing the Word: Language and Female Experience in Nineteenth-century Women's Writing* (Chicago, 1986), pp. 84–99. [Reprinted in this volume – see pp. 147–67. Ed.]

19. Politi, '*Jane Eyre* Class-ified', p. 64. [See this volume, p. 88. Ed.]

20. Although Edwards thinks Jane a 'spiritual aristocrat' (*Psyche as Hero*, p. 76), Politi and Eagleton are surely right to see her as, respectively, occupying 'the space ... of the unaccommodated *petit-bourgeois*' ('*Jane Eyre* Class-ified', p. 57) [p. 79 in this volume. Ed.] and as representative of a meritocratic bourgeois myth (*Myths of Power*, p. 26). I think it should be noted, however, that her marriage to Rochester constitutes a move into the rural gentry.

21. The narrative implications of phrenology and physiognomy are very well discussed in Karen Chase, *Eros and Psyche: The Representation of Personality in Charlotte Bronte, Charles Dickens and George Eliot* (London, 1984), pp. 47–65. [Reprinted in this volume – see pp. 52–67. Ed.]

22. Politi, '*Jane Eyre* Class-ified', p. 65. [See this volume, p. 89. Ed.]

23. Among these, the following are particularly worth attention: Gilbert and Gubar, *The Madwoman in the Attic*, pp. 336–71; Pauline Nestor, *Charlotte Brontë* (London, 1987), pp. 50–67; Rich, 'Motherless Woman'; Ruth Bernard Yeazell, 'More True Than Real: Jane Eyre's "Mysterious Summons"', *Nineteenth-Century Fiction*, 29 (1974), 127–43.

24. Jerome Beaty, '*Jane Eyre* and Genre', *Genre*, 10 (1977), 654.

25. Cf. Chase, *Eros and Psyche*, p. 11.

26. Doreen Roberts, '*Jane Eyre* and "The Warped System of Things"', in *Reading the Victorian Novel: Detail into Form*, ed. Ian Gregor (London, 1980), p. 138. [Reprinted in this volume – see p. 41. Ed.]

27. Chase, *Eros and Psyche*, pp. 66–91.

28. Nancy Pell, 'Resistance, Rebellion and Marriage: The Economics of *Jane Eyre*', *Nineteenth-Century Fiction*, 31:4 (March 1977), 397–420.

29. For a further consideration of these issues, see Penny Boumelha, 'George Eliot and the End of Realism', in *Women Reading Women's Writing*, ed. Sue Roe (Brighton, 1987), pp. 13–35.

7

Dreaming of Children: Literalisation in *Jane Eyre*

MARGARET HOMANS

'There was no possibility of taking a walk that day. ... I was glad of it. I never liked long walks, especially on chilly afternoons.'[1] With this opening assertion, Charlottë Bronte founds her novel on her heroine's scepticism about the experiences in nature that her sister's just-completed novel so ambiguously celebrates.[2] The literal is historically associated with nature, and especially in and just after the romantic period, it is against identification with nature that women writers stage their ambivalent defences against becoming identified with the literal and the object. Projected onto women by masculine texts, internalised and reproduced by women writers, an identification of the mother with nature might seem to offer women access to power, since, taking the form of nature, the literal is the final, maternal object of desire. Yet because the desired object is also so feared by androcentric culture, to accept that identification might be to stop writing and speaking intelligibly within the symbolic order. Both Charlotte and Emily Brontë figure this silence as death, because the mother's place in the symbolic order is to be absent. While *Wuthering Heights* entertains the possibility that the mother's place also has power and value of its own, *Jane Eyre* entertains only in order to defend against it the seductive possibility of a woman's becoming the literal.

Jane Eyre presents the fear of the objectification of the self in a variety of ways that make particularly explicit the connection between femininity and objectification. Jane fears that Rochester objectifies her when he wants to dress her in jewels and silks that correspond, not to her individual character, but to his abstract idea of Mrs Edward Fairfax Rochester.[3] Like Cathy shocked by the alienness of her mirror image, Jane is shocked twice by what she sees in the mirror, in the red-room when 'the strange little figure there gazing at [her] had the effect of a real spirit', and again on the morning of her wedding, when the mirror's 'robed and veiled figure, so unlike [her] usual self that it seemed almost the image of a stranger' represents both the appeal and the threat of having her subjectivity replaced by a beautiful object. This chapter, however, will examine the novel's exploration of the feminine temptation to become an object through two kinds of literalisation: the circumstances of childbearing and the Gothic literalisation of subjective states with which, in the novel, childbearing is often inauspiciously associated. (To draw on an already familiar example from *Wuthering Heights*, which makes a similar association, in Lockwood's 'dream' Brontë pairs the apparition of a ghost with what we later learn is the birth of Cathy's child-self.) In both the gothic and in childbirth, what was once internal acquires its own objective reality; and in both situations, the heroine is in a position to become identified with the object world on which her subjectivity is projected.

As Charlotte and Emily Brontë write it, the gothic both acknowledges and protests the place to which women are relegated in romantic myths of subjectivity and transcendence. In gothic novels generally, subjective states are so fully and literally projected into a social framework as to alter physical reality.[4] Specifically, the gothic literalises the romantic imagination, and it is this literalisation that produces its terror. When Heathcliff at the end of his life sees Cathy 'in every cloud, in every tree – filling the air at night, and caught by glimpses in every object by day' (ch. 33), the effective projection of his desire literalises Coleridge's figure for the way the imagination shapes the perceptual world, the 'fair luminous cloud/Enveloping the Earth'.[5] This pattern of literalisation operates in all gothic works, but it has special implications for women, which the Brontës make explicit. The romantic imagination that the gothic literalises is predominantly a masculine mode: Coleridge defines the imagination so that the poet is the patrilineal inheritor of a distinctly masculine God's self-assertion 'I AM'. Just as Mr Ramsay's metaphysical speculations depend upon and produce a feminine 'phantom kitchen table' for the puzzled Lily Briscoe, the desiring romantic imagina-

tion assumes feminine phantoms of desire. And just as Lily imperti-
nently imagines the table back into existence, the Brontës' female
gothic literalises romanticism's phantoms.[6]

The difficulty, especially as far as Charlotte Brontë is concerned,
is that literalisation is precisely what female figures embody in romantic myth. A woman writer's practice of literalisation, like Lily's
would seem to be a protest against romantic speculation; yet in a
larger sense, that protest has already been scripted within what it
protests. But if the Brontës' gothic rehearses women's fate within
the symbolic order, at least it does so self-consciously and therefore
sceptically.[7] It may be that the gothic became historically a predominantly female mode because it lends itself so well to women
writers' responses to the cultural identification of 'woman' with the
literal.[8] It could be that Charlotte Brontë uses the gothic, where all
sorts of literalisation occur, not because she is incapable of what
her culture would define as a liberating transcendence of the body,
but rather because it enables her to criticise the double position in
which culture places her. To the extent that a woman writes within
what we have retrospectively described as the symbolic order, she
accepts cultural definitions of femininity, yet those definitions
situate her as a woman outside the symbolic. Because as a woman
she has been excluded from the symbolic order, as a writer she feels
she must continually confront and defend against that exclusion.
While Woolf can celebrate Lily's literalising imagination (in part
because she also imagines other things for her woman artist to do),
Charlotte Brontë uses the gothic with ambivalence and uses her ambivalence to protest the objectification of the feminine that the
gothic enacts.

We can see this ambivalence at work in the way *Jane Eyre* frequently entertains gothic possibilities, then appears to undermine
them with rational explanations, and still later undermines those
rational explanations themselves.[9] Ultimately, as we will see, in a
final twist, Brontë undermines even that return to gothic literalisation. The most familiar example of this pattern is Jane's chastisement both of herself and of her reader when she finds herself
wondering about the demonic laughter that issues from Grace
Poole's attic room. 'Sometimes I saw her; she would ... go down to
the kitchen, and shortly return, generally (oh, romantic reader,
forgive me for telling the plain truth!) bearing a pot of porter. Her
appearance always acted as a damper to the curiosity raised by her
oral oddities' (ch. 12). But the laugh in the attic is only temporarily

explained away. Jane errs in denying the gothic's literalisation of speculation. That the source of those 'oral oddities' has an existence and a history more horrifying than the wildest fantasy demonstrates that her allegiance to 'the plain truth' offers no escape from the dangers of subjectivity, for it is precisely in the realm of 'the plain truth' that Jane's fears and subversive wishes take their most terrifying form. In Brontë's gothic, terror originates in the heroine's confinement to the world of objects.

This reading is confirmed by Brontë's curious and unconventional emphasis on Jane's fear of any apparition, whether good or bad. Apparitions horrify, not because they are evil, but because they appear at all. This is the case in Jane and Rochester's supernatural long-distance conversation at the end of the novel, but more strikingly in the novel's first gothic instance, the apparition of Mr Reed in the red-room. Thinking of stories about spirits returning to earth to avenge the oppressed, Jane relates, 'I wiped my tears and hushed my sobs, fearful lest any sign of violent grief might waken a preternatural voice to comfort me, or elicit from the gloom some haloed face, bending over me with strange pity. This idea, consolatory in theory, I felt would be terrible if realised' (ch. 2). This separation of 'theory' and 'realisation' allows Jane to establish that, for this text, any passage from subjective to objective, or from internal to external, is potentially terrifying. The introduction of these terms widens the implications of the use of the gothic and connects them explicitly to the larger issue of women's identification with the literal.

The gothic's literalisation of imaginative or other subjective states often coincides with representations of a rather different kind of literalisation, the experience or idea of childbirth. That women bear children and men do not is the simple origin of this complex and troubling tradition that associates women with the literal and with nature, an association that at once appeals to and repels women writers. Both novels foreground a curious connection between their most gothic elements and motherhood. The transitory experience of being a mother is the central and recurring metaphor for the abundant sense of danger in *Jane Eyre* (just as the plot of *Wuthering Heights* turns on the main character's death in childbirth and her subsequent transformation into a ghost). The specific connection between the literalisation of subjective states and childbirth's actual passage from internal to external takes place in dreams about children. Like other internal states in the gothic mode, dreams are literalised in the object world, and the ambiguous process of their literalisation mirrors and reinforces an ambivalence that is almost always integral to the imagery of childbearing in the two novels.

Neither Charlotte nor Emily Brontë was, at the time of writing, in a position to experience or even to anticipate actual motherhood, but my concern here is with a view of the subject of production that might more likely (though not necessarily) be shared by women than by men. Any literary woman of the nineteenth century would have assumed that marriage and motherhood would end her career. Further, the thought of the event of childbirth itself would have had highly ambiguous connotations for any pre-twentieth-century woman. In the nineteenth century, giving birth was not unlikely to be fatal to the mother or to the child or to both, and to fear childbirth or associate it with death would have been quite reasonable.[10] The commonplaceness of the dangers of childbirth is reflected in its casual treatment in romantic and other nineteenth-century fiction, where a mother's death in childbirth is often merely a convention for producing an interesting protagonist. Women who become mothers in novels tend to die psychically if they do not die literally; survivors usually subordinate their identities to those of their husbands or of their marriageable daughters. Within the conventions of fiction, childbirth puts an end to the mother's existence as an individual. And we have seen how a poetic myth of language such as Wordworth's in *The Prelude* likewise requires the death or absence of the mother.

This negative reading of childbearing is echoed in more recent psychoanalytic accounts that may be suggestive for the nineteenth century. Writing in 1945, Helene Deutsch describes the persistence of fears of childbirth despite medical advances in the last half of the nineteenth century that reduced childbirth mortality 'to a minimum'. She argues that the fear of actual death had all along been a screen for an expression of psychic fears, particularly of separation. That the unborn child both has and lacks its own identity complicates a pregnant woman's identity. The boundary between her identity and that of the child within her is quite literally permeable, psychically and physically. Her own sense of identity is quite naturally called into question: before birth there is an other, perhaps sensed as parasitical, resident within the self, while after birth a part of the self is gone. Fear of losing a part of the body's content is part of the separation fear, 'but it is only one component, among others, of a general fear of separation from the child conceived as a part of the woman's own ego, a fear that assumes the character of the fear of death'. This fear of loss of self, Deutsch argues, is augmented by a feeling of powerlessness in relation to the process that has been set in motion: 'Whether she wants to or not, she who has created this new life must obey its power, its rule is expected, yet invisible, implacable. Because of these very qualities it necessarily produces fear.'[11]

To say that the mother projects into the object world something that was once internal and that now has its own independent existence, and that that projection may produce fear, is also to describe the structure of the gothic (notice how gothic Deutsch's language is). Childbirth, thus construed, almost too vividly figures the gothic pattern in which unconscious projection takes actual form. What the male romantic mind does figuratively, the womb can do literally, and literal self-duplication invites the fear that what one has created will subsequently overpower and eradicate the self.

Jane Eyre establishes a complex series of connectives between danger or trouble and figures of childbirth or of mother–child relationships, comprising the prophetic dreams of children and also the narrative use of such figuration. This series originates in Jane's recollection of Bessie's folk belief that 'to dream of children was a sure sign of trouble, either to one's self or to one's kin' (ch. 21), and both Bessie's experience and Jane's verify the belief.[12] Initially the dream self is Jane, and the child and the trouble it portends are quite external to her, but in successive dreams the sense of self is divided, confusingly, between child and parent figures, or it shifts altogether from parent to child. Introducing this idea, Jane says that 'scarcely a night' for a week had passed 'that had not brought with it a dream of an infant: which I sometimes hushed in my arms, sometimes dandled on my knee, sometimes watched playing with daisies on a lawn. ... It was a wailing child this night, and a laughing one the next: now it nestled close to me, and now it ran from me. ... It was from companionship with this baby-phantom I had been roused on that moonlight night' (ch. 21) by the 'trouble' of Mason's outcry at Bertha's attack. Here Jane is clearly distinct from the child, and the trouble external to her. But it is also following this series of dreams that she is called to the sickbed of Mrs Reed, who deliriously dreams aloud of Jane as a troublesome child: 'I have had more trouble with that child than any one would believe. Such a burden to be left on my hands' (ch. 21). Mrs Reed wished that Jane would die of the fever at Lowood; she hated Jane as a baby 'the first time I set my eyes on it – a sickly, whining, pining thing! It would wail in its cradle all night long'. From her dream of self as adult and other as child, Jane now becomes the child and the other in someone else's subjective experience. Splitting the sense of self between child and adult, these dreams question and break down the boundary between subject and object, between self and other.

Following this dream inversion of self and other, childbirth enters the figurative structure of the novel as a way of describing the danger that the self will become something other than itself. Returning from Gateshead, fearfully certain that Rochester will marry Blanche Ingram, Jane describes her feelings thus: 'And then I strangled a new-born agony – a deformed thing which I could not persuade myself to own and rear – and ran on' (ch. 22). This newborn agony has a twin sister, another of Jane's metaphoric offspring, who at first does not appear to be either as undesirable or as threatening. The morning after her engagement Jane has a feeling of 'almost fear' on hearing herself addressed as Jane Rochester, and the night before the wedding she still senses and fears this radical split between her single and married selves. By the next day, she says, she will be on the road to London, 'or rather, not I, but one Jane Rochester, a person whom as yet I knew not', and whose name she refuses to affix to her trunks:

> Mrs Rochester! She did not exist: she would not be born till to-morrow, some time after eight o'clock A.M.; and I would wait to be assured she had come into the world alive before I assigned to her all that property. It was enough that in yonder closet, opposite my dressing-table, garments said to be hers had already displaced my black stuff Lowood frock and straw bonnet: for not to me appertained that suit of wedding raiment.
>
> (ch. 25)

Like Bessie's prophetic dreams of children, this metaphor of a child prophecies danger. As Mrs Rochester's clothes displace Jane's so does Jane fear that her desire to love and be the object of love will entirely displace her equally strong wish to maintain her independence. The birth metaphor employed here should not necessarily suggest displacement, as the exchange of one name for another so neatly does; yet apparently for Brontë the image of childbirth connotes primarily loss of self. Jane Eyre will have to die in giving birth to Mrs Rochester. Especially because the change of a married woman's name is determined by law, the situation corresponds to the aspect of Cathy's childbirth that is within the law, her production of a patrilineal heir who makes her own existence unnecessary. The 'trouble' with which all the novel's dreamt and figurative children are associated may originate in this vision of motherhood in which the mother vanishes as the child is born.

Although in fictive time, Jane's two best-known dream children precede her vision of Mrs Rochester as an unborn child, she narrates these events in reverse order, so that any reading of her dreams is coloured by the passage about Mrs Rochester. In these dreams, Jane is the surrogate mother of a child she seems not to know, but that they almost directly follow an image of birth suggests that the child does belong to the dreamer, who is unwilling to acknowledge it. In the first dream, the dreamer is travelling an unknown road, in the rain and dark, 'burdened with the charge of a little child: a very small creature, too young and feeble to walk, and which shivered in my cold arms and wailed piteously in my ear' (ch. 25). Thinking that Rochester is ahead on the road, the dreamer strains to overtake or call to him, 'but my movements were fettered' and Rochester vanishes. In the second dream, developing out of the first, Thornfield is a ruin through which the dreamer wanders. 'I thought that of all the stately front nothing remained but a shell-like wall, very high, and very fragile-looking. ... I still carried the unknown little child: I might not lay it down anywhere, however tired were my arms – however much its weight impeded my progress, I must retain it' (ch. 25). Hearing Rochester galloping away in the distance, she climbs the thin wall, frantic for one last glimpse of him; as the wall gives way beneath her, 'the child clung round my neck in terror, and almost strangled me'. She reaches the windy summit only to see Rochester vanishing, and dreamer and child fall as the wall crumbles. The dream child clearly represents some aspect of Jane's life, but what that might be is not clear. The child may be 'Mrs Rochester', the new self to which Jane pictures herself fatally giving birth at the moment of her marriage; it may be Jane's love for Rochester; it may also represent Jane's own neglected childhood, as suggested by the close parallel with Mrs Reed's description of Jane as a burdensome and wailing infant; the 'new-born agony' that Jane 'strangles' may also be present here.[13] However we interpret the child, what is significant is that subjectivity is divided between the dream self and the dream child. That there are several equally plausible readings suggests that what generates the sense of danger is not the particular part of the self the child represents, but that such a representation or division of the self into parts occurs at all. The dreams give Jane an intimation of what it would be like to become other than herself.

These two dreams in which Jane figures as the unwilling mother surrogate for a difficult child-self are complemented two nights later by a third dream in which the child is Jane and the mother is a benign spirit. The threat presented in the first two dreams seems to have been at once fulfilled and avoided. The self has become a child, yet the wedding has failed to take place, and the dream child now is manifestly not Mrs Rochester. Unable and unwilling to give birth to that troublesome child, Jane regresses to a version of her own childhood. She dreams that she is back at Gateshead, lying in the red-room and watching the same ghostly light that once terrified her, but now the ceiling resolves into clouds and that light into moonlight and then into the visionary mother:

> She broke forth as never moon yet burst from cloud: a hand first pen-etrated the sable folds and waved them away; then, not a moon, but a white human form shone in the azure, inclining a glorious brow earthward. It gazed and gazed and gazed on me. It spoke to my spirit: immeasurably distant was the tone, yet so near, it whispered in my heart –
> 'My daughter, flee temptation!'
> 'Mother, I will.'
>
> (ch. 27)

This dream of being the child of a loving and protective mother makes an ambiguous conclusion to the sequence of dreams and figures of children, since so far no child – real, figurative, or dreamt – has given or received anything but trouble. Although the dreamer rejoices, this dream must logically represent the fulfilment of the threat of the previous dreams, with the suggestion that the dream deceives as it soothes.

These dreams of children represent Jane's unconscious investiga-tion of the state of becoming other than herself or of deferring alto-gether to projections, and the process of this investigation is repeated in the literalisation or coming true of the dreams that char-acterises the gothic pattern. All the dreams come true in some way, but from one dream to the next they come true in increasingly literal ways. To be prophetic of trouble, according to Bessie's super-stition, the dream need only include the apparently arbitrary symbol of the child, and in the original series of dreams that brought out Jane's recollection of Bessie's story, the child represents danger whether it laughs or cries. But in the pair of dreams preceding the wedding, both child and mother are themselves vividly in trouble, so that the dreamt child is not simply an arbitrary symbol but a metaphor. That the dream child appears to represent some feature of Jane's life (and that Rochester riding away from Jane in the dream prefigures their separation three days later) suggests that the child as metaphor would match only Jane's particular situation.[14] Dreams also literalise each other: just as the second of the pair of dreams extends the action and implications of the first, the third dream, in which Jane explicitly dreams of herself as the child, realises the unpleasant implication of the first two dreams, that Jane is herself the child as well as the mother. Looking further back, the third dream also appears to spell out and explain the morally ambiguous ghost that confused Jane as a child in the red-room. Set in the same scene, the more recent vision soothes where Mr Reed terrified; but the vision of the shining human form 'inclining a glorious brow earthward' and speaking words of comfort literalises what the child had only imagined to be the ultimate terror. Her fear then was that her grief would 'waken a preternatural voice to comfort me, or elicit from the gloom some haloed face, bending over me with strange pity', and that is exactly what happens in the dream. The passage from 'theory' to 'realisation' was what was 'terrible' in the red-room, and the same turns out to be true here, in the passage from the dream to the next few days' actual experience. Jane finds the dream's figures enacted in the object world, and like other literalisations, these threaten her life.

In the waking scenes of flight and wandering that directly follow, the prophetic dream comes true in the literalisation of the dreamt mother: 'I have no relative but the universal mother, Nature: I will seek her breast and ask repose' (ch. 28). Mother Nature is a mother only figuratively, yet because Jane names the landscape in this way and insists on and extends the figure, the dreamt mother must be connected to this very tangible one. Naming nature 'mother', Jane accepts the tradition that identifies the feminine with the object world, an identification that at this point seems very appealing. The visionary mother encouraged Jane to flee temptation, and when Jane wanders into nature after leaving Rochester, the landscape appears maternal because it appears to help on her flight from temptation. This positive view of nature may represent what Nancy

Chodorow would identify as the daughter's continued close connection to her mother long past her entry into androcentric culture, a connection that, however, a daughter who is a figure for the novelist, whose main allegiance is to the father's symbol making, finds very difficult to sustain and finally rejects.[15]

As on every other occasion, the coming true of a dream, the discovery in the object world of what was at one time purely subjective, is actually more frightening than the subjective experience itself, even though Jane's tone at first directs us to find it consoling. Mother Nature betrays her daughter, but to be her daughter is dangerous enough, and betrayal is inherent in the relation. In the dream, Jane shifts her identity from adult to child without making the concomitant change from self to other that previous dreams intimated, and being this somewhat regressive child-self is clearly preferable to the loss of self that giving birth to Mrs Rochester would have represented. It appears now that the transformation of self into other was only deferred: simultaneous with the literalisation of her dream, Jane as a child of Mother Nature finds herself in the position of being identified with the literal, first deceived into seeking this identification, then almost forced into it. This experience's close connection with all of the dreams, where Jane has been a mother as well as a child, also suggests an identity between Jane and the mother figure herself, as a continuation of that perpetual shifting between subject and object that the dreams introduce. Either way, being like nature or being nature's child, the danger is the same identification with the literal that jeopardises both Jane's sense of self and her life.

Just before making this reference to Mother Nature, Jane describes her surroundings. Whitcross, where she alights after her destinationless coach ride away from Thornfield, appropriately signals her entry into a land of literalised dreams, because the name's meaning is as close to literal as any naming can be. Whitcross is not the name of a town but of a whitewashed stone pillar with four arms: a white cross. Like Dorothy Wordsworth's self-naming refuges, Whitcross names only itself. Yet whereas Dorothy Wordsworth's resistance to the symbolic order makes such a discovery fortuitous, Jane's allegiance to that order makes this discovery signal disaster. Jane has neither money, the symbol of symbols, nor any tie to human society, and lacking either a speakable past or an imaginable future, she has, like the self-referential Whitcross, no significance.[16] 'Strangers would wonder what I am doing, lingering here at the sign-post, evidently objectless and lost. I might be questioned: I could give no answer but what would sound incredible and excite suspicion' (ch. 28). That she describes her situation in terms of a lack of language explicitly names Jane's experience as literal. To be 'objectless' is to cease being a subject. That this passage concerning Jane's reduction to her physical being concludes with the reminder that matter is traditionally female deepens the danger of her position and defines that danger as a particularly feminine one.

Setting out from Whitcross, Jane arrives at a protective place in the heath, a soft hollow sheltered by high banks. As night very gently falls, 'Nature seemed to me benign and good; I thought she loved me, outcast as I was; and I, who from man could anticipate only mistrust, rejection, insult, clung to her with filial fondness. To-night, at least, I would be her guest – as I was her child: my mother would lodge me without money and without price' (ch. 28). The curious phrasing of the last sentence here suggests Jane's insight that she is not truly nature's child, but only nature's non-paying guest. That the passage proposes various images for nature (mother, innkeeper) creates a consciousness of figuration that serves to defend against, while the passage otherwise appears to endorse, the possibility that Jane is nature's child. Even more striking is the doubt implicit in 'Nature seemed to me benign and good; I thought she loved me'. This doubt is confirmed the next morning when the evening's relative comfort gives way to pressing exhaustion and hunger. Jane no longer refers to the landscape as a mother, the mother having abandoned the child who may have been deluded in imagining herself protected. In becoming actual, what seemed benign as a vision becomes neglectful, even malignant.

Jane discovers here on the moor, as does the dying Cathy in *Wuthering Heights*, that to become part of nature is to die. The solace nature offers is not just an illusion concealing death; that solace is itself death:

> What a still, hot, perfect day! What a golden desert this spreading moor! Everywhere sunshine. I wished I could live in it and on it. I saw a lizard run over the crag; I saw a bee busy among the sweet bilberries. I would fain at the moment have become bee or lizard, that I might have found fitting nutriment, permanent shelter here. ... Hopeless of the future, I wished but this – that my Maker had that night thought good to require my soul of me while I slept; and that this weary frame, absolved by death from further conflict with fate,

had now but to decay quietly, and mingle in peace with the soil of
this wilderness.

(ch. 28)

Jane's wish to 'live in it and on it' echoes Cathy's dying wish to be
'really with it, and in it' (ch. 15). That Cathy's 'it' refers at once to
nature and to a transcendent realm beyond death suggests that
Jane's 'it', which seems to refer here only to the moor, will soon
refer also to the world into which Cathy dies. That there is at this
point almost no difference between Mother Nature and her daughter almost completes the dreams' efforts to blur the distinctions
between mother and child, subject and object. In the context of the
dreams, to become the child is to become an object, while to
become part of this mother would also be to turn into an object.

Jane resists the fate that Cathy embraces because she retains her
consciousness of difference: she knows that to identify and mingle
with nature necessitates dying. Breaking into the middle of this
passage, interrupting that tempting continuity, is Jane's recollection
that she is not a child of nature but 'a human being, and had a
human being's wants: I must not linger where there was nothing to
supply them'. The true child of Mother Nature, one that finds
'permanent shelter' in her breast, is the lizard or the bee, never
the living woman. Jane's wish that she had died in the night and the
temptation as she walks to stop and 'submit resistlessly to the
apathy that clogged heart and limb' represent nature's residual pressure and conflict with 'life, ... with all its requirements, and pains,
and responsibilities', which prevents Jane from yielding. Nature is
now a dangerous tempter, in contrast to that mother within Jane's
mind who told Jane to 'flee temptation'. She returns to her starting
point at Whitcross, to begin again; soon she is again on the verge of
giving in to nature's temptation when she is recalled to consciousness by the chime of a church bell and then by the sight of a village
and cultivated fields that, by representing human life, help her resist
the literality of the wild moor.

If nature is no longer the mother and Jane no longer the child,
she can resist nature's appeal that she become part of the literal.
Toward the end of the second day of her wanderings, Jane, having
undergone extreme humiliation and physical suffering, finds that
she has 'once more drawn near the tract of moorland' (ch. 28). In
the same location, she seeks a version of the first evening's repose,
but here the consciousness of her difference sustains her in her

disillusionment with the dream vision's promises. She calls on Providence to guide her, not on Mother Nature to soothe her. Recognising that she may die, she prefers a death in nature to 'a workhouse coffin ... in a pauper's grave'. But in place of her earlier sympathetic identification with nature and her subsequent wish to 'mingle in peace with the soil of this wilderness', Jane now images a death in nature as a violent separation from the soil: crows and ravens will pick the flesh from her bones. As if in response to her state of mind, nature now repudiates Jane. Having passed beyond

> a few fields, almost as wild and unproductive as the heath from which they were scarcely reclaimed, ... it remained now only to find a hollow where I could lie down, and feel at least hidden, if not secure: but all the surface of the waste looked level. It showed no variation but of tint; green, where rush and moss overgrew the marshes; black, where the dry soil bore only heath. Dark as it was getting, I could still see these changes; though but as mere alternations of light and shade: for colour had faded with the daylight.
>
> (ch. 28)

Difference is necessary for human signification, and this wild, unvarying sterility represents nature's closure to such meaning. Nature is more than fatal here; it is unwilling to help Jane in any project, even her death. In the earlier 'golden desert' vision of this same fatal moorland, in which Jane briefly envies the bee and the lizard, it turns out that nature's vitality was an illusion produced by light, hiding the moor's true barrenness. This last picture of the moorland completes the literalisation of the original maternal vision, the metaphor still adhering in 'the dry soil bore only heath'. This landscape's life-threatening sameness makes it the extreme form of all the novel's literalisations, wherever figural structure gives way to actuality. All literalisations here tend toward death.[17]

Jane survives this confrontation with the fatally literal by means of various kinds of figuration that protect her from psychic and physical death. Directly after her vision of the undifferentiated landscape, the plot offers her a chance of life, a turn of events that appears to be not only paralleled but actually generated by a rhetorical turn from almost literal naming to dense figuration: 'My eye still roved over the sullen swell, and along the moor edge, vanishing amidst the wild scenery; when at one dim point, far in among the marshes and ridges, a light sprang up' (ch. 28). This light returns the reader to the complex world of multiple signification that imparts textual life where literal meaning denies it. Cautious now of illusions, Jane at first thinks it is an '*ignis fatuus*'; but what is important about her effort to interpret this sight is that she speculates at such length. If it is not an illusion, it may be a bonfire. When it remains steady, she decides it is a candle in a window, but she subjects even that interpretation to further interpretation. Like Emily Brontë's Lockwood, who cures his flu by substituting tame metaphors for wild moors, Jane rescues herself by making nature into figures. The candle next becomes 'my star' of 'hope'; finally it repeats an image from one of Jane's visionary paintings, subordinating the actual landscape to a wholly different and entirely internal realm of psychic signification. It is as if, appropriately, Jane were saved by her ability to create figures. Painting herself back into life, she reverses the process of literalisation.

From the vantage point of this reading of *Jane Eyre*, I wish to return briefly to *Wuthering Heights* to clarify, by contrasting the two novels, my reading of their structures of literalisation and figuration and of their thematics of childbirth. Much as Jane's dreams of herself as child come true in the form of her subjection to nature, Cathy dreams herself as a child, and that dream comes true in the form of the child to which she regresses and later in the form of the ghostly child-self who appears to Lockwood.[18] But Cathy seeks what Jane actively resists: a merging with nature that is also a return to childhood and that is, incidentally for Cathy but crucially for Jane, also death. Jane reverses the process of literalisation embodied in the coming true of her dreams, and she resists altogether the literalisation embodied in childbirth, while Cathy embraces both.

Jane's almost becoming part of the fatally literal in nature began with her unwillingness to give birth to Mrs Rochester. When Jane Eyre contemplates giving metaphorical birth to Mrs Rochester, she justifiably fears that the law will cause the 'child' to replace and supersede the 'mother'. This is exactly what happens to Cathy, when her reproduction of an heir for the Lintons makes her own identity unnecessary within the law. Because childbirth is defined in *Jane Eyre* as entirely within the law, its only meaning is the mother's self-replacement and death. The novel does not acknowledge the extralegal definition of motherhood that in *Wuthering Heights* makes Cathy's reproduction of her child-self a happy restoration. For Cathy, in giving birth, also remains partly outside the law, as we have seen, reproducing the lawless childhood self that she yearns to become again. Similarly, Jane temporarily regresses from being a mother figure to being a child, though for her this occurs through refusing to 'give birth' in a way that would perpetuate and subordinate her to the law. Like Cathy (and even more explicitly), Jane becomes a child of Mother Nature; but again because it has no place for the outlaw, the novel presents this return to childhood and the death it would bring with it in nothing like the positive terms of *Wuthering Heights*. The stories of the two heroines, then, because they make different assumptions about the structure and the meaning of childbirth as a form of literalisation, conclude in different consequences: while Cathy's production of a child fulfils her desire to be permanently a child, Jane's failure to give birth to her figurative child allows her to survive and grow. In both cases, the potential of motherhood is a transformation of the self or subjectivity into a literal object, a transformation that Cathy desires and Jane at first courts but finally refuses. While Jane comes to understand the danger that to become the child of her dreams would be to merge with objective nature and to transfer the self from subject to object, the view of the same transference expressed by Cathy's situation is almost wholly positive.

The threat that Charlotte Brontë has Mother Nature pose to Jane's identity and existence expresses her sense of the danger to all women of the identification of nature as mother. The temptation to become part of a feminised nature, to become a feminised object like nature, amounts in Brontë's view to a temptation to die, for it would be to join the dead mother, to accept exclusion from what her culture defines as human. By a curiously defensive logic, because Mother Nature is already dead, she might kill the writer who is a daughter, so the writer must kill Mother Nature first. Both Emily and Charlotte Brontë see that a woman, a mother, has been buried in the landscape of romanticism, and both know they have been complicitous in placing her there yet again. In order to assert her allegiance to her culture's dominant myth of language, Charlotte Brontë dramatises the near-murder of a woman at the hand of Mother Nature. Like Lockwood's snowstorm, this threat justifies Jane's subsequent betrayal of nature. The writer must betray the mother. Emily Brontë may protest this murder by bringing the mother to life again, but she does so only briefly, and only from the perspective of a mad and dying mother. Although the first Cathy in *Wuthering Heights* would view Jane's behaviour as a

betrayal of Mother Nature, Emily Brontë's view is not wholly contained in the story of the first Cathy. Just as Jane, having almost
identified herself with nature's otherness, leaves it by multiplying
significations and by thinking of her own figurative art, *Wuthering
Heights* continues past Cathy's death to offer a daughter's history
more in keeping with the rules of law. Like the story of the second
Cathy in relation to the first, Charlotte Brontë offers a correction of
a prior story, a story in which the attractions of the mother's place
were even more adventurously explored.

From Margaret Homans, *Bearing the Word: Language and Female
Experience in Nineteenth-century Women's Writing* (Chicago,
1986), pp. 84–99.

NOTES

[*Bearing the Word* was published in the series *Women in Culture and
Society*, edited by Catherine Stimpson, which aimed to move beyond 'the
populism of the feminist criticism of the 1970s', and towards a more sophisticated combination of formalist, psychoanalytical and historical approaches in feminist work. Homans' book begins with an ambitious
attempt to reconceptualise the relation between female language and experience in the nineteenth century, by bringing together Lacanian psycholin-
guistics and the model of female development proposed by the American
object-relations psychologist Nancy Chodorow. Women in western culture
have, Homans argues, been associated with the literal, men with the figurative; and these associations are writ large in the dominant nineteenth-
century myth of language, which saw language as a kind of mastery and
women as the absent or silent objects of male quest, part of nature rather
than of culture, incapable of acts of figuration of their own. This myth of
language is, according to Homans, one which 'women writers of the nineteenth century ... ambivalently accept and contest' (p. 161). For if, on the
one hand, they seem to acquiesce in their culture's view of their own silent
and subordinate position, they can also, she suggests, be seen as developing
their own distinctive and creative relation to the medium in which they
work. Whereas for men signifiers substitute for referents, women retain a
capacity for a literal or presymbolic, 'maternal' language, immanent with
presence rather than indicative of absence: they are able to speak 'two languages at once' (p. 33). In a series of thought-provoking readings, *Bearing
the Word* goes on to explore the ways in which, in a number of works by
nineteenth-century women writers, 'the shift from figurative to literal and
back again is heavily charged with mythic and thematic significance'
(p. 30), and metaphors of childbirth are deployed to richly ambiguous
effect. The essay reprinted here immediately follows a chapter in which

Homans discusses the ways in which *Wuthering Heights*, whilst associating
the literal with death, also 'celebrates ... resistance to systems and to the
father's law, celebrates a return to childhood that is a return to nature'
(p. 84). In this respect, she argues, Emily Brontë's work stands in suggestive
contrast to that of her sister: a contrast which she goes on to elaborate in
this reading of *Jane Eyre*. Ed.]

1. Charlotte Brontë, *Jane Eyre* (New York: Norton, 1971), ch. 1. All
   references to the novel are from this edition, cited in the text by
   chapter number.

2. *Jane Eyre* was begun just a few months after the completion of
   Wuthering Heights, and we know that the sisters read their ongoing
   work aloud to each other.

3. It is this sort of feminine objectification, brought about by the pressure to conform to socially acceptable notions of femininity, that concerns Sandra Gilbert and Susan Gubar in their readings of *Jane Eyre*
   as well as of *Wuthering Heights*. See in particular their discussion of
   Jane's various mirror images (*The Madwoman in the Attic: The
   Woman Writer and the Nineteenth-Century Literary Imagination*
   [New Haven, CT, 1979], p. 359).

4. This reading is indebted to Mary Poovey's interpretation of the gothic
   mode as the novel's way of incorporating the romantic period's privi-
   leging of subjectivity and imagination ('The Novel as Imaginative
   Order', PhD diss., University of Virginia, 1976). See also G. R.
   Thompson, 'Introduction: Romanticism and the Gothic Tradition', in
   The Gothic Imagination: Essays in Dark Romanticism, ed. G. R.
   Thompson (Pullman, WA, 1974), pp. 1–10.

5. Coleridge, 'Dejection: An Ode', lines 54–5.

6. The term 'female gothic' was first introduced by Ellen Moers in her
   reading of Mary Shelley, Emily Brontë, Christina Rossetti and others
   in her chapter 'Female Gothic' in *Literary Women* (New York, 1977),
   pp. 137–67. This reading enables our inquiry into Charlotte Brontë's
   particular version of the female gothic.

7. Although both Charlotte and Emily Brontë use gothic elements in
   their novels, and although the structure of gothic literalisation is essentially the same in *Wuthering Heights* and *Jane Eyre*, *Jane Eyre* is
   more sceptical than *Wuthering Heights* about gothic literalisation and
   about its implications for women, for Emily envisages the possibility
   of reclaiming the literal and literalisation for an original female power
   in a way that Charlotte does not.

8. In a reading of female gothic that in some respects thematically parallels my own, and that like mine draws on the work of Nancy
   Chodorow, Claire Kahane argues that the female gothic (defined

mainly by Anne Radcliffe's works) represents the daughter's struggle to separate from the boundaries of a pre-Oedipal mother, who is typically figured in gothic fiction both as nature and as a gloomy, mysterious castle. She writes: 'the female child, who shares the female body and its symbolic place in our culture, remains locked in a ... tenuous and fundamentally ambivalent struggle for a separate identity. This ongoing battle with a mirror image who is both self and other is what I find at the centre of the Gothic structure.' My argument about the complex results of Charlotte Brontë's ambivalence about the cultural identification of woman with the literal and with nature investigates, with respect to myths and structures of language, something like what Kahane explores thematically and with particular emphasis on the reader's experience. See Kahane, 'The Gothic Mirror', *Centennial Review*, 24 (1980), 43–64; revised and reprinted in *The (M)other Tongue: Essays in Feminist Psychoanalytic Interpretation*, ed. Shirley Nelson Garner, Claire Kahane, and Madelon Sprengnether (Ithaca, NY, 1985), pp. 334–51 (quotation, p. 337).

9. At least two commentators on the novel have argued that Brontë modifies the gothic elements she introduces, testing them against the reality principle so that they will deepen her novel's emotional realism rather than making it too fantastic to be believed. I am adding to, not disagreeing with, these arguments. See Robert B. Heilman, 'Charlotte Brontë's "New" Gothic', in *From Jane Austen to Joseph Conrad*, ed. Robert C. Rathburn and Martin Steinmann, Jr (Minneapolis, 1958), pp. 118–32 and Ruth Bernard Yeazell, 'More True Than Real: Jane Eyre's "Mysterious Summons"', *Nineteenth-Century Fiction*, 29 (1974), 127–43.

10. The Brontës' mother died when they were young children, probably of complications resulting from bearing six children in seven years. Helene Moglen discusses Charlotte's response to the deaths of her mother and of her maternal older sister, Maria (see *Charlotte Brontë: The Self Conceived* [New York, 1976], pp. 21–32). She argues that Charlotte's fears about childbirth (actual and metaphoric, her own and her mother's) constrained both her life and her literary production. Although Mrs Brontë's death may well have left her daughters with a powerful nostalgia for mothering, a nostalgia that can be traced in what is known of Charlotte's life, the response to the mother's death within the literary text is an overriding drive to dissociate the writing self from the idea of the mother because of the various threats she poses to writing.

   For discussion and documentation of maternal and infant mortality in the nineteenth century, see, for example, Adrienne Rich, *Of Woman Born* (New York, 1976), pp. 30, 143–5, 161; Roy P. Finney, *The Story of Motherhood* (New York, 1937), pp. 191–223; or A. J. Rongy, *Childbirth Yesterday and Today* (New York, 1937), pp. 176–88. Susan Gubar summarises the history of views of childbirth and suggests their implications for more recent women writers in 'The Birth of the Artist as Heroine: (Re)production, the Kunstlerroman Tradition, and the Fiction of Katherine Mansfield', in *The Representation of Women in Fiction*, ed. Carolyn Heilbrun and Margaret Higonnet (Baltimore, MD, 1983), pp. 19–59.

11.   Helene Deutsch, *Motherhood*, vol. 2 of *The Psychology of Women: A Psychoanalytic Interpretation* (New York, 1945), p. 215. It is important to stress that Deutsch's conservative and pessimistic view is not the only one, but that it seems to describe the view of the Brontës' novels better than does, say, Nancy Chodorow's interpretation (*The Reproduction of Mothering: Psychoanalysis and the Sociology of Gender* [Berkeley, CA, 1978]).

12.   Charlotte Brontë apparently had dreams of this kind herself and shared Jane's belief in them, based on an actual superstition: see Lucile Dooley, 'Psychoanalysis of Charlotte Brontë, as a Type of the Woman of Genius', *American Journal of Psychology*, 31 (1920), 242. Like much genuine folklore, whatever logical origin the belief may have had has been obscured and now seems arbitrary. Freud's translation of small children in dreams as the genitals could point to a hypothetical origin for the actual superstition, but the novel avoids offering any explanation of whatever sort.

13.   There has been much debate over the interpretation of the child in Jane's dreams, and almost all readings are justifiable; but there can be no single interpretation. See, for example, William E. Siebenschuh, 'The Image of the Child and the Plot of *Jane Eyre*', *Studies in the Novel*, 8 (1976), 304–17; and Moglen, *Charlotte Brontë*, pp. 125–7. Gilbert and Gubar read the dreams of children and the Mrs Rochester passage as representing the 'fragmentation' of Jane's self, the major thesis of their reading of the novel, though the aim of their discussion is different from mine (*The Madwoman*, pp. 357–9).

14.   If the passage from symbol to metaphor moves in the direction of relative literalisation, the sequence is finally completed much later on (though not with reference to the mother and child figure that concerns us here) by the uncanny literal repetition of Jane's vision in the object world. The shell-like battlements that she climbs in the second dream, burdened with the child, are precisely realised in Thornfield's ruin by fire. Typical of *Jane Eyre*'s handling of the gothic is the fact that, when the dream picture of Thornfield comes true so literally, Jane very casually relegates to a subordinate clause her acknowledgement of the uncanniness of the situation, as if the gothic's turn from visionary fear to the world of substance were a demystification, and not a further mystery: 'The front was, as I had once seen it in a dream, but a shell-like wall, very high and very fragile looking.'

15. See Adrienne Rich's more positive account of Jane's relations with a series of surrogate mothers: 'Jane Eyre: the Temptations of a Motherless Woman' (1973), reprinted in *On Lies, Secrets and Silence: Selected Prose 1966–1978* (New York, 1979), pp. 89–106.

16. Of course, to say that the white cross, or Jane's lack of money, figures Jane's reduced state, and to remember that while the white cross may not signify a town it does signify in a different way by pointing to four destinations, is already to acknowledge that literal meaning is never quite representable, yet this is as close as a written text can come to literality.

17. Readers using the Penguin edition find this point made even more strongly by a misprint: 'black, where the dry soil bore only death'. There is no authority for this reading in any of the editions supervised by the author.

18. Indeed, Lockwood's 'dream' of Cathy is itself prophetic in something of the same way that dreams of children are in *Jane Eyre*. It 'comes true' in the gothic sense that Heathcliff knows the objective reality of what Lockwood takes to be 'imagination', and in the literary sense that it prefigures the novel's actual violence, its scenes of exiled wanderers, and its orphans. Numerous writers have considered this latter aspect of the dream: for example, Edgar F. Shannon, Jr, *Nineteenth-Century Fiction*, 14 (1959), 95–109; and Ronald E. Fine, 'Lockwood's Dream and the Key to *Wuthering Heights*', *Nineteenth-Century Fiction*, 24 (1969), 16–30.

8

The Anathematised Race: The Governess and *Jane Eyre*

MARY POOVEY

The governess was a familiar figure to midcentury middle-class Victorians, just as she is now to readers of Victorian novels.[1] Even before Becky Sharp and Jane Eyre gave names to the psychological type of the governess, her 'plight' was the subject of numerous 1830s novels; by the 1840s, the governess had become a subject of concern to periodical essayists as well. In part, the attention the governess received in the 1840s was a response to the annual reports of the Governesses' Benevolent Institution, the charity founded in 1841 and reorganised in 1843.[2] But the activities of the GBI were also responses to a widespread perception that governesses were a problem of – and for – all members of the middle class. For many women, the problem was immediate and concrete; after all, as one editor of the *English Woman's Journal* remarked in 1858, every middle-class woman knows at least one governess, either because she has been taught by one or because she has 'some relative or cherished friend ... actually engaged in teaching, or having formerly been so engaged'.[3] For most men, the governess represented a more abstract – but no less pressing – problem. As a competitor for work in an unregulated and increasingly overcrowded profession, the governess epitomised the toll capitalist market relations could exact from society's less fortunate members.

168

Modern historians do not generally dispute that governesses suffered increasing economic and social hardships after the 1830s. The bank failures of that decade combined with the discrepancy between the numbers of marriageable women and men and the late marriage age to drive more middle-class spinsters, widows, and daughters of respectable bankrupts into work outside the home. At the same time that the economic pressure to work increased, the range of activities considered socially acceptable for middle-class women decreased; whereas in the 1790s, middle-class women had worked as jailors, plumbers, butchers, farmers, seedsmen, tailors, and saddlers, by the 1840s and 1850s, dressmaking, millinery, and teaching far outstripped all other occupational activities.[4] Of these occupations, private teaching was widely considered the most genteel, largely because the governess's work was so similar to that of the female norm, the middle-class mother. The overcrowding these conditions produced within the teaching profession drove salaries down and competition for places up; at the same time, employers could and often did demand an increasingly wide range of services from would-be governesses, ranging from childcare for the very youngest children to instruction in French, music, and paper-flower-making for older daughters.

Despite these very real hardships, however, modern historians also point out that, given the relatively small number of women affected by the governess's woes, the attention this figure received in the 1840s and 1850s was disproportionate to the problem.[5] The 1851 Census lists 25,000 governesses, for example, but at the same time there were 750,000 female domestic servants, whose working conditions and wages were often more debilitating but markedly less lamented than the distress of the governess. In this chapter, I address some of the reasons why the governess received so much attention during these decades. I argue that the social stress the governess suffered aroused so much concern when it did at least partly because the economic and political turmoil of the 'hungry forties' drove members of the middle class to demand some barrier against the erosion of middle-class assumptions and values; because of the place they occupied in the middle-class ideology, women, and governesses in particular, were invoked as the bulwarks against this erosion.[6] The governess is also significant for my analysis of the ideological work of gender because of the proximity she bears to two of the most important Victorian representations of woman: the figure who epitomised the domestic ideal, and the figure who threatened to destroy it. Because the governess was like the middle-class mother in the work she performed, but like both a working-class woman and man in the wages she received, the very figure who theoretically should have defended the naturalness of separate spheres threatened to collapse the difference between them. Moreover, that discussions of the governesses' plight had dove-tailed, by the mid-1850s, with feminist campaigns to improve both employment opportunities for women and women's education reveals the critical role representations of the governess played, not, as conservatives desired, in defending the domestic ideal, but in capitalising on the contradiction it contained.

The periodical essayists of the 1840s justified the attention they devoted to the distressed governess by emphasising the central role she played in reproducing the domestic ideal. As a teacher and example for young children, they argued, the governess was charged with inculcating domestic virtues and, especially in the case of young girls, with teaching the 'accomplishments' that would attract a good husband without allowing the sexual component of these accomplishments to get the upper hand. The governess was therefore expected to preside over the contradiction written into the domestic ideal – in the sense both that she was meant to police the emergence of undue assertiveness or sexuality in her maturing charges and that she was expected not to display wilfulness or desires herself.[7] Theoretically, the governess's position neutralised whatever temptation she, as a young woman herself, might have presented to her male associates; to gentlemen she was a 'tabooed woman', and to male servants she was as unapproachable as any other middle-class lady.[8]

If the governess was asked to stabilise the contradiction inherent in the middle-class domestic ideal by embodying and superintending morality, then she was also expected to fix another, related bound-ary: that between 'well-bred, well-educated and perfect gentle-women', on the one hand, and, on the other, the 'low-born, ignorant, and vulgar' women of the working class.[9] The assumption implicit in these conjunctions, as in the middle-class preference for governesses from their own class, was that only 'well-bred' women were morally reliable. In this reading of contemporary affairs, the unfortunate circumstances that bankrupted some middle-class fathers were critical to the reproduction of the domestic ideal, for only such disasters could yield suitable teachers for the next genera-tion of middle-class wives.

One reason the governess was a figure of such concern to her middle-class contemporaries, then, was simply that she was a middle-class woman in a period when women were considered so critical to social stability. Especially in the 'hungry forties', women became both the focus of working-class men's worries about competition for scarce jobs and the solution advanced by middle-class men for the social and political discontent hard times fostered. If only women would remain in the home, men of all classes argued, work would be available to men who needed it and both the family wage and morality would be restored. The assumptions implicit in this argument are those I have already discussed: that morality is bred and nurtured in the home as an effect of maternal instinct, and that if lower-class women were to emulate middle-class wives in their deference, thrift, and discipline, the homes of rich and poor alike would become what they ought to be – havens from the debilitating competition of the market.

A second reason the governess was singled out for special attention was that she did not seem to be fulfilling this critical social task. In fact, contemporaries openly worried that the governess was not the bulwark against immorality and class erosion but the conduit through which working-class habits would infiltrate the middle-class home. One source of this anxiety was the widespread belief that more tradesmen's daughters were entering the ranks of governess, therefore heralding the 'degradation of a body so important to the moral interest of the community'.[10] Against such 'degradation', middle-class commentators proposed a range of defences, including most of the solutions formulated to end the governesses' plight.[11] Whatever their practical value, all of the suggested remedies functioned to defend the class barrier that was also assumed to mark a moral division; even the Governesses' Benevolent Institution reinforced the distinction between ladies 'with character' and other women by providing the former with a separate residence and source of charity.[12]

A second source of the anxiety about governesses surfaces in discussions of the hardships of their situation. As these hardships were most vividly imagined, they were not primarily physical or economic but emotional; the threat they posed was to the governess's self-control and, even more ominously, to her sexual neutrality. This danger surfaces most explicitly in fictional representations of the governess, and I pursue it in a moment in relation to one of the period's most famous governess novels, Charlotte Brontë's

Jane Eyre.[13] In periodical essays about the governess, allusions to her sexual susceptibility are more indirect, but precisely because of this indirection, they direct our attention to the governess's place in the complex system of associations in which the domestic ideal was also embedded. Two of the figures to which the governess was repeatedly linked begin to suggest why her sexlessness seemed so important – and so unreliable – to her contemporaries. These figures are the lunatic and the fallen woman.

The connection contemporaries made between the governess and the lunatic was, in the first instance, causal. According to both the author of the 1844 'Hints on the Modern Governess System' and Lady Eastlake's 1847 review of the GBI's annual report, governesses accounted for the single largest category of women in lunatic asylums.[14] Lady Eastlake attributes this unfortunate fact to the 'wounded vanity' a governess suffers, but the author of 'Hints' connects this 'wound' more specifically to sexual repression. Citing 'an ordinary case', this author describes a young girl trained for her governess position in 'one of those schools which are usually mere gymnasia for accomplishments and elegant manners'. There her 'animal spirits' are indulged, and her youthful 'elasticity' becomes a 'craving for pleasures'. Once she leaves the school, however, and takes up her governessing work, this 'craving' is subject to the frustration and denial her position demands.

> She must live daily amidst the trials of a home without its blessings; she must bear about on her heart the sins she witnesses and the responsibilities that crush her; without any consent of her will, she is made the *confidante* of many family secrets; she must live in a familial circle as if her eyes did not perceive the tokens of bitterness; she must appear not to hear sharp sayings and *mal-a-propos* speeches; kindly words of courtesy must be always on her lips; she must be ever on her guard; let her relax her self-restraint for one moment, and who shall say what mischief and misery might ensue to all from one heedless expression of hers?[15]

If the allusion to some mischievous 'expression' hints at the governess's latent feelings, this author will not elaborate the nature of these feelings; instead, the writer turns to the 'nervous irritability, dejection, [and] loss of energy' that result from repressing them (*FM*, 575). The 'twisted coil of passion and levity', the author concludes, 'may be moved into sobriety by the help of forbearance and long-suffering', but too often the very girls who have sprung up 'like plants in a hot-house', fade before their 'bloom' is gone. 'It is no exaggeration to say that hundreds snap yearly from the stalk, or ˜˜olong a withered, sickly life, till they, too, sink, and are carried ᴗᴜt to die miserably in the by-ways of the world' (*FM*, 575, 574).

The image of the short-lived or barren plant elaborates the causal connection between the governess and the lunatic by metaphorically tying both to a vitality stunted, silenced, driven mad by denial and restraint. This vitality may not be explicitly represented as sexuality here, but its sexual content *is* present in the images to which this last phrase alludes. The representation of the governess 'carried out to die miserably in the by-ways of the world' metonymically links the governess to the victim of another kind of work that was also represented as 'white slavery' at midcentury – the distressed needle-woman 'forced to take to the streets'.[16] The association between the two figures is further reinforced by the fact that the governess and the needlewoman were two of the three figures that symbolised working women for the early and mid-Victorian public; the third was the factory girl.[17] Significantly, both of the working-class members of this trio were specifically linked by middle-class male commentators to the danger of unregulated female sexuality. Henry Mayhew's determination to expose (and, by extension, control) the 'prostitution' he identified among needlewomen in 1849 expresses the same concern to curtail female promiscuity that Lord Ashley voiced in the 1844 parliamentary debate about factory conditions.[18] For both Mayhew and Lord Ashley, the relevant issue was any ex-tramarital sexuality, not just sex for hire; Mayhew's interviews make it clear that for him any woman who lived or had sexual rela-tions with a man outside of marriage was a prostitute.

That representations of the governess in the 1840s brought to her contemporaries' minds not just the middle-class ideal she was meant to reproduce, but the sexualised and often working-class women against whom she was expected to defend, reveals the mid-Victorian fear that the governess could not protect middle-class values because she could not be trusted to regulate her own sexual-ity. The lunatic's sexuality might have been rhetorically contained by the kind of medical categories I have already discussed, after all, but the prostitute's sexual aggression was undisguised; to introduce either such sexuality or such aggression into the middle-class home would have been tantamount to fomenting revolution, especially in a period in which both were imaginatively linked to the discontent expressed by disgruntled members of the working class and by the 'strong-minded women' who were just beginning to demand reform. The conjunction of economic, moral, and political anxieties that could be mobilised by the image of an army of aggressive, impoverished governesses emerges in the warning advanced by the author of 'Hints': if someone does not remedy the current injustices, this writer worries, 'the miseries of the governess may even swell that sickening clamour about the "rights of women" which would never have been raised had women been true to themselves' (FM, 573).

This author's wishful plea that women be 'true to themselves' explicitly enjoins middle-class employers and employees to unite in defence of the domestic ideal that the governesses' distress threatens to disturb. Implicitly, however, the plea for women to unite has more subversive implications because it calls attention to the fact that middle-class women have something in common, which is epitomised in the governesses' plight. This more controversial reading of the governesses' situation was made explicit in 1847 by Elizabeth Rigby, later Lady Eastlake, in her review of Vanity Fair, Jane Eyre, and the 1847 report of the Governesses' Benevolent Institution. Like many other essayists, Lady Eastlake's express concern was the fate of governesses who could no longer find work, for, as she phrases it, their situation more 'painfully expresses the peculiar tyranny of our present state of civilisation' than any other social ill.[19] The governess was so affecting to Lady Eastlake, as to many male commentators, because she epitomised the helplessness unfortunate individuals experienced, not just from ordinary poverty but from the volatile fluctuations of the modern, industrialising economy; the toll these fluctuations exacted had become starkly visible in the depression of the 1840s, and contemporaries feared such hardship lay behind working-class discontent. But to Lady Eastlake, the governess was a special kind of victim, for, unlike lower-class men, she was born to neither discomfort nor labour. 'The case of the governess', she explains, 'is so much the harder than that of any other class of the community, in that they are not only quite as liable to all the vicissitudes of life, but are absolutely supplied by them.' What was distressing to Lady Eastlake in this fact was that the governess's plight could be any middle-class woman's fate. Lady Eastlake recognised, however reluctantly, that the governess revealed the price of all middle-class women's dependence on men: 'Take a lady, in every meaning of the word, born and bred, and let her father pass through the gazette, and she wants

nothing more to suit our highest *beau ideal* of a guide and instruc-
tress to our children. We need the imprudencies, extravagancies,
mistakes, or crimes of a certain number of fathers, to sow that seed
from which we reap the harvest of governesses' (*QR*, 176).

Such a recognition could have led Lady Eastlake to identify fully
with the 'lady' whose imprudent, extravagant, or criminal father has
squandered her security; it could have led her, as it did women like
Barbara Bodichon, to urge women to unite against the dependence
that tied them to their fathers' luck and business sense. Instead,
however, Lady Eastlake explicitly rejects such a conclusion; she
defends against her identification with the governess by simply
asserting the necessity of women's dependence, which she bases on
the natural difference between men's work and the 'precious' work
of women. 'Workmen may rebel', Lady Eastlake writes, 'and tradesmen may combine, not to let you have their labour or their wares
under a certain rate; but the governess has no refuge – no escape; she
is a needy *lady*, whose services are of too precious a kind to have any
stated market value, and is therefore left to the mercy, or what they
call the *means*, of the family that engages her' (*QR*, 179).

In the law that places the governess's 'precious' work above
market value but beneath a fair wage, Lady Eastlake sees that moral
superintendence is simultaneously devalued and exploited. Still, she
insists that things must be this way: after all, the difference between
work whose value can be judged and work that is too 'precious' to
be subjected to market evaluation is what saves ladies from being
like men. But if the difference between working men and leisured
ladies is obvious to Lady Eastlake, the definition of ladies becomes
problematic when one must establish some difference *among* them.
The problem, as she formulates it, is that the difference among ladies
is difficult to see because it is not based on some natural distinction.
The difference among ladies, she complains,

> is not one which will take care of itself, as in the case of a servant. If
> she [the governess] sits at table she does not shock you – if she opens
> her mouth she does not distress you – her appearance and manners
> are likely to be as good as your own – her education rather better;
> there is nothing upon the face of the thing to stamp her as having
> been called to a different state of life from that in which it has
> pleased God to place you; and therefore the distinction has to be kept
> up by a fictitious barrier which presses with cruel weight upon the
> mental strength or constitutional vanity of a woman.
>
> (*QR*, 177)

Because neither sex nor class 'stamp[s]' the governess as different from the lady who employs her, Lady Eastlake is once more drawn toward identifying with her. Yet even though she realises the barrier between them is 'fictitious' and 'cruel', Lady Eastlake will not lower it for a moment. Instead, she turns away again, this time decisively, by appealing to another kind of nature – 'the inherent constitution of English habits, feelings, and prejudices': 'We shall ever prefer to place those immediately about our children who have been born and bred with somewhat of the same refinement as ourselves. We must ever keep them in a sort of isolation, for it is the only means for maintaining that distance which the reserve of English manners and the decorum of English families exact' (*QR*, 178).

Lady Eastlake's appeal to 'the inherent constitution' of the English is meant to resolve the paradox whereby two persons who are by class and sex the same must be treated differently. Her invocation of national character therefore extends the work we have already seen this concept perform. Like the discussions of Dickens I have already examined, Lady Eastlake's appeal to the unassailable authority of national character generalises middle-class 'reserve' and 'decorum' to all 'English families'. Beyond this, however, it also rationalises a difference among members of the middle class that is otherwise unaccountable: the difference of circumstances or luck.

Lady Eastlake's discussion of governesses follows her reviews of two recently published governess novels, *Vanity Fair* and *Jane Eyre*.[20] The substance of these reviews highlights both the conservatism and the potential subversiveness of Eastlake's position. In general, Lady Eastlake approves of Thackeray's novel, despite the immorality of Becky Sharp, but she declares the heroine of *Jane Eyre* to be 'vulgar-minded', a woman 'whom we should not care for as an acquaintance, whom we should not seek as a friend, whom we should not desire for a relation, and whom we should scrupulously avoid for a governess' (*QR*, 176, 174). Eastlake formulates her objections in religious language, but she focuses specifically on the threat this heroine poses to the barrier she will soon admit is 'fictitious' – the barrier between one wellborn (if penniless) lady and another. 'It is true Jane does right', Lady Eastlake begrudgingly admits, in discussing Jane's decision to leave Rochester,

> and [she] exerts great moral strength, but it is the strength of a mere heathen mind which is a law unto itself ... Jane Eyre is proud, and

therefore she is ungrateful too. It pleased God to make her an orphan, friendless, and penniless – yet she thanks nobody, and least of all Him, for the food and raiment, the friends, companions, and instructors of her helpless youth. ... The doctrine of humility is not more foreign to her mind than it is repudiated by her heart. It is by her own talents, virtues, and courage that she is made to attain the summit of human happiness, and, as far as Jane Eyre's own statement is concerned, no one would think that she owed anything either to God above or to man below.

(*QR*, 173)

As Lady Eastlake continues, her religious argument explicitly becomes a warning against the political upheavals threatened by working-class discontent. What has happened here is that the difference of circumstance that Lady Eastlake acknowledges to be a matter of chance has become a matter of class, which is a difference she assumes to be authoritative because it is appointed by God. 'Altogether the auto-biography of Jane Eyre is pre-eminently an anti-Christian composition', she asserts.

There is throughout it a murmuring against the comforts of the rich and against the privations of the poor, which, as far as each individual is concerned, is a murmuring against God's appointment. ... There is a proud and perpetual assertion of the rights of man ... a pervading tone of ungodly discontent which is at once the most prominent and the most subtle evil which the law and the pulpit, which all civilised society in fact has at the present day to contend with. We do not hesitate to say that the tone of mind and thought which has overthrown authority and violated every code human and divine abroad, and fostered Chartism and rebellion at home, is the same which has also written Jane Eyre.

(*QR*, 173–4)

If this objection targets the class issues contemporaries associated with the governess, then Lady Eastlake's other complaint about *Jane Eyre* centres on the second anxiety this figure aroused. The protagonist's 'language and manners ... offend you in every particular', she asserts, especially when Rochester 'pours into [Jane's] ears disgraceful tales of his past life, connected with the birth of little Adèle', and the governess 'listens as if it were nothing new, and certainly nothing distasteful' (*QR*, 167, 164). What offends Lady Eastlake here is the 'perpetual disparity between the account [Jane Eyre] herself gives of the effect she produces, and the means shown us by which she brings that about – the gap between Jane's professed innocence and the sexual knowledge the author insinuates in the language and action of the novel. What this implies is that the author of the novel knows more about sexual matters than the character admits and that the novel is 'vulgar' because it makes the hypocrisy of women's professed innocence legible.

Despite Lady Eastlake's strenuous complaint about *Jane Eyre's* 'gross vulgarity' – or, rather, precisely because of this complaint – she draws out the similarities rather than the differences between herself and the author of the novel. If Lady Eastlake sees sexuality in Jane's 'restlessness', after all, there is little to distinguish her from the writer who created this sexuality in the first place. Just as Lady Eastlake inadvertently exposes her likeness to the governess, then, so she betrays her resemblance to the author she disdains. If we turn for a moment to Brontë's novel, we can begin to identify some of the implications of this similarity and some of the reasons discussions of the governesses' plight sparked other controversies that eventually challenged the domestic ideal.

Jane Eyre may be neither a lunatic nor a fallen woman, but when she refuses Rochester's proposal in chapter 27 that she become his mistress, her language specifically calls to mind the figures to whom the governess was so frequently linked by her contemporaries. Despite her passion, Jane says, she is not 'mad', like a lunatic; her principles are 'worth' more than the pleasure that becoming Rochester's mistress would yield.[21] The two women metaphorically invoked here are also dramatised literally in the two characters that precede Jane Eyre as Rochester's lovers – the lunatic Bertha and the mistress Céline Varens. But if the juxtaposition of these characters calls attention to the problematic sexuality that connects them, the way Brontë works through Jane's position as governess seems to sever the links among them. Read one way, Brontë's novel repeats such conservative resolutions of the governesses' plight as Lady Eastlake's, for Jane's departure from Rochester's house dismisses the sexual and class instabilities the governess introduces, in a way that makes Jane the guardian of sexual and class order rather than its weakest point. When considered in terms of the entire novel, however, Brontë's treatment of the governess problem does not seem so conservative. In introducing the possibility that women may be fundamentally alike, Brontë raises in a more systematically critical way the subversive suggestions adumbrated by Lady Eastlake.

The issues of sexual susceptibility and social incongruity that contemporaries associated with the governess are inextricably bound up with each other in Jane's situation at Thornfield Hall: Jane is vulnerable to Rochester's advances because, as his employee, she lacks both social peers and the means to defend herself against her attractive, aggressive employer. But Brontë symbolically neutralises both of these problems by revising the origin, the terms, and the conditions of Jane's employment. While Jane seeks employment because she has no one to support her, Brontë makes it clear that, in this case, the social incongruity that others might attribute to her position as governess precedes Jane's taking up this work. It is, in part, a family matter; Jane is 'less than a servant', as her cousin John Reed sneers, because she is an orphan and a dependent ward (p. 44). In part, Jane's 'heterogeneity' comes from her personality; she is called 'a discord' and 'a noxious thing', and she thinks that her temperament makes her deserve these names (p. 47).

The effect of making Jane's dependence a function of family and personality is to individualise her problems so as to detach them from her position as governess. Brontë further downplays the importance of Jane's position by idealising her work. Not only is there no mother to satisfy at Thornfield and initially no company from which Jane is excluded, but Adèle is a tractable, if untaught, child, and Jane's actual duties are barely characterised at all. Beside the physical and psychological deprivations so extensively detailed in the Lowood section of the novel, in fact what Jane terms her 'new servitude' seems luxurious; the only hardship she suffers as a governess is an unsatisfied craving for something she cannot name – something that is represented as romantic love.

When Rochester finally appears at Thornfield, Brontë completes what seems to be a dismissal of Jane's employment by subsuming the economic necessity that drove Jane to work into the narrative of an elaborate courtship. Rochester's temperamental 'peculiarities', for which Mrs Fairfax has prepared us, lead him to forget Jane's salary at one point, to double, then halve it, at another. By the time Blanche Ingram and her companions ridicule the 'anathematised race' of governesses in front of Jane, Brontë has already elevated her heroine above this 'race' by subordinating her poverty to her personality and to the place it has earned her in Rochester's affections. 'Your station', Rochester exclaims, 'is in my heart.' The individualistic and psychological vocabulary Rochester uses here pervades Brontë's characterisation of their relationship: 'You are my sympathy', Rochester cries to Jane at one point (p. 342); 'I have something in my brain and heart', Jane tells the reader, 'that assimilates me mentally to him' (p. 204).

When Rochester proposes marriage to Jane, the problems of sexual susceptibility and class incongruity that intersect in the governess's role ought theoretically to be solved. In this context, Mrs Fairfax's warning that 'gentlemen in [Rochester's] station are not accustomed to marry their governesses' (p. 287), Blanche Ingram's admonitory example of the governess dismissed for falling in love (pp. 206–7), and Jane's insistence that she still be treated as a 'plain, Quakerish governess' (p. 287) all underscore the alternative logic behind Jane's situation – a logic that eroticises economics so that class and financial difficulties are overcome by the irresistible (and inexplicable) 'sympathy' of romantic love. But if so translating the class and economic issues raised by the governess resembles, the psychologising gesture I have just examined in *David Copperfield* [in the previous chapter of *Uneven Developments*], Brontë's novel here takes a different turn. For the very issues that foregrounding personality and love should lay to rest come back to haunt the novel in the most fully psychologised episodes of *Jane Eyre*: Jane's dreams of children.[22]

According to Jane's exposition in chapter 21, emotional affinity, or 'sympathy', is a sign of a mysterious but undeniable kinship: 'the unity of the source to which each traces his origin' (p. 249). But Jane's discussion of sympathy here focuses not on the bond of kinship, which she claims to be explaining, but on some *disturbance* within a family relationship. Specifically, Jane is recalling her old nursemaid Bessie telling her that 'to dream of children was a sure sign of trouble, either to oneself or to one's kin' (p. 249). Jane then reveals that Bessie's superstition has come back to her because every night for a week she has dreamed of an infant, 'which I sometimes hushed in my arms, sometimes dandled on my knee, sometimes watched playing with daisies on a lawn. ... It was a wailing child this night, and a laughing one the next: now it nestled close to me, and now it ran from me' (p. 249). This revelation is immediately followed by Jane's discovering that the obvious 'trouble' presaged by her dream is at her childhood home, Gateshead: John has gambled the Reed family into debt and is now dead, probably by his own hand, and Mrs Reed, broken in spirit and health, lies near death asking for Jane.

The implications of this 'trouble' surface when this reference is read against the other episodes adjacent to the dream. Jane's journey to Gateshead follows two scenes in which Rochester wantonly taunts Jane with his power: in chapter 20 he teases her that he will marry Blanche Ingram, and in chapter 21 he refuses to pay her her wages, thereby underscoring her emotional and financial dependence. Once at Gateshead, Jane discovers that Mrs Reed has also been dreaming of a child – of Jane Eyre, in fact, that 'mad', 'fiend'-like child who was so much 'trouble' that Mrs Reed has withheld for three years the knowledge that Jane has other kin and that her uncle, John Eyre, wants to support her (pp. 260, 266–7). Mrs Reed's malice has thereby prolonged Jane's economic dependence while depriving her of the kinship for which she has yearned. Jane explicitly denies feeling any 'vengeance ... rage ... [or] aversion' toward Mrs Reed, but her very denial calls attention to the rage she expressed when she was similarly helpless at Lowood. Foregrounding the structural similarities among the scenes conveys the impression that John Reed's suicide and the stroke that soon kills Mrs Reed are displaced expressions of Jane's anger at them for the dependence and humiliation they have inflicted on her. These symbolic murders, which the character denies, can also be seen as displacements of the rage at the other figure who now stands in the same relation of superiority to Jane as the Reeds once did: Rochester. That both the character and the plot of the novel deny this anger, however, leads us to the other 'trouble' adjacent to this dream of a child: Bertha's attack on her brother, Richard Mason.

As soon as Mason enters the narrative, he is rhetorically linked to Rochester: he appears when and where Rochester was expected to appear, and in her description of him Jane compares him explicitly to Rochester (pp. 218, 219). Like the sequence I have just examined, Mason's arrival punctuates a series of painful reminders of Jane's dependence and marginality; he interrupts the engagement party (when Jane, obsessed with watching Rochester and Blanche, specifically denies that she is jealous, p. 215), and his arrival is immediately followed by the gypsy scene, in which Rochester so completely invades Jane's thoughts that she wonders 'what unseen spirit' has taken up residence in her heart (p. 228). When the gypsy reveals that s/he is Rochester, Jane voices more rage toward her 'master' than at any other time: 'It is scarcely fair, sir', Jane says; 'it was not right' (p. 231). Jane's hurt is soon repaid, however, even if what happens is not acknowledged as revenge. Jane suddenly, and with a marked carelessness, remembers Mason's presence. The effect on Rochester is dramatic. Leaning on Jane as he once did before (and will do again), Rochester 'staggers' and exclaims, 'Jane, I've got a blow – I've got a blow, Jane!' (p. 232). The 'blow' Jane's announcement delivers is then graphically acted out when Bertha, who is Jane's surrogate by virtue of her relation to Rochester, attacks Mason, whose textual connection to Rochester has already been established. As before, anger and violence are transferred from one set of characters to another, revenge is displaced from Jane's character, and agency is dispersed into the text.

The text – not as agent but as effect – turns out to be precisely what is at stake in these series, for in each of them Rochester's most serious transgression has been to usurp Jane's control over what is, after all, primarily her story. In the gypsy scene he has told her what she feels, in words as 'familiar ... as the speech of my own tongue' (p. 231), and in the scene immediately following Bertha's assault on Mason, he has usurped her authority even more, first commanding her not to speak (p. 239), then asking her to imagine herself 'no longer a girl ... but a wild boy' – to imagine she is Rochester, in other words, while he tells *his* story to her as if she were telling her own story to herself (pp. 246–7). The precarious independence Jane earned by leaving Gateshead has been figured in the ability to tell (if not direct) her own story; thus, the measure of autonomy gained by translating Jane's economic dependence into a story of love is undercut by Rochester's imperious demand that she listen to him tell his story and hers, that she be dependent – seen and not heard, as women (particularly governesses) should be.

Jane's second reference to dreaming of children extends and elaborates this pattern of enforced dependence and indirect revenge. Once more, Jane's narration of the dream is temporally displaced from the moment of her dreaming. When she does disclose to Rochester and the reader what frightened her, Jane also reveals that when Bertha awakened her, Jane had twice been dreaming of a child. In the first dream, 'some barrier' divided her and Rochester. 'I was following the windings of an unknown road', Jane explains; 'total obscurity environed me; rain pelted me; I was burdened with the charge of a little child. ... My movements were fettered, and my voice still died away inarticulate; while you, I felt, withdrew farther and farther every moment' (p. 309). In the next dream, of Thornfield Hall in ruins, the child still encumbers Jane. 'Wrapped up in a shawl', she says,

> I still carried the unknown little child: I might not lay it down anywhere, however tired were my arms – however much its weight

impeded my progress, I must retain it. I heard the gallop of a horse. ... I was sure it was you; and you were departing for many years, and for a distant country. I climbed the thin wall with frantic, perilous haste. ... The stones rolled from under my feet, the ivy branches I grasped gave way, the child clung round my neck in terror, and almost strangled me. ... I saw you like a speck on a white track, lessening every moment. ... The wall crumbled; I was shaken; the child rolled from my knee, I lost my balance, fell, and woke.

(p. 310)

To this 'preface' Jane then appends the story of the 'trouble' that followed: Bertha's rending Jane's wedding veil. This is immediately followed by the much more devastating 'trouble' of Mason's denunciation in the church, Rochester's revelation that he is already married, and the obliteration of Jane's hopes to formalise her 'kinship' with Rochester.

Alone in her bedroom, Jane surveys her ruined love – which she likens to 'a suffering child in a cold cradle'; once more she denies that she is angry at Rochester ('I would not ascribe vice to him; I would not say he had betrayed me', p. 324), but even more explicitly than before, the plot suggests that the person who has hurt Jane is now indirectly suffering the effects of the rage that follows from such hurt: Jane's letter to John Eyre, after all, led her uncle to expose to Mason her planned marriage, and Jane's desire for some independence from Rochester led her to write her uncle in the first place. In this instance, of course, Jane initially suffers as much as – if not more than – Rochester does: not only is she subjected to the humiliating offer of his adulterous love, but she also forces herself to leave Thornfield and she almost dies as a consequence. Jane's suffering, however, turns out to be only the first stage in her gradual recovery of kinship, independence, money, and enough mastery to write both her story and Rochester's. By contrast, Rochester is further reduced by the novel's subsequent action; when he is blinded and maimed in the fire Bertha sets, the pattern of displaced anger is complete again.[23]

Why does dreaming of children signify 'trouble' in these sequences, and why does the trouble take this form? When Jane dreams of children, some disaster follows that is a displaced expression of the anger against kin that the character denies. In the sense that narrative effect is split off from psychological cause, *Jane Eyre* becomes at these moments what we might call a hysterical text, in which the body of the text symptomatically acts out what cannot make its way into the psychologically realistic narrative. Because there was no permissible plot in the nineteenth century for a woman's anger, whenever Brontë explores this form of self-assertion the text splinters hysterically, provoked by and provoking images of dependence and frustration.

Dreaming of children, then, is metonymically linked to a rage that remains implicit at the level of character but materialises at the level of plot. And *this* signifies 'trouble' both because the children that appear in these dreams metaphorically represent the dependence that defined women's place in bourgeois ideology (and that was epitomised in the governess) *and* because the disjunction that characterises these narrative episodes shows that hysteria is produced as the condition in which a lady's impermissible emotions are expressed. What Jane's dreams of children reveal, then, in their content, their placement, and their form, is that the helplessness enforced by the governess's dependent position – along with the frustration, self-denial, and maddened, thwarted rage that accompanies it – marks every middle-class woman's life because she is not allowed to express (or possess) the emotions that her dependence provokes. The structural paradigm underlying the governess's sexual vulnerability and her social incongruity – her lunacy and her class ambiguity – is dependence, and this is the position all middle-class women share.

From one perspective, Brontë neutralises the effects of this revelation and downplays its subversive implications. By making Jane leave Thornfield, Brontë seems to reformulate her dilemma, making it once more an individual, moral, emotional problem and not a function of social position or occupation. As soon as Jane stops being a governess, she is 'free' to earn her happiness according to the paradoxical terms of the domestic ideal: even the sceptical Lady Eastlake conceded that the self-denial Jane expresses in renouncing Rochester's love and nearly starving on the heath gives her a right to earthly happiness. When Jane discovers she has both money and kin, then, the dependence epitomised by the governess's position seems no longer to be an issue – a point made clear by the end to which Jane puts her newfound wealth: she liberates Diana and Mary from having to be governesses and so frees them to a woman's 'natural' fate – marriage.

From another perspective, however, Brontë's 'resolution' of the governess's dilemma can be seen to underscore – not dismiss – the problem of women's dependence. That only the coincidence of a rich uncle's death can confer on a single woman autonomy and power, after all, suggests just how intractable her dependence really was in the 1840s. Brontë also calls attention to the pervasiveness of this dependence in the very episode in which Jane ceases to be a governess, the episode at Whitcross. As soon as Jane is not a governess, her irreducible likeness to other women returns with stark clarity – and in the very form that relieving Jane of her economic dependence should theoretically have displaced: the sexual vulnerability and class uncertainty epitomised in the lunatic and the fallen woman. 'Absolutely destitute', 'objectless and lost', Jane is mistaken for an 'eccentric sort of lady', a thief, and a figure too 'sinister' to be named: 'you are not what you ought to be', sneers the Riverses' wary servant (pp. 349, 355, 361).

The return of these other women at the very moment at which Jane is least of all a governess functions to reinscribe the similarity between the governess and these sexualised women. At the same time, it lets us glimpse both why it was so important for contemporaries like Lady Eastlake to insist that the governess was different from other women and why it was so difficult to defend this assertion. For the fact that the associations return even though Jane is *not* a governess suggests the instability of the boundary that all the non-fiction accounts of the governess simultaneously took for granted and fiercely upheld: the boundary between such aberrant women as lunatic, prostitute, and governess and the 'normal' woman – the woman who is a wife and mother.

That the governess was somehow a threat to the 'natural' order superintended by the middle-class wife is clear from essayists' insistence that the governess's availability kept mothers from performing their God-given tasks. This interruption of nature, in turn, was held responsible for the 'restless rage to push on' that was feeding class discontent (*FM*, 572). If 'ladies of the middle rank resume[d] the instruction of their own children, as God ordained they should,' the author of 'Hints' asserted, 'if mothers would obey their highest calling, many who now fill their places would be safer and happier in their lower vocation' (*FM*, 581). At stake, according to this writer, is not only the happiness of those 'daughters of poor men' who are now 'crammed by a hireling' instead of being taught domestic skills, but also the 'depth and breadth of character' all women should display. 'Surely it must be acknowledged', the author continues, 'that women whose lesson of life has been learned at mothers' knees, over infants' cradles, will be more earnest and

genuine than those taught by a stranger, however well qualified'
(*FM*, 581).

This intricate weave of assumptions about class relations and
female nature reproduces the ideological equation I have already
examined: that morality and class stability will follow the expression of maternal instinct – a force grounded in God's order and the
(middle-class) female body. In this representation, maternal instinct
is paradoxically both what distinguishes the mother from the governess and what naturally qualifies the former to perform the
services the latter must be trained to provide.

> New difficulties and responsibilities meet [the governess] every day;
> she is hourly tried by all those childish follies and perversities which
> need a mother's instinctive love to make them tolerable; yet a for-
> bearance and spring of spirits is claimed from the stranger, in spite of
> the frets she endures, which He who made the heart that knew that ma-
> ternal affection only could supply, under the perpetual contradictions
> of wilful childhood. This strength of instinct has been given to every
> mother. It enables her to walk lightly under a load which, without it,
> she could not sustain.
>
> (*FM*, 744)

Positioning the governess against a normative definition of
woman as wife and mother reinforced the complex ideological
system I have set out in this book. This juxtaposition shored up the
distinction between (abnormal) women who performed domestic
(in this case maternal) labour for wages and those who did the same
work for free, as an expression of a love that was generous, non-
competitive, and guaranteed by the natural force of maternal 'instinct'. The image of an arena of 'freedom' for women was, in turn,
central to the representation of domesticity as desirable, and this
representation, along with the disincentive to work outside the
home that it enforced, was instrumental to the image of women as
moral and not economic agents, antidotes to the evils of competition, not competitors themselves. Finally, the picture of a sphere of
relative freedom was crucial to establishing some boundary to the
market economy; the wife, protected and fulfilled by maternal instinct, was living proof that the commodification of labour, the
alienation of human relations, the frustrations and disappointments
inflicted by economic vicissitudes stopped at the door of the home.
From this complex ideological role, we can see that laments about
the governess's plight in the 1840s belonged primarily to a dis-

course about domestic relations – which was necessarily a discourse about gender, class, and the nature of labour as well.

The problem was that governesses – especially in such numbers and in such visibly desperate straits – gave the lie to the complex of economic and domestic representations that underwrote this ideology. Not only did the governess's 'plight' bring the economic vicissitudes of the market economy into the middle-class home, thereby collapsing the separation of spheres, but the very existence of so many governesses was proof that, whatever middle-class women might want, not all of them could be (legitimate) mothers because they could not all be wives. As the 1851 Census made absolutely clear, there simply were not enough men to go around. Moreover, there was something dangerously unstable even about the putatively reliable force of maternal love. Moralists admitted that 'love' was a notoriously difficult emotion to define and that the distinction between one kind of love and another required constant defence. What, they worried, could prevent 'the key-stone of the stupendous arch which unites heaven to earth, and man to heaven' from becoming *'morbid sentimentality – an ungovernable, tumultuous passion'* – especially if the person who should incarnate the former was distinguished from the victim of the latter only by maternal instinct, which even the most optimistic moralists admitted was unstable.[24] According to the logic of these fears, the governess not only revealed what the mother might otherwise have been; she also actively freed mothers to display other desires that were distinctly *not* maternal. This set up the unsettling possibility that a mother's 'jealousy' and her energies might find an object other than the one 'nature' had decreed. 'If more governesses find a penurious maintenance by these means', Lady Eastlake warned, 'more mothers are encouraged to neglect those duties, which, one would have thought, they would have been as jealous of as of that first duty of all that infancy requires of them' (*QR*, 180).

These warnings suggest that, even though the unemployed mother functions as the norm in the essays I have been examining and in the symbolic economy of which they are a part, motherhood had to be rhetorically constructed *as* the norm in defiance of real economic conditions and as a denial of whatever additional desires a woman (even a mother) might have. My reading of *Jane Eyre* suggests that articulating the 'problem' of female sexuality upon class difference was not always sufficient to repress the contradiction written into the domestic ideal. Brontë's novel reveals that the figure from whom the mother had to be distinguished was not just the lower-class prostitute but the middle-class governess as well, for the governess was both what a woman who should be a mother might actually become and the woman who had to be paid for doing what the mother should want to do for free. If the fallen woman was the middle-class mother's opposite, the middle-class governess was her next-of-kin, the figure who ought to ensure that a boundary existed between classes of women but who could not, precisely because her sexuality made her like the women from whom she ought to differ.[25]

This is the ideological economy whose instabilities Brontë exposes when she 'resolves' the problem of the governess by having Jane marry Rochester. Jane's marriage imperils this symbolic economy in two ways. In the first place, despite her explicit dis-avowal of kinship, Jane has effectively been inscribed in a series that includes not just a lunatic and a mistress, but also a veritable united nations of women. In telling Jane about these other lovers, Rochester's design is to insist on difference, to draw an absolute distinction between some kinds of women, who cannot be legiti-mate wives, and Jane, who can. This distinction is reinforced by both racism and nationalist prejudice: that Bertha is West Indian 'explains' her madness, just as Céline's French birth 'accounts for' her moral laxity. But Jane immediately sees that if she assents to Rochester's proposal, she will become simply 'the successor of these poor girls' (p. 339). She sees, in other words, the likeness that Rochester denies: *any* woman who is not a wife is automatically like a governess in being dependent, like a fallen woman in being 'kept'.

Emphasising the likeness among women is subversive not merely because doing so highlights all women's dependence – although this is, of course, part of the point. Beyond this, the fact that the like-ness Brontë stresses is not women's selflessness or self-control but some internal difference suggests that the contradiction repressed by the domestic ideal is precisely what makes a woman womanly. This internal difference is figured variously as madness and as sexu-ality. Jane's own descriptions of herself show her growing from the 'insanity' of childhood rebellion to the 'restlessness' of unspecified desire: 'I desired more', she says, '... than I possessed' (p. 141). In the passage in chapter 12 in which Jane describes this 'restlessness', she compares it specifically to the 'ferment' that feeds 'political re-bellions' and she opposes it explicitly to the self-denial that caring for children requires. This passage returns us once more to Jane's dreams of children, for the manifest content of the majority of those dreams reveals how carrying a child burdens the dreamer, impeding her efforts to reach her lover or voice her frustrated love. 'Anybody may blame me who likes', Jane says of the 'cool language' with which she describes her feelings for Adèle, but caring for the child is not enough; 'I believed in the existence of other and more vivid kinds of goodness, and what I believed in I wished to behold' (pp. 140, 141). Even when Jane has her own child at the end of the novel, her only reference to him subordinates maternal love to the sexual passion that Rochester's eyes have consistently represented.[26]

Positioning Jane within a series of women and characterising her as 'restless' and passionate transforms the difference among women that Dickens invoked, to 'cure' the problematic sexuality written into the domestic ideal, into a difference within all women – the 'difference' of sexual desire. This similarity thus subverts the putative difference between the governess and the lunatic or mistress, just as it obliterates the difference between the governess and the wife. Having Jane marry Rochester – transforming the governess into a wife – extends the series of aberrant women to include the figure who ought to be exempt from this series, who ought to be the norm. The point is that, as the boundary between these two groups of women, the governess belongs to both sides of the opposition: in her, the very possibility of an opposition collapses.

The second sense in which Jane's marriage is subversive follows directly from this relocation of difference. If all women are alike in being 'restless', then they are also like – not different from – men. Charlotte Brontë makes this point explicitly in chapter 12, in the passage I have been quoting. 'Women are supposed to be very calm generally', Jane notes, 'but women feel just as men feel; they need exercise for their faculties, and a field for their efforts as much as their brothers do; they suffer from too rigid a restraint, too absolute a stagnation, precisely as men would suffer; and it is ... thoughtless to condemn them, or laugh at them, if they seek to do more or learn more than custom has pronounced necessary for their sex' (p. 141). The implications of this statement may not be drawn out consistently in this novel, but merely to assert that the most salient difference was located within every individual and not between men and women was to raise the possibilities that women's dependence was customary, not natural, that their sphere was kept separate only by artificial means, and that women, like men, could grow through work outside the home. Even though Jane marries Rochester, then, she does so as an expression of her desire, not as the self-sacrifice St John advocates; the image with which she represents her marriage fuses man and woman instead of respecting their separate bodies, much less their separate spheres. 'Ever more absolutely bone of his bone and flesh of his flesh', Jane represents herself as taking the law of coverture to its logical extreme.

What Lady Eastlake objected to in *Jane Eyre* is exactly this subversive tendency. But despite her objection, Eastlake's intermittent – and irrepressible – recognition that the governess's plight is, theoretically at least, that of every middle-class woman repeats Brontë's subversive move. Moreover, Eastlake's charge that the 'crimes of fathers' sow the crop of governesses fingers men as the villains behind women's dependence even more specifically than Brontë was willing to do.[27] This charge – that men are responsible for the fetters women wear – also appears in the bitter myth recounted in 'Hints on the Modern Governess System'. ''Twas a stroke of policy in those ranty-pole barons of old', the author writes, 'to make their lady-loves idols, and curb their wives with silken idleness. Woman was raised on a pinnacle to keep her in safety. Our chivalrous northern knights had a religious horror of the Paynim harems. They never heard of Chinese shoes in those days, so they devised a new chain for the weaker sex. They made feminine labour disgraceful' (*FM*, 576). The implicit accusation here is that women had to be idolised and immobilised for some men to think them safe from other men's rapacious sexual desire and from their own susceptibility. Just as some medical men attempted to regulate medical practice so as to control fears about sexuality, so our 'chivalrous northern knights' curtail women's honourable labour to protect men from the appetite they represent as uncontrollable and destructive.

Neither Lady Eastlake nor the author of 'Hints on the Modern Governess System' developed this indictment of men into an extended argument; instead, they continued to see the problem in terms of a natural difference between the sexes and the inevitability of women's dependence. So fixed did these writers imagine women's dependence to be, in fact, that the only solution they could devise was to defer their criticism of men, to make women responsible for remedying the trouble they identified: Lady Eastlake yokes her plea that upper-class employers pay their governesses higher wages to an argument that middle-class women – not to mention those in lesser ranks – resume their maternal duties; the author of 'Hints' explicitly states that 'the modern governess system is a case between woman and woman. Before one sex demands its due from the other, let it be just to itself' (*FM*, 573).

From Mary Poovey, *Uneven Developments: the Ideological Work of Gender in Mid-Victorian England* (London, 1989), pp. 126–48.

NOTES

[The book from which this essay is taken originally appeared, like Margaret Homans' book, in the *Women in Culture and Society* series, published by the University of Chicago Press (it was published in England the following year by the feminist press Virago). Like Margaret Homans', it is a work of considerable theoretical sophistication; but it is a work of a very different kind. Poovey's object of study is 'neither the individual text ... nor literary history, but something extrapolated from texts and reconstructed as the conditions of possibility for those texts' (p. 15). She is particularly concerned with the ways in which 'what may look coherent and complete in retrospect was actually fissured by competing emphases and interests', and the same ideological formulations were given rather different emphases by different institutions, individuals or groups. This 'unevenness' in the construction and deployment of representations of gender enabled, she argues, 'the emergence in the 1850s of a genuinely – though incompletely articulated – oppositional voice' (p. 4). Poovey's approach draws on the methodologies of three contemporary interpretative paradigms (poststructuralist versions of formalism, Marxism and psychoanalysis), each of which shares the assumption that 'signifying practices always produce meanings in excess of what seems to be the text's explicit design' (p. 16). Each of her five chapters focuses on a specific controversy that developed during the 1840s and 1850s, in each of which, very differently, the ideological formulation of gender was contested, and its instabilities revealed. In the chapter from which this extract is taken, she shows how the debate over the employment of women as governesses mobilised and engaged with two powerful stereotypes of womanhood – that of the sexless, virtuous 'angel in the house', and that of the aggressive, carnal woman of the streets. It is within the context of this debate that she places *Jane Eyre*, arguing that, in constantly threatening to collapse this opposition, the novel's presentation of its governess-protagonist points toward intuitions of a potentially subversive kind. Ed.]

1. For discussions of nineteenth-century governess novels, see Wanda E. Neff, *Victorian Working Women: An Historical and Literary Study of Women in British Industries and Professions: 1832–1850* (1929; reprint, New York, 1966), pp. 153–74; Jerome Beaty, '*Jane Eyre* and Genre', *Genre*, 10 (Winter 1977), 619–54; and Robert A. Colby,

Fiction with a Purpose: Major and Minor Nineteenth-Century Novels (Bloomington, IN, 1967), pp. 178–212. More theoretical discussions of the governess include: Shoshana Felman, 'Turning the Screw of Interpretation', *Yale French Studies*, 55/56 (1977), 94–207; and Jane Gallop, *The Daughter's Seduction: Feminism and Psychoanalysis* (Ithaca, NY, 1982), pp. 141–8.

2. For the history of the Governesses' Benevolent Institution, see *The Story of the Governesses' Benevolent Institution* (Southwick, Sussex, 1962). The GBI (which was still in existence in 1962) was the second institution to address the governesses' plight. The first, the Governesses' Mutual Assurance Society, founded in 1829 to help governesses save for sickness, unemployment and old age, did not fare well and dissolved in 1838. The GBI also got off to an uncertain start, and, largely because it had managed to save only about £100 in its first two years, was substantially reorganised in 1843 under the Rev David Laing, chaplain of Middlesex Hospital and pastor of the Holy Trinity Church of Saint Pancras. The stated goals of the GBI were 'to raise the character of governesses as a class, and thus improve the tone of Female Education; to assist Governesses in making provision for their old age; and to assist in distress and age those Governesses whose exertions for their parents, or families have prevented such a provision' (*Story of the GBI*, p. 14). What is interesting about these goals is the way they combine provisions that encourage professional identification and cooperation with more explicitly moral (and implicitly class-specific) aims ('raise the character'). The GBI gave its first annuity in May 1844, and by 1860, 99 governesses were receiving annuities from the GBI, though the annual reports made it clear how dramatically the need exceeded the monies the GBI had at its disposal. See [Jessie Boucherette], 'The Profession of the Teacher: The Annual Reports of the Governesses' Benevolent Institution, from 1843 to 1856', *English Woman's Journal*, 1 (March 1858), 1–13. Other activities of the GBI included the opening in 1845 of a home in Harley Street to provide cheap, respectable lodgings for governesses who were temporarily unemployed; the establishment at about the same time of a free employment register; and, in 1849, the establishment of a permanent home for aged governesses in the Prince of Wales Road.

3. Boucherette, 'Profession of the Teacher', p. 1.

4. Leonore Davidoff and Catherine Hall, *Family Fortunes: Men and Women of the English Middle Class, 1780–1850* (Chicago, 1987), pp. 312–13.

5. See M. Jeanne Peterson, 'The Victorian Governess: Status Incongruence in Family and Society', in Martha Vicinus, *Suffer and Be Still: Women in the Victorian Age* (Bloomington, IN, 1972), p. 4;

and Martha Vicinus, *Independent Women: Work and Community for Single Women, 1850–1920* (Chicago, 1985), pp. 23, 26.

6. Peterson, 'The Victorian Governess', pp. 3–19.

7. For a discussion of the increasingly problematised conceptualisation of Victorian children, see Mark Spilka, 'On the Enrichment of Poor Monkeys by Myth and Dream; or, How Dickens Rousseauisticised and Pre-Freudianised Victorian Views of Childhood', in *Sexuality and Victorian Literature*, ed. Don Richard Cox (Knoxville, TN, 1984), pp. 161–79.

8. The phrase 'tabooed woman' comes from Lady Eastlake (Elizabeth Rigby), '*Vanity Fair* – and *Jane Eyre*', *Quarterly Review*, 84 (1848), 177; hereafter cited as *QR*. See also 'Hints on the Modern Governess System', *Fraser's Magazine*, 30 (November 1844), 573; hereafter cited as *FM*.

9. *The Governess: Or, Politics in Private Life* (London, 1836), p. 310. One of the few departures from the conceptualisation of the governess as 'genteel' appears in an article entitled 'The Governess Question', *English Woman's Journal*, 4 (1860). In this essay, the author argues that the governess's position is not considered genteel and is never likely to be elevated in status. 'Whatever *gentility* may once have attached to the profession of the governess has long since vanished, and it is impossible to name any occupation, not positively disreputable, which confers so little respectability, – respectability in the worldly sense. ... The governess, however well-conducted, remains a governess; may starve *genteely*, and sink into her grave friendless and alone' (pp. 163, 170). This is explicitly a polemical article, however, 'addressed to parents, who, not having the means of giving their daughters any fortune, seem seized with an epidemic madness to make them governesses' (p. 163). It is, in other words, designed to discourage lower-middle-class women from entering the governesses' ranks by disparaging the social status of this work.

10. The phrase about 'degradation' appears in [Sarah Lewis], 'On the Social Position of Governesses', *Fraser's Magazine*, 37 (April 1848), 414. See also *FM*, 581.

11. See *QR*, 180; *FM*, 573; [Lewis], 'Social Position', 413–14.

12. Peterson also makes this point. See 'Victorian Governess', p. 17.

13. For an autobiographical report of a governess's sexual vulnerability, see Ellen Weeton, *Miss Weeton's Journal of a Governess*, ed. J. J. Bagley (New York, 1969), I, pp. 209–327. The sexual exploitation to which the governess was potentially exposed surfaces obliquely at the end of an 1858 essay in the *English Woman's Journal*. 'Depths of horror', the author (Jessie Boucherette) warns, 'into which men

cannot fall' await the unemployed governess ('Profession of the Teacher', p. 13).

14. See *QR*, 177; and *FM*, 573.

15. *FM*, 574.

16. The phrase 'white slavery' is the title of a letter about governesses published in the London *Times* and cited by Barbara Leigh Smith Bodichon, *Women and Work* (London, 1857), p. 17. The phrase 'needlewomen forced to take to the streets' was used by Henry Mayhew in his 1849–50 *Morning Chronicle* series on London, 'Labour and the Poor'. See *The Unknown Mayhew: Selections from the 'Morning Chronicle', 1849–50*, ed. E. P. Thompson and Eileen Yeo (Harmondsworth, 1973), p. 200.

17. See Elizabeth K. Helsinger, Robin Lauterbach Sheets, and William Veeder (eds), *The Woman Question: Social Issues 1837–1883*, vol. 2 of *The Woman Question: Society and Literature in Britain and America, 1837–1883* (New York, 1983), p. 115.

18. Henry Mayhew, 'Second Test – Meeting of Needlewomen Forced to Take to the Streets', in *Unknown Mayhew*, pp. 200–15; and Anthony Ashley Cooper (Lord Ashley, later the seventh Earl of Shaftesbury), in *Hansard's Parliamentary Debates*, 3rd series, 15 March 1844, cc. 1088–9, 1091–6, 1099–100.

19. *QR*, 181.

20. Other early reviews of *Jane Eyre* include: George Henry Lewes' in *Fraser's Magazine*, 36 (December 1847), 690–3; John Eagles' essay in *Blackwood's Magazine* (October 1848), 473–4; [H. R. Bagshawe], '*Jane Eyre, Shirley*', *Dublin Review*, 28 (March 1850), 209–33; [G. H. Lewes], 'The Lady Novelists', *Fraser's Magazine*, 58 (July 1852), 129–41; and [E. S. Dallas], 'Currer Bell', *Blackwood's Magazine*, 82 (July 1857), 77–94.

21. *Jane Eyre*, ed. Queenie Leavis (Harmondsworth, 1966), p. 344. All future references will be cited in the text by page numbers.

22. Other essays on these dreams include Margaret Homans, 'Dreaming of Children: Literalisation in *Jane Eyre*', in *Bearing the Word: Language and Female Experience in Nineteenth-century Women's Writing* (Chicago, 1986), pp. 84–99 [reprinted in this volume – see pp. 147–67. Ed.]; Maurianne Adams, 'Family Disintegration and Creative Reintegration: the Case of Charlotte Brontë and *Jane Eyre*', in *The Victorian Family: Structure and Stresses*, ed. Anthony S. Wohl (London, 1978), pp. 148–79.

23. See Sandra M. Gilbert and Susan Gubar, *The Madwoman in the Attic: The Woman Writer and the Nineteenth-Century Literary Imagination* (New Haven, CT, 1979), pp. 336–71.

24. 'Love', *The Governess: A Repertory of Female Education*, 2 (1855), 94. This periodical was founded in 1854 and continued publication at least until 1856. In addition to essays on educational theory, it included both practical help for governesses (directions and patterns for 'fancy needle work', sample lesson plans, and quizzes for periods of English history) and a correspondence section that elicited extremely pragmatic complaints and suggestions from governesses (as to the poisonous properties of the colouring agent in modelling wax, for example). In 1855 the editors of the periodical described it as Christian but non-sectarian and as 'the *first* – and for twelve months. ... the *only* periodical on the subject of Female Education' (*The Governess: A Repertory of Female Education*, iii).

25. Nancy Armstrong, in *Desire and Domestic Fiction: A Political History of the Novel* (New York, 1987), p. 79, discusses the problematic position the governess occupied. The unstable boundary between the governess and the mother was explicitly explored by Mrs Henry Wood in *East Lynne*, when the (disfigured) mother returns home as the governess for her own children.

26. The only reference to Jane's child is this sentence: 'When his first-born was put into his arms, he could see that the boy had inherited his own eyes, as they once were – large, brilliant, and black' (*Jane Eyre*, p. 476).

27. Jane's father is only obliquely held responsible for her situation – but her maternal grandfather is more directly to blame. Jane's father, a poor clergyman, wooed her mother into marriage against her father's wishes, and it was the old man's inexorable anger that caused him to leave all his money to Jane's uncle, thus leaving her penniless and dependent when her parents died.

9

Femininity – Missing in Action

ELISABETH BRONFEN

Three types of femininity presided over the literary imagination of the nineteenth century: firstly, the diabolic outcast, the destructive, fatal demon woman, secondly, the domestic 'angel of the house', the saintly, self-sacrificing frail vessel, and thirdly a particular version of Mary Magdalene, as the penitent and redeemed sexually vain and dangerous woman, the fallen woman. It is significant, however, that the feminine perfection, excess because it lies beyond the human, and its counterpart, the feminine monster, excess in that it falls short of the cultural code's limit, can be seen as medium for the death drive. The first type, demonstrating, in imitation of the Virgin Mary and Christian martyrs, how physical weakness, self-sacrifice and self-denial taken to the sheer materiality of the body fading into absence serve as proof of physical and spiritual purity, can be seen as embodying fantasies of a masochistic turning inward of the death drive that results in a self-negation and self-obliteration. Though these fading, ethereal women types, of which Little Nell and Little Eva would be examples, contradict the Virgin Mary's attribute of body wholeness beyond any physical inhabitation by death, they too serve as mediators and intercessors for men's souls. Their death purifies the sins of the living and, as angels, they help the living prepare for heaven by leading them to death. The suffering and diseased feminine invalid, dying of self-effacing inanition can, Dijkstra notes, be seen as 'the perfect representative of woman as Christ figure'.[1]

The second type can be understood, instead, in the sense of a fear of Woman as being an incarnation of a sadistic turning outward of the death drive, transferring aggressive violence from the self to the feminine lover, to which he reciprocates by destroying her. Positioned in between the innocent, ethereal feminine type, staging an excessive absence of artifice or a fading of body, and the witch, the demonic feminine type staging an excessive presence of the dangers of the body and the duplicity of artifice, the seduced, penitent and redeemed 'fallen woman' is also an agent or medium of the death drive. Not only because her 'fall' implies an introduction to Eve's sin, and thus physical as well as spiritual decay, but also because her cultural representation often presented death as the necessary climax to the fallen woman's trajectory. Whether the semantic coding of the feminine involves the purity of the fading loss of body, the danger of an excessive bodiliness or the conjunction of the two, the death drive which is given presence is secured into absence when death translates the typified woman into the perfect allegorical type, where body is completely missing.

Countless examples could be given to illustrate how the death of a woman helps to regenerate the order of society, to eliminate destructive forces or serves to reaggregate the protagonist into her or his community. A common pattern emerges even if the cultural values that are connected with the dead woman and debated in connection with her death vary. When the topos of martyrdom serves as model for the narrative, then the death of the innocent, virtuous woman, as in the case of Clarissa, appears inculpatory as well as edifying and soothing to the spectators, who undertake a pilgrimage to the dying body. The potential for change is shifted away from the self on to the signifier of the sacrificed body so as to be transferred into the existing order without fundamentally changing it.

Another kind of recuperation, in respect to threatening, because undomesticated or irrational aspects of nature, occurs when a figure like Carmen, unable or unwilling to comply with assigned role behaviour, is punished or sacrificed. A woman may also consciously break conventions or commit a crime punished with death, such as adultery, infanticide or murder, as an expression of liberating subjectivity, of assuming authorship and responsibility for her destiny. The following analysis of Charlotte Brontë's *Jane Eyre* (1847) is meant to be a paradigmatic illustration of the conjunction of femininity, semantically encoded as a metonymy for death, with the feminine character's ambivalent position – divided, shifting, contradictory – as the uncanny figure traced by death, in order to show how this conjunction culminates in the sacrifice of the feminine agent of disturbance.

In the course of her education from orphanage to marriage, Jane Eyre occupies various positions of social liminality that include encounters with death. I will focus only on the two equally liminal feminine figures who embody extremities of death's agency: the orphan Helen Burns, whose desire for death stages a 'masochistic' violence against the self, a total subjugation before cultural laws, and Bertha Rochester, the bodily living though socially dead wife, who embodies defiance of cultural laws that translates into a 'sadistic' violence against others. In her own liminality as orphan and maiden, Jane is divided between these two figures of death, as her two 'Others', and, provoked by an identification, she can confront aspects of the death drive within herself. Yet she must also mitigate this Otherness to survive and to enter a fixed position in her social order. The logic of the text implies that in their extremity these two women are not only objects of punishment, but must ultimately also be destroyed. While Bertha reflects in extremity Jane's excessive passion, her destructive impulses of hatred and vengeance which must be corrected, Helen reflects her shy, frightened self-abnegation which must be transformed to boldness. Jane learns from each of her doubles that value which will mitigate the extremity of the other.

Jane's first impression of Helen is of an ignominiously punished girl who bears her degradation with gravity and composure, whose gaze is directed 'beyond her punishment', beyond 'what is really present' (p. 84). Living the posture of a martyr she not only completely submits to the laws of Lowood School, endures her punishment patiently and forgives the cruelty of her teachers, but also fully acknowledges the legitimacy of their chastisement. This leads her to see herself as 'wretchedly defective', slatternly, careless, lacking method (p. 88).

In two senses she lives more in reference to death than to life, is divided between and inhabited by two agencies of death. Her propensity to dream lets her privilege the past, lost and absent world of her childhood, the 'dead' memory images, over the present, so that she is metaphorically more with the dead, 'beyond' the living. At the same time, her total obedience to her punishers obliterates all narcissistic self-preservation and lets her identify so exclusively with the guilt they induce, that her superego, Freud's

punishing conscience, has been entrenched with destructive components to such a degree that it becomes the site of 'a pure culture of
the death drive'. Because the logical consequence of her stigmatisa-
tion as 'defective' would be a destruction of herself and because the
objects of her desire are not among the living, what Helen in fact
desires is death as an agency of radical Otherness, beyond or more
than the paternal law, beyond Lacan's 'phallic' referent. This excessive and exclusive embrace of death lets narcissistic impulses like
revenge and degradation appear inconsequential – 'I live in calm,
looking to the end' (p. 91). In this active not passive self-denial she
strikes Jane as a 'martyr, a hero', against her own posture of 'slave
or victim' (p. 99), a warning against the indulgence of resentment
and fury.

Her ultimate form of death, consumption, enacts, at the body,
her belief in the supremacy of the spiritual, and her disinterest in
her corruptible 'frame of flesh'. Her gradual etherealisation also
serves as the symptom of a guilt-induced turning of the death drive
against herself. Given that Helen dies in Jane's arms while the other
sleeps, and that Jane wakes to find her body missing, may indicate
that, though she has embraced the aspects of death which Helen incorporates, she must also renounce this in its extremity. Not only is
her direct knowledge of death barred – she hears of her embrace of
the corpse belatedly. She will also use her memory of Helen's dying
to understand subsequent deaths, notably that of her foster mother
Mrs Reed, to assert her own survival, and will replace, at the end of
her own liminality, the unmarked grassy mound with a 'grey
marble tablet' bearing Helen's name and the word 'Resurgam'. This
final mark is a social aggregation of a woman who remained marginalised during her life. It is the gift of a signifier that marks her
existence but only as an absent body.[2]

In contrast to Helen's self-renunciation and excessive spirituality
enacted in a self-destructive fading of the body, Bertha Rochester is
an agent of the death drive as a sadistic impulse turned outward
with an emphasis on the big, corpulent, virile body conjoined with
extreme vengeance and passion. Where Helen obeys the law to such
an excessive degree that she literally becomes its vanishing point,
Bertha is that which disrupts the law and is abjected, an agency of
Freud's murderous Id. Her form of self-articulation, her preternatural laugh, her eccentric murmurs, her threatening 'snarling, snatch-
ing sound', in fact recall Kristeva's concept of the 'semiotic chora'.
For her husband she is all that lies below acceptable femininity, the

feminine body as dangerous Other to man; a cunning and malignant lunatic, a maniac, a monster, a wild beast, a goblin, a fury. Because she 'castrated' him socially, 'sullied' his name, 'outraged' his honour, 'blighted' his youth and threatens his life, she is a superlative figure of death.

Like the perfect feminine body of Helen, excessive in that her spiritualisation places it beyond the human, this monstrous feminine body, polluted because Creole, because 'bad, mad and embruted' – equally excessive in that it falls short of the 'expected' code – can be maintained in the social order only as a dead body. In the first stage Bertha, like Helen, occupies the liminal position of a social death, not dead-in-life as the latter, but rather living though interred in an attic, termed 'dead and buried' by her husband in an effort to have her 'identity ... buried in oblivion' (p. 336). Her abode is perceived by Jane as a 'home of the past – a shrine of memory', as the 'haunt of Thornfield Hall's ghost', a vault, 'a corridor in some Bluebeard's castle' (p. 138). Where Helen 'fed' off her dead ancestors, Bertha feeds off the living, bites and draws blood from her brother, repeatedly threatens the life of her husband, and embodies a return of what they would like to repress, yet what, in Jane's words 'could neither be expelled nor subdued by the owner' (p. 239). In her perception, Bertha is a figure of ambivalence, appearing alternately as a foul, ghastly spectre or vampire, between living and dead, and as a figure of which she can't at first sight tell whether it is 'beast or human ... it snatched and growled like some strange wild animal: but it was covered with clothing' (p. 321). In this position of nominally dead woman, Bertha is also analogous to Jane, whose foster mother spread the news of her death of a typhus fever at Lowood in order to prohibit an inheritance.

Bertha can be seen as Jane's darkest double, as her ferocious secret self, who appears whenever an experience of anger or fear arises on Jane's part that must again be repressed. Acting for and like Jane, she enacts the violence Jane would like but can't express, especially in respect to marriage.[3] I would like to shift the focus away from Bertha's literal madness and sexual threat to the fact of her figural 'death', and suggest that she also articulates Jane's fears and desires about her own mortality. Significantly her presence at Jane's bed on the night before her marriage induces the 'second' loss of consciousness in Jane's life and points back to the scene in the red-room, Mr Reed's death chamber, where she falls insensible because she fears the dead man's ghost; because she fears the uncanny presence of death as an intimation of her own physical demise. Bertha's existence introduces a fatal division into the harmonious unity between Jane and Rochester, turns Jane's cherished wishes of marriage into 'stark, chill, livid corpses that could never revive' (p. 324) and prolongs her own social liminality.

Like Helen's, Bertha's death is also symptomatic of the aspect of death she incorporates; namely of the unstructured, diffuse aggressive drives that must be controlled and restrained for culture to exist. In an effort to totalise her destruction of her external world, Bertha sets fire to Thornfield Hall and standing on the roof, triumphing over her fatal creation, 'waving her arms above the battlements and shouting', she recedes from her husband's call to safety, synonymous with the social death of interment, to embrace real death instead; 'she yelled and gave a spring, and the next minute she lay smashed on the pavement' (p. 453). While for Helen death is the liberation from potential suffering, procured by her sense of social defectiveness, and her body as 'corruptible and cumbrous', Bertha's death is a last exertion of that body equally termed by others as socially defective and physically corrupt. For both, the second, real death puts closure on their liminality and the disruption their presence caused. From the logic of the plot, they signify those aspects of femininity along with unmitigated death, that ground notions of 'normal' femininity as well as grounding the survivor's attitude to mortality, while, owing to their extremity, they must also be eliminated.

Precisely by virtue of their respective deaths, Jane can triumph over her inwardly and outwardly directed aggressive impulses. These 'sacrifices' allow her to externalise securely her own proclivity towards destruction by focusing her own violence on these two 'victims' or extreme versions of herself, and burying it along with each of the two feminine corpses. To signify the end of her own liminality, Jane emerges from her position of ambivalence by drawing a safe boundary between herself and the two women whose bodies figuratively and then literally marked the site of death's presence in life, so that their demise secures Jane's triumph over her own ambivalent position in her world as well as her anxiety about and her desire for death.

While Helen and Bertha remain positioned within social liminality and divided, in Lacan's sense, between the paternal, social law and the radical Otherness of death, Jane, survivor, heiress and wife, ultimately takes on a fixed position within the masculine symbolic order. She functions as a hero in Lotman's typological sense, in that she enters into death, in her encounter with two feminine figures of death, only to be socially 'reborn'. What is enacted as the novel's plot unfolds is that society requires a violent but recuperative regulation of the violence of death's presence as this is condensed, along with other aspects of difference such as 'non-white race', 'physical and mental illness' at the bodies of two 'defective,' not assimilable feminine members. What is implied is that Jane's psychic and social education requires not only an encounter with death, in the form of identificatory doubles, but also a destruction of death enacted successfully by virtue of their sacrifice.

The two feminine figures of death, once sacrificed, provoke regeneration, though not without leaving scars – in the form of the gravestone Jane erects for Helen, in the form of the burnt mansion that incites public gossip about Bertha Rochester. The social signifiers that result from a 'sacrificial' death (and one could include Jane Eyre's own narrative as confession), assign a fixed position within the newly established social order to the disruption each woman traced, but can do so only by translating the marginalised into figures of Otherness, of excessive purity or excessive pollution. They are uncanny scars because they can 'mark the spot' and acknowledge the presence of these two feminine bodies previously positioned ambivalently between life and death only once the bodies of both are definitely missing.

Jane Eyre illustrates the most conventional association of femininity with death – the innocent, passive, fading woman as signifier for the desired Otherness of the sublime and the powerful, self-assertive woman as signifier for the threatening Otherness of the body, of nature, of sexuality. Apart from standing for contradictory values Woman, however, also stands for ambivalence as value, and in that sense she is not just a figure of death but the rhetorical figuration of death in narrative. Her ambivalence is such that she merges various psychic registers, serving as the source of the imaginary, as the body that allegorically figures ideas of Otherness in the symbolic, yet whose Otherness also positions her in the non-semiotic real, as the limit of signification, the exteriorised factor which grounds the system. As a metonymy for that which has no fixture, the sacrificed woman translates the disruptive into the system, giving it a fixed position, regardless of whether the normative order is assured or critiqued. However, as aspects of the self or the community are expulsed in the condensation of death and femininity at the body of the Other, we are left with an uncanny sense of ambivalence. Does the recuperated homogeneity contain difference and/or its negation? Is the Other safely outside, or still uncannily present despite all efforts at closure? Is Woman conjoined with death as a way to articulate real difference or to exclude Otherness and difference? The pleonasm 'feminine death' also stands for the force which simultaneously supports and undercuts attempts to construct oppositions like uncanny interiority/canny exteriority.

From Elisabeth Bronfen, *Over Her Dead Body: Death, Femininity and the Aesthetic* (Manchester, 1992), pp. 218–23.

NOTES

[Elisabeth Bronfen's book is an ambitious and wide-ranging study of the recurrent association, since the mid-eighteenth century, between femininity and death in Western art. Drawing upon semiotic, deconstructionist and (mainly Lacanian) psychoanalytic theory, Bronfen argues that the figure of a dead woman, as a representation of the death of the other, serves for patriarchal culture as a disguised expression of that knowledge of mortality which 'it is too dangerous to articulate openly but too fascinating to repress' (p. xi). The fear of death translates into a fear of woman, who for man is death; and 'an elimination of the feminine figure is a way of putting closure on aspects of mortality allegorically embodied through her' (p. 205). The chapter from which this extract is drawn begins with a discussion of the Lacanian account of subjectivity, according to which woman, as object of desire, 'is a symptom for man's yearning for full identity, for ego coherence and for narcissistic pleasure' but also 'points out the lack fundamental to human existence … the limitations which it must acknowledge even as it attempts to deny them' (pp. 212–13). Thus, she simultaneously promises the recovery of illusory wholeness and reminds of mortality: 'she is the site where the repressed anxiety about death re-emerges in a displaced, disfigured form' (p. 215). It is in the light of this theory that Bronfen reads *Jane Eyre*, finding within it a classic expression of this ambivalent cultural fascination with death. Jane's story of survival is, she argues, premised on the deaths of two radically opposing others – the saintly, self-denying Helen Burns, and the monstrous, murderous Bertha Rochester – figures who represent, respectively, 'a masochistic turning inward' and 'a sadistic turning outward' of the death drive. As figures of 'excessive purity' and 'excessive pollution', they are marked, definitively, as other: extreme versions of self which Jane must repudiate and kill off in order to 'triumph over her own ambivalent position in her world'. But their presence in the novel is, Bronfen suggests, an uncannily disruptive one: even in death they leave scars and traces (a tombstone, a ruin) which speak of that which underwrites such triumph – the 'violent ... regulation' that accommodation to the social order demands. References are to the Penguin edition of *Jane Eyre*, ed. Queenie Leavis (Harmondsworth, 1966), and are cited in the text by page numbers. Ed.]

1. Bram Dijkstra, *Idols of Perversity: Fantasies of Feminine Evil in Fin-de-Siècle Culture* (Oxford, 1986), p. 33.

2. For a different discussion of Jane's death, see Robert Keefe, *Charlotte Brontë's World of Death* (Austin, TX, 1979).

3. See Sandra M. Gilbert and Susan Gubar, *The Madwoman in the Attic: The Woman Writer and the Nineteenth-Century Literary Imagination* (New Haven, CT, 1979).

10

Charlotte Brontë's 'Tale Half-Told': The Disruption of Narrative Structure In *Jane Eyre*

PETER ALLAN DALE

Toward the close of *Jane Eyre*, just after the orphaned and outcast heroine has discovered that she has inherited a fortune and is about to discover what matters far more to her, that she has inherited a family as well, she interrupts the sentence of recognition with a tantalising dash and, while we wait, digresses for a paragraph on the nature of expectation.

> 'But what then? Surely – '
> I stopped: I could not trust myself to entertain, much less to express, the thought that rushed upon me – that embodied itself, – that, in a second, stood out a strong, solid probability. Circumstances knit themselves, fitted themselves, shot into order: the chain that had been lying hitherto a formless lump of links, was drawn out straight, – every ring was perfect, the connection complete. I knew, by instinct, how the matter stood, before St John had said another word: but I cannot expect the reader to have the same intuitive perception, so I must repeat his [St John's] explanation.[1]

By an 'instinct', an 'intuitive perception', Jane knows the form and the end of what St John has begun but not yet finished telling her about the kinship between them. Where she is mistaken is in the belief that her readers lack her capacity for thus intuiting the order of events, the shape of the story, before it is made explicit. What, after all, were attentive and experienced readers to expect when three chapters earlier they read that the Riverses had an uncle who, like Jane's own long-lost uncle, was distant, wealthy, unmarried, and named John, an uncle who had no kindred but themselves 'and one other person' (p. 457) to whom he had left all his money? And what, after all, were readers with an ear for homophones to expect would be likely to happen to a disinherited person named Eyre?

In fact, the process of mind that Jane is here ascribing to herself, the process by which one anticipates the unrevealed structure of events to come, is the ordinary process of reading literature, as modern criticism from Northrop Frye to Umberto Eco has done so much to bring home to us. Every particular narrative initiates certain expectations because it is in some significant degree derived from a code or grammar of narratology with which the 'competent reader' is familiar. 'To speak of the structure of a sentence', writes Jonathan Culler,

> is necessarily to imply an internalised grammar that gives it that structure. ... To read a text as literature is not to make one's mind a *tabula rasa* and approach it without preconceptions; one must bring to it an implicit understanding of the operations of literary discourse which tells one what to look for.[2]

Accordingly, readers of *Jane Eyre*, like Jane herself in the passage quoted, imaginatively 'rush' forward to complete the story they expect as soon as they have gathered sufficient clues to the mythos on which they have embarked.

I begin with this passage because it seems to me in its effect to epitomise one of the most characteristic aspects of Charlotte Brontë's art. She is intensely sensitive to the structures of expectation in our lives – 'foregone determinations' (p. 405), as she calls them at a critical point in her narrative – and to the consequences of disrupting those structures. Among early Victorian novelists there is probably no greater master of suspended expectation, or what we might, in our current vocabulary, prefer to call 'indeterminacy'. Fascinated by the rushing forward of the mind toward some preconceived end, she seems at the same time somehow terrified of its arrival there. For her, as for Scheherazade, the end implies a reckoning that she longs to postpone, a necessary alignment of the self with one structure or another. Reassuring as such alignment may be, it may also seem a kind of death, a closing off of the imaginative search for still more satisfying alternatives. Such imaginative projection upon 'an indefinite future period' (p. 118) has its own special appeal. As Jane tells us, 'my sole relief was ... to open my inward ear to a tale that was never ended – a tale my imagination created, and narrated continuously; quickened with all of incident, life, fire, feeling, that I desired and had not in my actual existence' (p. 132). What we will be exploring is the way in which Brontë's narrative establishes certain fundamental patterns of desire which 'actual existence' will not allow to be properly completed. The result is, indeed, a tale that is never ended or, more accurately, is so equivocally ended as to evade an explicit recognition of the imagination's limits.

We must begin by identifying the kind of mythos or narrative structure that governs the reader's expectations in *Jane Eyre*, and here we immediately run into a problem because there is not one simple unified structure defining the story's progression but rather two structures, a religious and a romantic one, which seem to be competing with one another for the reader's attention.

   At the most general level, the shape of our expectations is established by the initial exclusion of Jane from family and hearth at Gateshead. Trying to come in from her 'wandering' outside, the child Jane meets the insurmountable opposition of her aunt/stepmother. Aunt Reed 'really must exclude me from privileges intended only for contented, happy, little children' (p. 3). Shortly the exclusion becomes still more definitive as Jane is 'severed' (p. 45) from Gateshead and sent to the institutionalised privation of Lowood where she will again be excluded from any real participation in the community. From Lowood she goes to Thornfield where she finds herself excluded (by class) from both the servant and the genteel society of the hall and eventually (by conscience) from Thornfield itself. The story of Jane's life, in short, is the story of being constantly on the outside wanting in. Here, in one of Gaston Bachelard's 'great, simple images' of human consciousness, the tension of exclusion demands the resolution of inclusion. In the 'dialectics of outside and inside',[3] we expect the heroine must eventually find some inside, some proper and permanent home. That expectation reaches a crisis when Jane, having fled Thornfield, finds herself lost on a storm-swept moor. 'More desolate, more desperate than ever' (p. 427), she must find an inside or die. Coming providentially upon Moor House, she urgently begs admission, and we readers beg with her, anxious as we are for the completion of the expected order. Of course, she is admitted, and Moor House turns out to be more home than either she or we had any right to expect. The master of the house is St John Rivers, her unknown cousin, who with his two sisters offers her that from which she has been so conspicuously excluded throughout the narrative: home, family, and filial love. With a symmetry that seems to belie the realist claim to truth-telling with which Brontë prefaced the second edition of the novel, Jane gives us at this point an excess of order – three good cousins and their maternal housekeeper finally bring in the wanderer whom three bad cousins and their mother began the book by excluding. To recur to the passage with which we started: 'every ring [is] perfect, the connection complete'.

Or so it would seem, but of course the story is not over. The very excess of order in a narrative that to this point has shown itself consummately aware of the 'unfathomed gulf', the 'formless cloud and vacant depth' (p. 93) that underlie all appearance of order, is unsettling, is too much like irony, which, indeed, it is. No sooner does Jane begin to feel herself comfortably installed at Moor House – 'I at last find a home' (p. 458) – than St John raises a problem that should hardly come as a surprise to the attentive reader:

> 'It is all very well for the present', said he: 'but seriously, I trust that when the first flush of vivacity is over, you will look a little higher than domestic endearments and household joys.'
> 'The best things the world has!' I interrupted.
> 'No, Jane, no: this world is not the scene of fruition; do not attempt to make it so. ...'
>
> (p. 499)

When Jane refuses to look 'higher' than worldly 'completeness', St John does not hesitate to threaten her with the most frightening and final of exclusions. Reading to her from the twenty-first chapter of Revelation, 'slowly, distinctly' he quotes: 'the fearful, the unbelieving ... shall have their part in the lake which burneth with fire and brimstone, which is the second death' (p. 532). This serves sharply to remind us of what we may well have lost sight of during Jane's sojourn at Thornfield. Her story from the outset has been, after all, significantly concerned with the question of whether she is an adequate Christian. We may, for example, go back to the Reverend Brocklehurst's first interview of her. Having determined that she is 'wicked', Brocklehurst, in a carefully designed anticipation of St John's later warning, is made to impress upon Jane that she is headed directly for the 'pit full of fire'. To his crucial question, 'What must you do to avoid it?' (p. 34), Jane has, from a religious point of view, no satisfactory answer – no more than she will have to St John's comparable question ten years later.

What I want to argue is that this question of what one must do to avoid damnation (or achieve salvation) is very much at the centre of the novel, that it implies the narrative's essential structure of expectation, the end toward which the narrative is assumed to be headed. The fundamental narrative type defining *Jane Eyre* is that which Robert Lee Wolff identifies as the most prevalent in early Victorian fiction: the spiritual pilgrimage.[4] The 'inside' or 'home', which from the very beginning of the novel we are conditioned to expect for Jane, is the heavenly home of true faith. Like Christian/Christiana in Bunyan's narrative, Jane is, above all, a pilgrim in search of salvation, as she departs from the wicket gate (Gateshead), manoeuvres through deadly snares, clambers over significant stiles, crosses sloughs, sojourns in Castle Doubtful, and always expects, in Bunyan's words (and St Peter's [1 Pet. 1:4]), that *'Inheritance, incorruptible, undefiled, and that fadeth not away'*.[5] Now I certainly do not claim any originality for discerning a prominent religious motif in the novel. A number of modern critics have drawn our attention to this religious dimension, and one, Jane Millgate, has explicitly made the point I have just implied, that Bunyan's 'presence is everywhere apparent' in the novel.[6] The unusual and, as I believe, controversial aspect of my argument is its contention that the religious structure is the *dominant* one in the narrative, the one which, above all, conditions – or should condition – reader expectation. If this is once accepted, then we are in a position to understand the particular kind of suspension or disruption of order that characterises the novel's close.

That the modern reader does not, in fact, regard the religious structure as central to the narrative is evident from the commentary of the great majority of recent critics. Modern readers, by and large, find that the structure that finally governs the novel is a romantic one, with the word 'romantic' working in essentially two directions. On the one side, it means simply that what we most expect from Jane's story is a satisfactory love relationship. By this reading the inclusion or home toward which she is headed is, in her own significantly ambiguous word, the 'catastrophe' of marriage (p. 249). On another, deeper level, 'romantic' takes on a meaning philosophically associated with the literary period that the word conventionally labels, a romantic narrative being, in this sense, one that specifically privileges the individual artist's assertion of spiritual or psychological independence from the strictures of traditional religious belief, as, for example, when Wordsworth places imagination at the centre of the universe or Shelley proposes an ideal of psychic and sexual unity as the goal of human endeavour.

We need not look far for such romantic readings of *Jane Eyre*; they are, indeed, among the most stimulating we have. Robert B. Heilman's famous essay on Brontë's 'new Gothic', for example, is concerned to make the point that what matters most in the novel is the celebration of deep psychic forces that transcend what we may call the 'old Gothic' preoccupation with the status of the eternal soul.[7] Earl A. Knies, from another point of view, finds 'all the conflicts of the novel' romantically resolved when Jane is at last married to Rochester and psychologically 'at peace ... with herself'.[8] Even Millgate, after taking care to bring out the presence of Bunyan 'everywhere', concludes that Jane's destiny is radically different from Christian/Christiana's: her 'final arrival' is at the 'destination of mature independence and integrity' (p. xxix).

More recently we have had feminist interpretations which significantly improve upon these earlier readings by recognising not resolution but continued conflict at the novel's close, but which seem to me still essentially 'romantic' in my second sense, if not in my first. Sandra M. Gilbert and Susan Gubar, for example, find Jane's story a 'passionate drive toward freedom' from patriarchal authority and, in this, a 'parody' of *Pilgrim's Progress* in so far as it is the patriarchal system of Christianity which opposes that freedom.[9] I fully agree that the novel contains a conflict between religious belief and the romantic drive for freedom of passion. Where I disagree is in the description of that conflict as parodic, for so to account for it is, in effect, to resolve it. If the narrator has so far distanced herself from the constraints of religion as to be able to parody them, she has gone far enough for us to be able to say, as Gilbert and Gubar are saying, that the romantic impulse has displaced and triumphed over the religious, that the book, finally, is *about* how the heroine frees herself from the expectations imposed upon her by God the father (even if she does not go the whole distance and free herself from the impositions of his earthly vicar, man the husband).

If we want a romantic novel in the sense that any of these readers is urging upon us, we are much closer to the mark with Emily

Brontë's *Wuthering Heights*. Here the novelist actually does end by asserting the value of human personality, imaginative expression, and human love as superior to that of otherworldly concerns. The servant Joseph, a co-religionist of Brocklehurst and St John, is, indeed, a parody of religious strictures from which Catherine Earnshaw and Heathcliff free themselves to a degree quite beyond what we find in Jane. I would speculate further that Charlotte wrote *Jane Eyre* at least in part to correct her sister's excessively romantic faith in the power of people in their situation (raised, that is, as they had been) to achieve genuine imaginative or psychological freedom from what she calls the 'law given by God' (p. 404).

What the religious structure of the narrative tells us to expect is that Jane, like Christian/Christiana, will progress providentially, from unbelief to belief. Her expected course is instilled in her (and us) at the narrative's beginning by Bessie's song:

> There is a thought that for strength should avail me,
>   Though both of shelter and kindred despoiled:
> Heaven is a home, and a rest will not fail me;
>   God is a friend to the poor orphan child.
>
> (p. 21)

At Lowood, as a child with no particular religious conviction, Jane finds herself called upon to conform to the Evangelical Calvinism of its master, Brocklehurst. She resists and turns instead to friendship with Helen Burns, who manages to keep alive a humane Arminianism in Lowood's chilly spiritual atmosphere. But whatever solace Helen's creed offers Jane, it disappears with the death of its conveyer. Confronted with her closest friend's death, Jane, not unlike Tennyson at a similar juncture, loses sight of God altogether and plunges into her first full-fledged spiritual crisis, a crisis that marks her transition to a mature self-consciousness about the state of her soul:

> ... my mind made its first earnest effort to comprehend what had been infused into it concerning heaven and hell: and ... it recoiled, baffled; and for the first time, glancing behind, on each side, and before it, it saw all round an unfathomed gulf ... and it shuddered at the thought of tottering, and plunging amid that chaos.
>
> (p. 93)

This doubt, this 'tottering' on the edge of unbelief, marks the end of the first stage of Jane's spiritual journey. The next stage, her sojourn ten years later at Thornfield Hall, far from resolving the crisis, compounds it as she turns from doubt to outright apostasy. Rochester and the purely secular love he offers her become, in effect, her religion: in the words of Rochester's song (meant, certainly, as an ironic echo of Bessie's earlier one), 'I have at last my nameless bliss: / As I love – loved am I!' (p. 343). Of the dangers of this new faith, Jane, writing in retrospect, explicitly warns us:

> My future husband was becoming to me my whole world; and, more than the world: almost my hope of heaven. He stood between me and every thought of religion, as an eclipse intervenes between man and the broad sun. I could not, in those days, see God for his creature: of whom I had made an idol.
>
> (p. 346)

What follows is the dramatic collapse of this false belief, a catastrophe for which we are amply prepared by the remarks on idolatry just cited. Awaiting the return of her bridegroom from a journey, Jane receives a night visitation from Bertha Mason, who tears her wedding veil and symbolically reveals to Jane an aspect of her own self. Looking into her mirror, Jane sees the reflection of Bertha wearing her veil. She describes the incident to Rochester: 'Fearful and ghastly to me – oh, sir, I never saw a face like it! It was ... a savage face. ... Sir, it removed my veil from its gaunt head, rent it in two parts, and flinging both on the floor, trampled on them' (p. 358). Jane's 'vision' of Bertha as herself is, in terms Jane uses earlier, that of 'crime ... incarnate', of the 'mocking demon', which is 'masked in an ordinary woman's face and shape' (p. 264). The symbolic discovery that the demon is in some sense her own idolatrous self is fit prelude to the reality of the disrupted marriage and the flight from Thornfield. Jane once more finds herself on the spiritual outside facing despair.

> My hopes were all dead – struck with a subtle doom, such as, in one night, fell on all the first-born in the land of Egypt. I looked on my cherished wishes, yesterday so blooming and glowing; they lay stark, chill, livid – corpses that could never revive.
>
> (p. 374)

There is one further point we need to observe with a view to the novel's ending. The experience of fervid expectation of the 'bliss' of marriage leading up to the disaster of separation is couched in terms that ironically echo the book of Revelation and the apocalyptic marriage that there symbolises Christian redemption:

'There was no putting off the day that advanced – the bridal day; and all preparations for its arrival were complete… It was not only the hurry of preparation that made me feverish; not only the anticipation of the great change – the new life which was to commence. … As I looked up … the moon appeared; … her disk was blood-red. … a horseman came on, full gallop. …'

[Rochester asks] 'Are you apprehensive of the new sphere you are about to enter? – of the new life into which you are passing?'

(pp. 347–53)

Surely here (Bk. 2, ch. 10), Brontë underlines Jane's apostasy by having her speak in a way that must seem to the orthodox reader something like blasphemy. Rochester becomes in these passages, as he does throughout Jane's relationship with him at Thornfield, a type of Christ, and marriage with him a parody (and here I think the word is appropriate) of the apocalyptic 'marriage' announced at the close of Scripture. The promise of that spiritual marriage and its likely denial to Jane, we recall, will be the burden of St John Rivers's later pointed reading of Revelation to her.

We shall look more closely in the next section at the nature of Jane's apostasy and at Brontë's further ironic use of scriptural language. For the moment, however, we need to notice the fact that Jane, as a mature narrator, clearly wants the reader to believe that whatever religious failings she may have experienced in earlier phases of her life are now behind her. Thus, for example, after describing the religious crisis that followed Helen's death, she steps back from the immediate narrative present to project herself fifteen years into the future when someone is able to inscribe 'Resurgam' on Helen's tomb (p. 97), the affirmation, that is, of faith in resurrection. Jane does not tell us who this someone is but implies it is herself. Again, in retrospectively recognising the idolatry of her love for Rochester in the passage cited a moment ago, she speaks of this as something characteristic of 'those days' – that is, by implication, not of 'these days' in which she is writing. It would appear, then, that our erring pilgrim has at some point come out of the wilderness and arrived at her expected spiritual destination.

But at what point? This for me is the great problem raised by the narrative. If this is, indeed, a story of the soul's journey to salvation, we expect some time actually to witness the moment at which the narrator turns to God, the critical moment of conversion. The absence of that moment is a phenomenon which Barbara Hardy noticed long ago, but which no one has properly explained. Like me, Hardy considers that the central structure of the narrative is the religious one: 'In *Jane Eyre* the religious explanation determines motive and action. ...'[10] The novel is about Jane's providential journey from unbelief to belief, but according to Hardy there is something missing in this journey. Brontë, Hardy writes, fails to give us any account of the actual growth of religious belief in her heroine:

> ... there is a gap in the novel. ... [Brontë shows] two distinct stages in Jane's feelings and beliefs and leave[s] the middle stage of transition undramatised. ... What we do not come to see is exactly how Jane comes to accept ... faith, even though such faith is at the root of her decision to leave Rochester. She has presumably moved away from her early doubts about Heaven. ... but the actual growth of ... religious feeling is the one thing the novel takes for granted and does not demonstrate.
>
> (pp. 65–6)

Hardy's explanation for this 'gap' or omission is that Brontë's psychological interests lie elsewhere, that she is more concerned to show Jane's development of a mature and independent character than to show her conversion, which, in any case, says Hardy, Victorian readers would have assumed and not needed to see. Again, we have the romantic reading, but in this case made at the expense of our faith in Brontë's control over what she is writing. The dominant (religious) form is 'inappropriate' to the end toward which Brontë is headed: 'Jane's *character* seems to demonstrate the strength of the individual and human relationships, but the *action* demonstrates the need for heavenly resources' (p. 69). This notion of an inadvertent conflict between 'character' and 'action' or plot in the novel is a good deal more plausible than the sort of romantic reading noticed above that effectively disposes of the religious structure as a problem in the novel. Yet, I am far from convinced that the discontinuity in the narrative, which Hardy so nicely locates, is, as she believes, unintended, the result of a confusion of purpose. Rather, it seems to me that the omission of the experience of conversion is quite purposeful, that it represents a deliberate withholding of an expected satisfaction from the reader.

Far from taking for granted the psychological growth of the heroine toward faith and the climactic spectacle of conversion, the Victorian reader would have expected nothing less from a narrative that throughout shows us a girl and woman in danger of losing her immortal soul. It is difficult to believe that Brontë, familiar as she was with contemporary religious fiction and religious crisis, could have been unaware of these expectations; that she either inadvertently omitted the process of conversion or simply allowed the reader to assume it.

The third and final volume of the novel is where the question of belief is meant to be settled. Two points in particular in the closing chapters give us situations that seem to cry out for Jane to speak of her faith. The first of these occurs in the penultimate chapter when Rochester tells her of what amounts to his own conversion experience. He had acknowledged the 'hand of God in [his] doom' (p. 571), he says, and was content to die in the hope of everlasting life, when in a moment of extreme longing he involuntarily called out Jane's name. The result is a sort of miracle. A voice calls out, 'I am coming: wait for me!' (p. 572). Jane, of course, has heard his 'mysterious summons' (p. 573) at Moor House, and the words he tells her he heard are precisely the words she uttered upon hearing the call. A supernatural occurrence, surely, and the obvious thing for Jane to do at this moment is to tell Rochester about it and for both of them to celebrate the wonders of God's providence. At the very least we expect her to say something to *us* about the miraculous ways in which God works. Yet she withholds the information from Rochester, while with us she is strangely noncommittal:

> Reader. ... I listened to Mr Rochester's narrative; but made no disclosure in return. The coincidence struck me as too awful and inexplicable to be communicated or discussed. If I told anything, my tale would be such as must necessarily make a profound impression on the mind of my hearer; and that mind, yet from its sufferings too prone to gloom, needed not the deeper shade of the supernatural. I kept these things, then, and pondered them in my heart.
>
> (p. 573)[11]

The explanation for not revealing the coincidence to Rochester is, as Brontë must have recognised, a tremendous *non sequitur*. The suffering mind, 'prone to gloom' – not only Rochester's but her own – wants precisely the reassurance of supernatural and benevolent intervention that she withholds.

The second and still more critical occasion on which the narrative seems to demand a confession of faith occurs after Jane and Rochester have 'wended homeward' (p. 573) to marriage, the expected close of the novel's romantic structure. Six months into her marital bliss she receives a letter from St John with a pertinent expectation: 'he hopes I am happy, and trusts I am not of those who live without God in the world ...' (p. 575). Now, surely, she must turn to us and say not simply 'Reader, I am happy', which we know, but 'Yes, reader, I live with God in my heart and daily praise him for the good he has done me'. But she does not. On the contrary, in the very next sentence she reminds us of what many might consider an egregious result of living without God in the world: 'You have not quite forgotten little Adèle, have you, reader?' (p. 575).

The confession of faith that we feel must close the religious narrative does come at last, but not from Jane. It comes, rather, from St John, who writes from his deathbed in India, 'My master ... has forewarned me. Daily he announces more distinctly, – "Surely I come quickly"; and hourly I more eagerly respond, – "Amen; even so come, Lord Jesus!"' (p. 579). These are the closing words of the novel, and they are also among the closing words of the Bible. Jane is quoting St John Rivers quoting St John the Evangelist. With these words we are, at the closing, decisively back within the structure of *Pilgrim's Progress*: there the true believer dies to resounding allusions to Revelation, as Bunyan seeks to draw his narrative into the ending of Scripture and thus take us from the end of his earthly story to the story that is presumably without end:

> Then I heard in my Dream, that all the Bells in the City rang again for joy. ... I also heard the men themselves say, that they sang with a loud voice, saying, *Blessing, Honor, Glory, and Power, be to him that sitteth upon the Throne, and to the Lamb for ever and ever.*
>
> (p. 172)

Yet the fact remains that St John Rivers's vision of the Heavenly City is not the ending we expected. It is not the erring pilgrim but someone else who utters the final confession of faith, someone, indeed, whose faith, like that of Bunyan's Greatheart to whom he is compared (p. 578), we never worried about.

What has happened is that the expected closure of conversion has been displaced. Instead of Jane's final confession of faith we have a conspicuous silence on her part while another character affirms the Christian ending. The result is a strange disorder in the religious narrative. We both have and have not what we expected. We have a confession of faith and inclusion (or likely inclusion) in the heavenly home but not for the pilgrim in whom we are most interested. The anticipated ending has, as it were, slipped away from Jane, or, perhaps better, she from it. In so far as we do leave the novel (as most readers do) with a comfortable sense of resolution, a sense that God is in his heaven and all is right with Jane Eyre, we are the victims of a sort of narratorial sleight of hand that leads us to assume a salvation that may, in fact, never have occurred.

Victorian readers, more accustomed than we are to the expected pattern of the religious narrative, perceived, more readily than we apparently do, the problem at the story's close. The *Christian Remembrancer*, for example, complained that all Jane's Christianity is 'concentrated' in Helen Burns, and that 'with her it expires'.[12] The popular Evangelical novelist Emma Jane Worboise felt so strongly about this 'questionable aspect' of the novel (Allott, p. 91) that she rewrote the story in her own unexceptionably Christian terms as *Thornycroft Hall* (1864). Here the Jane figure, Ellen Threlkeld, rejects the Rochester figure, an incorrigible philanderer, marries the St John Rivers figure, and, needless to say, makes abundant confession of faith along the way.[13] Such criticisms and corrections as these, while they may strike us as extraordinarily obtuse, do nonetheless emphasise what we find difficult to see, that *Jane Eyre* raises strong expectations with regard to its heroine's progress which it significantly fails to fulfil. Worboise's particular way of straightening the narrative out helps show us that the 'proper' ending to Jane's story is marriage to St John, not a return to Rochester, for only in such a marriage would she have 'confessed' – symbolically, if not discursively – her final acceptance of God's will. When the point is put in this unpalatable way, we can see more clearly the tension Brontë wants at once to expose and somehow to disguise.

Thornycroft Hall, like countless other popular novels of the period, mingles religious and romantic interests. The question of the heroine's religious salvation cannot be dissociated from the question of whom she marries. There are in Worboise's book essentially two marital possibilities, one that appeals to the passions, another that appeals to the soul. The former is, in fact, never a temptation for her heroine (another improvement upon Jane). The latter means marrying a man of a disposition as forbiddingly ascetic as we find in St John Rivers, and this she chooses without serious hesitation. For her there is no moral or emotional incongruity whatsoever in such a marriage.

Yet, if we think about it, a more rigorous Christianity would not find so comfortable a congruity between religion and romance. In

Bunyan, after all, Christian leaves his wife behind to undertake his pilgrimage, and Christiana undertakes hers after her husband is dead. Clearly, the point Bunyan is concerned to make is that salvation comes first and has nothing to do with human love – that it may, indeed, be lost as a result of too great an investment in human love. It is, of course, St Paul's point as well, who inveighs against those who change 'the truth of God into a lie' by worshipping 'the creature more than the Creator' (Rom. 1:25) and warns particularly of the dangers of marriage:

> He that is unmarried careth for the things that belong to the Lord, how he may please the Lord: But he that is married careth for the things that are of the world, how he may please his wife. There is a difference also between a wife and a virgin. The unmarried woman careth for the things of the Lord, that she may be holy both in body and in spirit: but she that is married careth for the things of the world, how she may please her husband.
>
> (1 Cor. 7:32–4)

Worboise, for all her Evangelicalism, is evidently not sufficiently concerned with St Paul's reservations about romance to allow them to interfere with a good novelistic ending.

Brontë, on the other hand, does feel these reservations and feels them deeply, as we may see in Jane's fear of marrying St John, her desire to accompany him on his mission only in Christian celibacy. What Jane has perceived – and what Ellen Threlkeld and countless of her Evangelical sisters ignore – is that there is a stark inconsistency in relating to so Pauline a preacher as St John in so un-Pauline a way as he is proposing. What such a relationship would mean to Jane is a constant reminder that her duty or desires (as the case may be) as a wife are incompatible with her duties to God. With St John there would be absolutely no way to escape this conflict, for in everything he said or did he would condemn as a preacher the love he would offer as a husband. 'Can I bear the consciousness', says Jane, 'that every endearment he bestows is a sacrifice made on principle?' (p. 517). She wisely seeks to avoid the strain of such a relationship by accepting the preacher and refusing the husband.

We must beware of not taking St John's asceticism seriously enough. Brontë had clearly internalised the prohibition he represents. Few things were more present to her imagination than the possibility that the creed he lives by is the true, the expected one. As she wrote to her friend Ellen Nussey,

> My eyes fill with tears when I contrast the bliss of a saintly life ...
> with the melancholy state I now live in; uncertain that I have ever felt
> true contrition, wandering in thought and deed, longing for holiness
> which I shall *never, never* attain, smitten at times to the heart with
> the conviction that —'s ghastly Calvinistic doctrines are true, dark-
> ened, in short, by the very shadows of spiritual Death! ... If the
> Doctrine of Calvin be true I am already an outcast. ...[14]

Among the misgivings that she felt about her 'unsaintly' life, clearly
the most persistent was the fear that what she meant by love and
experienced as love was radically incompatible with Christianity. If
we go well back before the novels into her early adulthood, we find
this inhibition already fully developed. When she was twenty-one
she wrote to a friend,

> What shall I do without you? How long are we likely to be sepa-
> rated? Why are we to be denied each other's society? ... Why are we
> to be divided? Surely, it must be because we are in danger of loving
> each other too well – of losing sight of the *Creator* in idolatry of the
> *creature.*[15]

The allusion here to the idolatry of the creature, one notes, is a
paraphrase of St Paul, a paraphrase, as we have seen, she later used
in treating Jane's relation to Rochester. If we go forward to the end
of her career and the last novel, *Villette*, we find a heroine, like Jane
a descendant of Christian/Christiana, who begins her pilgrimage,
literally, in the shadow of St Paul (i.e., St Paul's Cathedral) and
completes it waiting for a lover who will never arrive, who is
named Paul, and under whose shadow she will undoubtedly live
out the remainder of her days.[16] In short, there is always anxiety
over the conflict of love and religion; always, the tendency to
believe that when love goes away, when she is left alone and be-
reaved as she was so many times in her short life, it is as retribution
for an excess of love for the creature. The third volume of *Jane
Eyre*, far from giving us a resolution of this conflict, forces it, in
Jane and St John's relationship, to an extremity. For St John, marriage to his cousin satisfies at once 'God and nature' (p. 514); for
Jane, however, it is a 'monstrous' 'martyrdom' (p. 517), an abandonment of 'half myself' to a 'premature death' (p. 516).

Given Brontë's self-conscious refusal to accept the sort of
Christian-cum-romantic resolution offered by Worboise and more
conventional fiction, where is Jane at last to go? Back to Rochester,
it appears. But does not the conflict between human and divine love

continue to apply in his case? One may argue that it does, but less oppressively, for Rochester is no Pauline ascetic who, like St John, constantly reminds her of the division within herself. Or one may argue still more boldly that the return to Rochester represents a final abandonment of the 'half' of herself that had initially driven her from him, an abandonment now made possible by the realisation of the consequence of a truly Christian marriage with such as St John. In this reading, Jane is drawn to Rochester 'involuntarily' (as she says), instinctively, by a force within herself (her sexuality, as Heilman [p. 129] and others maintain) that obscures and subordinates her religious misgivings. She forgets the 'law given by God' because it is *natural* to do so, and nature, particularly the naturalness of mating, has for Jane an irresistible appeal. Those birds that, as a child, she is constantly reading about in *Bewick's History* (p. 4) become emblems of that appeal, so that when she leaves Rochester they represent what she can scarcely bear to abandon and eventually must return to: 'Birds began singing in brake and copse: birds were faithful to their mates; birds were emblems of love' (p. 410). This is the side of her that would prefer to remain outside, to 'mingle in peace with the soil of this wilderness' (p. 415), although, as the metaphor suggests, that peace means the finality of an entirely natural, unresurrected death.

Such a consummation would give her story the ending that we moderns would perhaps wish it to have, but this notoriously 'restless' narrator cannot rest here. The return to Rochester does not, in fact, resolve the conflict between nature and God brought to a head in Jane's relation with St John. Caught up in the melodramatic rescue of Jane from St John by Rochester's 'mysterious summons', we tend to forget that Jane returns to her 'master' without in any way having overcome the problems that initially drive her from him. Rather, in the return the conflict is sublimated to the point where the reader (and, one imagines, Jane herself) almost loses sight of it. Rochester, his own conversion to Christianity notwithstanding, calls to her as 'the alpha and omega of [his] heart's wishes' (p. 572; cf. Rev. 1:8), and she responds with her own resounding echo of Revelation: 'I am coming'. As the two are reunited, the language in which Jane describes their renewed relationship is really no less blasphemous than her earlier metaphorical association of their impending sexual union with the marriage of the Lamb. His call comes to her 'like an inspiration', a 'wondrous shock of feeling ... like the earthquake which shook the foundations of Paul and Silas's prison' (p. 539). When they meet, he is again her 'dear master' to whom she has now returned, as he immediately understands, very much 'in the flesh' (p. 555). And she affirms again the exclusiveness of her love: 'All my heart is yours, sir; it belongs to you; and with you it would remain, were fate to exile the rest of me from your presence for ever' (p. 568). Could there be a more complete expression of the idolatry of the creature, for is Jane not saying here what for even the most liberal of Christians is the unsayable, that not only in life but in death her entire heart will belong to her lover? Nor is this confusion or conflation of love objects the expression simply of the strong emotion of the moment of reunion. What she felt for Rochester then, Jane takes care to tell us, she still feels now at the time of writing. 'I hold myself supremely blest ... because I am my husband's life as fully as he is mine. No woman was ever nearer to her mate than I am: ever more absolutely bone of his bone, and flesh of his flesh' (p. 576). The invocation of Genesis 2:23 with the implication that with Rochester Jane has recovered paradise on earth cannot in the context of this novel cause us to forget how far Jane departs in these remarks from Paul's advice to men and women in the fallen world; and lest we forget, the very next page, the last page in most editions, gives us St John Rivers paraphrasing, as if against Jane's closing paean to love, that very uncompromising injunction of the other master:

> If any man will come after me, let him deny himself, and take up his cross daily, and follow me. For whosoever will save his life shall lose it: but whosoever will lose his life for my sake, the same shall save it. For what is a man advantaged, if he gain the whole world, and lose himself, or be cast away?
>
> (Luke 9:23–5)

The fundamental 'insanity' (p. 459) of her passion, in short, remains a problem to the very close of the novel, not so apparent a problem as before Bertha (and all she stands for) is providentially disposed of, but nonetheless a problem. It comes back to us, as I say, in a sublimated and unconscious form through a disorder in language that subtly displaces the expected reference of powerful scriptural signifiers with thoroughly secular (and sexual) signifieds. This disorder, it seems to me, parallels and further explicates the aporia already noticed between two possible endings, romantic and religious.

The words 'cast away' in the quotation from Luke above bring us back to the central issue of the religious narrative: is the pilgrim saved at last? If we have been attending carefully, we do not hear the affirmative answer we expect or, for that matter, the negative one we do not expect. What we hear at last is a very uncertain trumpet. According to Jane's own account of what it takes to reach the promised religious end, a decisive choice for the Creator over the creature, she remains as alienated from that end at the close of her narrative as she was at the beginning. Yet she is still somehow at peace in her 'lesser' romantic home, and from the perspective of the religious narrative – a perspective, as we see, insisted upon at the close – we find this peace almost passes our understanding.

Either her apparent repose is ironic, that is, she enjoys it only by ignoring or suppressing the religious objections she has so painstakingly raised against it in the course of the narrative, or it is revolutionary in the sense that she is defiantly challenging the 'foregone determinations' of the contemporary religious code. Neither possibility seems to me adequately to account for her situation at the end. Rather, as a character, a creature of Brontë's, she is being made to hover between ironic and revolutionary possibilities of meaning. Her story is, in this unexpected manner, the endless one she longed to write. She is, finally, caught between what are for her two mutually incompatible structures of experience, the religious and the romantic. As Brontë would subsequently show in her more realistic retelling of the same story in *Villette* – more realistic because the gesture toward an apparent romantic peace is at last refused – this is a situation that is in itself a version of hell, a purely psychological hell of having a home in neither this world nor the other:

> I think if Eternity held torment, its form would not be fiery rack, nor its nature, despair. I think that on a certain day amongst those days which never dawned, and will not set, an angel entered Hades – stood, shone, smiled, delivered a prophecy of conditional pardon, kindled a doubtful hope of bliss to come; ... spoke thus – then towering, became a star, and vanished into his own Heaven. His legacy was suspense – a worse boon than despair.
>
> (pp. 644–5)

Finally, we may briefly consider a distant but intriguing parallel to the book upon which she has drawn so heavily and in so doing give her particular reality a broader historical perspective. In

Pilgrim's Progress the neatness of the ending of the First Part is disrupted, as many have noticed, by the anticlimactic return of one of Christian's tempters. After Christian has entered the Celestial City and the Shining Ones have sung the glories of Emanuel, 'Ignorance' strangely returns to the scene and attempts to enter the City. He is immediately arrested and escorted to a nearby door that leads straight to hell. 'Then I saw', says the dreamer, 'that there was a way to Hell, even from the Gates of Heaven' (p. 173). The special attention given Ignorance here is not an idle afterthought on Bunyan's part, as some have argued, but a final warning against what he may have taken to be the most serious threat to the Puritan hegemony embodied in his narrative structure. 'Ignorance', as others have shown, probably represents the natural religion or Deism which was, in the late seventeenth century, effectively subverting orthodox Christianity, especially that of the Calvinist sort.[17] It must have seemed to Bunyan that his readers needed an especially strong and well-placed reminder of the fate of this antagonistic belief precisely because of its insidious appeal to the best in our human nature:

> Christian *The wise man says*, He that trusts his own heart is a fool.
> Ignorance That is spoken of an evil heart, but mine is a good one.
> ... my heart and life agree together, and therefore my hope [of heaven] is well grounded.
> Christian *Who told thee that thy heart and life agree together?*
> Ignorance My heart tells me so.
> Christian ... *Thy heart tells thee so!* Except the word of God beareth witness in this matter, other testimony is of [no] value.
>
> (p. 154)

What is happening at the close of Bunyan's narrative is that an alternative and more liberal structure of belief (and implicitly, of narrative) is pressing upon and disrupting that structure which he has sought to embody in his story. This revolutionary structure he recognises, but recognises specifically to discard. By the time we come to Brontë, 'Ignorance' – that is, reliance on the heart rather than on the Word – is obviously a much more plausible threat to the dominant religious structure. It must be given more latitude, and the issue of its defeat left in greater doubt. The only triumph allowed the dominant structure is the triumph of the last word/Word, and St John Rivers can only utter it; he has no power to enforce it, no Shining Ones to cart Jane off to a Christian hell.

The question of whether she is going there is left, really, to the reader to answer, and that is also part of the historical reality the novel defines. *Jane Eyre* implies a contemporary reader who is no longer able to accept so definitive an authorial closure as Bunyan offers even when that closure invokes the Word itself. This leaving of the ending to the reader may strike us as an especially modern gesture, a deconstructive challenge to the proposition that we have any right to expect or intuit any 'foregone determination' of experience. But it is more interesting, it seems to me, to see it as the artist's recognition of a problem with a particular historical structure of expectation. The inevitability of that structure has ceased to command implicit assent, but, at the same time, it is too much part of the artist's consciousness to be transcended. It can, through the duplicitous effects of art, be suspended, but, as we see, this aesthetic suspension is very unstable. In the continued absence of an acceptable alternative structure of experience, it becomes 'worse ... than despair'.

From *Modern Language Quarterly*, 47 (1986), 108–29.

NOTES

[Peter Allan Dale brings to *Jane Eyre* a knowledge both of structuralist narrative theory and of Victorian religious literature and thought. Drawing on the former, he suggests that every narrative 'initiates certain expectations because it is in some significant degree derived from a code or grammar of narratology with which the "competent reader" is familiar', and that Charlotte Brontë plays in a sophisticated way upon this fact. But unlike many narratological analyses, Dale's is a historicist one: he is concerned less with a generalised reader, unchanged over time, than with that early Victorian 'reader' to whom *Jane Eyre* was addressed. That reader, he argues, would have found in the novel not one but two kinds of narrative structure, each evoking its own particular set of expectations which question those called forth by the other both in obvious and subtle ways. One, the romance structure – the story of independence asserted and desire fulfilled – is still familiar to us today. But the other, the 'religious structure' – the narrative of spiritual pilgrimage, towards or away from salvation – has become more alien: and it is this which Dale sees as 'the fundamental narrative type defining *Jane Eyre*'. The novel's first readers would, he suggests, have expected Jane's story to be one of progression from unbelief to belief. But they would have been disconcerted by the absence within it of that which their familiarity with such narratives would have led them to expect – a critical moment of conversion, an explicit confession of faith.

These absences, Dale contends, are not accidental, but deliberate: indeed, they are underlined by the fact that it is not the protagonist, but another whose path is radically different from hers, who makes the expected appeal to God at the novel's end. The result is 'a strange disorder in the religious narrative': one which questions and complicates the ostensibly happy ending of Jane's story, and one which the Victorian reader would have perceived much more sharply than we. Against the grain of many twentieth-century readings, which see Jane's story as bespeaking a successful reconciliation between religion and romance, Dale argues for a novel that for its original readers at least was both more troubled and more troubling, and 'hovered' between opposing possibilities of meaning in a disconcerting way. Ed.]

1. *Jane Eyre*, ed. Jane Jack and Margaret Smith (Oxford, 1969), p. 490. All quotations from *Jane Eyre* are taken from this edition.

2. Jonathan Culler, *Structuralist Poetics: Structuralism, Linguistics and the Study of Literature* (Ithaca, NY, 1975), pp. 113–14.

3. Gaston Bachelard, *The Poetics of Space*, trans. Maria Jolas (Boston, 1969), p. 72. See especially chs 1 and 2.

4. See Robert Lee Wolff, *Gains and Losses: Novels of Faith and Doubt in Victorian England* (New York, 1977), pp. 1–26; see also Margaret M. Maison, *The Victorian Vision: Studies in the Religious Novel* (New York, 1961), pp. 1–8.

5. John Bunyan, *The Pilgrim's Progress, from this World to That which is to Come*, ed. James Blanton Wharey (Oxford, 1928), p. 12.

6. Jane Millgate, 'Jane Eyre's Progress', *English Studies*, 50 (1969), xxi. The centrality of the novel's religious structure has lately been developed in the context of Victorian fiction in general by Thomas Vargish, *The Providential Aesthetic in Victorian Fiction* (Charlottesville, VA, 1985). My own reading finds Jane's story less unambiguously 'providential' than his, but his emphasis on the controlling presence of contemporary religious expectations in the novel's structure is obviously one with which I am sympathetic.

7. Robert B. Heilman, 'Charlotte Brontë's "New" Gothic', in *From Jane Austen to Joseph Conrad*, ed. Robert C. Rathburn and Martin Steinmann, Jr (Minneapolis, 1958), pp. 123, 129.

8. Earl A. Knies, *The Art of Charlotte Brontë* (Athens, OH, 1969), p. 136.

9. Sandra M. Gilbert and Susan Gubar, *The Madwoman in the Attic: The Woman Writer and the Nineteenth-Century Literary Imagination* (New Haven, CT, 1979), pp. 369–70, 342.

10. Barbara Hardy, *The Appropriate Form: An Essay on the Novel* (London, 1964), p. 65.

11. The last sentence echoes Luke 2:19. In Luke 'These things' are the glorification of God at the coming of His Son.

12. *Christian Remembrancer*, 15 (April 1848), pp. 396ff.; quoted in Miriam Allott (ed.), *The Brontës: the Critical Heritage* (London, 1974), p. 91.

13. See Elizabeth Jay, *The Religion of the Heart: Anglican Evangelicalism and the Nineteenth-Century Novel* (Oxford, 1979), pp. 61, 246–53.

14. Quoted in Winifred Gérin, *Charlotte Brontë: The Evolution of Genius* (Oxford, 1967), p. 101.

15. Quoted in Elizabeth Gaskell, *The Life of Charlotte Brontë* (1857; reprinted London, 1978), p. 122.

16. The 'Marchmont' episode of *Villette* presents an epitome of Lucy Snowe's future problems in the situation of Miss Marchmont who wonders whether in 'loving the creature so much' she has 'blasphemed the Creator' (*Villette*, ed. Herbert Rosengarten and Margaret Smith [Oxford, 1984], p. 55); all quotations from *Villette* are taken from this edition.

17. John W. Draper, 'Bunyan's Mr Ignorance', *Modern Language Review*, 22 (1927), 18–19.

11

Closing the Book: The Intertextual End of *Jane Eyre*

CAROLYN WILLIAMS

Asked to recall the end of *Jane Eyre*, many readers first remember the resolution of the plot, reported in Jane's conclusive address to her audience: 'Reader, I married him'. But that memorable line only begins the last chapter. The novel ends on quite another note, and in another voice:

> As to St John Rivers, he left England: he went to India. He entered on the path he had marked for himself; he pursues it still. A more resolute, indefatigable pioneer never wrought amidst rocks and dangers. Firm, faithful, and devoted; full of energy, and zeal, and truth, he labours for his race: he clears their painful way to improvement: he hews down like a giant the prejudices of creed and caste that encumber it. He may be stern; he may be exacting; he may be ambitious yet; but his is the sternness of the warrior Greatheart, who guards his pilgrim convoy from the onslaught of Apollyon. His is the exaction of the apostle, who speaks but for Christ when he says – 'Whosoever will come after Me, let him deny himself, and take up his cross and follow Me.' His is the ambition of the high master-spirit, which aims to fill a place in the first rank of those who are redeemed from the earth – who stand without fault before the throne of God; who share the last mighty victories of the Lamb; who are called, and chosen, and faithful.
>
> St John is unmarried: he never will marry now. Himself has hither-to sufficed to the toil; and the toil draws near its close: his glorious sun hastens to its setting. The last letter I received from him drew

from my eyes human tears, and yet filled my heart with Divine joy:
he anticipated his sure reward, his incorruptible crown. I know that a
stranger's hand will write to me next, to say that the good and faithful servant has been called at length into the joy of his Lord. And
why weep for this? No fear of death will darken St John's last hour:
his mind will be unclouded; his heart will be undaunted; his hope
will be sure; his faith steadfast. His own words are a pledge of this: –
'My Master', he says 'has forewarned me. Daily he announces more
distinctly, – "Surely I come quickly!" and hourly I more eagerly
respond, – "Amen; even so come, Lord Jesus!"'[1]

Of course this does not sound like the character 'Jane Eyre', as
readers over the years have complained – from formalists who have
felt that the ending is 'tacked on', to feminists who have felt that
the novel swerves, at its end, toward the patriarchal rhetoric it had
presumed to reject. Both these objections are legitimate, and yet the
ending of the novel continues to evoke a powerful response, which
suggests that its effect has still not been adequately explained.
Precisely what makes this closing passage so problematic, so odd,
and so interesting?

First and most simply, in terms of dramatic and thematic content,
it focuses on the 'other man', the rejected suitor, and through him it
focuses on another way of life, the very way most pointedly *not*
taken by Jane. Thinking about the dramatic resolution of the last
chapter, we might pose the question raised by the ending this way:
Why is the privileged place of closure occupied by St John Rivers?
Why does Jane end her story with 'one brief glance at the fortunes
of those whose names have most frequently recurred in this narrative' rather than with her last 'word respecting [her] experience of
married life'? Why not close on the subject of a conjugal relation so
perfect that she can say 'I am my husband's life as fully as he is
mine' (p. 475)? After all, marriage to a character so lavishly drawn
as Jane's alter ego has profound autobiographical significance:
within the romantic rhetoric of the novel, Jane marries another part
of herself, so to speak – her 'likeness' or her 'second self' – and in
the marriage she thus achieves the 'delightful consciousness' which
'brought to life and light [her] whole nature' (p. 461).[2] Within the
rhetoric of romantic congruence, in other words, another character
can metaphorically reflect the central autobiographical 'I'; but St
John Rivers, who has been unsympathetic in the highest degree, is
not such another. Instead of turning toward the alter ego – and thus
figuratively returning us to Jane's own chosen life – the novel

swerves at its end into an apparent altruism that seems profoundly out of character. What could be gained by this turn toward another character, toward the world outside Jane's sequestered life – indeed, toward the other world itself?

Then again, in terms of narrative discourse – in terms of narration, that is, as opposed to plot or story – this choice at closure is even more puzzling. For the novel not only ends in an extended reference to the character of St John Rivers but, even more surprising, it ends ostensibly in 'his own words' (p. 477). Quotation of this sort has a special force in first-person narration. If one goal of a first-person narrative is to establish a particular 'voice', to beguile you, 'dear reader', into believing that you are hearing from this particular 'person' and no other, then ending in the voice of another would be a radical gesture in any first-person novel; but ending in the voice of another seems an especially radical gesture in *Jane Eyre*, given the life history of Jane's struggle to exert the claims of a special self.

Finally, the closing paragraphs are curious because they end the novel in a web of dense intertextuality. What is the effect of so many quotations and allusions, here at the end? And what is the effect of these particular references? What is the relation of the female first person to the high canonical literature here invoked? One clue may perhaps be found in the fact that only the first intertextual reference issues directly from Jane's own narrative voice. She draws on *The Pilgrim's Progress* for a comparison when she calls St John 'the warrior Greatheart, who guards his pilgrim convoy from the onslaught of Apollyon'. The second intertextual reference, from the gospel of Mark (8:34), is then offered hypothetically as the words of the exemplary, exacting apostle. Those words are ventriloquially thrown, originating in Jane's narrative voice but attributed to St John as the apostolic inheritor. The third intertextual reference then takes us even further from Jane's voice toward St John's. It is represented as a direct quote from St John's 'last letter'. But it seems that St John's words are not 'his own words' at all. He is himself echoing the words of another. In the quotation from the gospel of Mark, St John hypothetically would echo the words of Christ demanding self-denial and *imitatio* from anyone who would follow him. St John's 'exaction' is in large part a function of this echo-effect; he 'speaks but for Christ', speaks literally *as* Christ. Then at the very last, St John echoes the words of his namesake, St John the Divine, in conversation with the voice of Christ. I will return, at the end of this argument, to the figure of an intertextual chain of voices. For now let us fully appreciate another aspect of this extraordinary closing gesture.

The last words of the novel are exactly the same as the last words of the Christian Bible. Jane Eyre ends the story of her life with the last words of the Revelation of St John the Divine, excepting only its concluding benediction ('The grace of the Lord Jesus Christ be with you all. Amen.'). Here are those last words:

> 7. Behold, I come quickly. ... 8. And I John saw these things, and heard them. ... 10. And he saith unto me. ... 12. ... behold, I come quickly; and my reward is with me, to give every man according as his work shall be. 13. I am Alpha and Omega, the beginning and the end, the first and the last. ... 16. I Jesus have sent mine angel to testify unto you these things in the churches. I am the root and the offspring of David, and the bright and morning star. 17. And the spirit and the bride say Come. And let him that heareth say, Come. And let him that is athirst come. ... 20. He which testifieth these things saith, Surely I come quickly. Amen. Even so, come, Lord Jesus.
> (*Revelation* 22)

For Jane to end her story by quoting these last words of the book about last things, which is itself the last book of the Book of Books – this is having the last word, with a vengeance. And yet it seems as if it is not Jane herself who has this last word, even in her own story. 'I Jane' seems to have disappeared into 'I John'. This cannot precisely be the case, of course, since the fabric of first-person narration is never ruptured; what is conveyed is conveyed, to the last, through the fiction of that 'person'. What can it mean, then – but more important, *how* can it mean – for a female autobiographer to close the book of her life with the very words that close The Book, the canonical Scripture of her Protestant culture? And if she does choose to close with those words, why give them away? Why write them as the words of another? In the process of the following argument, I hope to shed light on all these questions; and in the end, I hope to show how this closing of her book might work in terms of the novel's strong, articulate, and ambivalent feminism.

ENGENDERING THE NARRATIVE: MOTHER NATURE AND GOD THE FATHER

Jane is an orphan, of course, the quintessential figure of indeterminate identity, who must discover and construct her place in the world. Like her status incongruence as a governess on the social level of the plot, her orphanhood works on the epistemological level to open the question of her identity and 'place'.[3] But the romantic 'I' without parents is free to imagine them, for not only the quest romance but also the family romance has been internalised.[4] Instead of discovering formerly unknown, but 'real', parents (as Tom Jones does, for example), Jane produces figurative representations of the primary, gendered others from whom the self derives and in relation to whom the self defines itself. Since Jane is at once an orphan and a first-person narrator, in other words, we may see in her narrative a succession of fantasied attempts to realise those engendering figures.

Jane's narrative engenders itself by producing figural parents from whom she differs, primal 'others' who are projected in the text precisely in order to be 'contradicted'. She associates these primal others, these parent-figures, with different systematic principles of plotting or storytelling, and her own particular voice is generated as she steers between them. 'Contradiction' is not simply a structural principle, but a mobile and productive strategy of voice in *Jane Eyre*. The narrative voice self-consciously positions itself as the separating daughter, and it enacts its own production of meaning and voice in difference from both parent-figures, Mother Nature and God the Father.[5] Jane invokes these figures at crucial moments in the story, as agents of narrative transformations; they serve as pivot points around which the narrative turns. These parent-figures, in other words, serve doubly in the construction at once of a psychology of the female subject and of a gendered scheme of narrative production or generation.

For an example, let us glance at another crucial scene of separation before focusing on Jane's transformative separation from Rochester. Early in the novel Bessie's song promises a heavenly Father who will 'take to his bosom the poor orphan child'.[6] And Helen Burns recommends Jane to trust in that same heavenly Father, who will receive them as true siblings in another world. On the night of Helen's death 'the light of the unclouded summer moon' guides Jane to her deathbed, where the two discuss the prospects of heavenly reunion (p. 111). At that point in the plot, Jane finds Helen's invocation of another world incomprehensible. She asks the crucially sceptical questions: 'Where is God? What is God?' Helen answers 'God is my father'. She further promises that God is Jane's father, too, and that His heaven will be their future home: 'You will come to the same region of happiness: be received by the same mighty universal Parent, no doubt, dear Jane' (p. 113). But Jane remains sceptical about the existence of that other world.

Thus, Jane's separation from Helen, an alter ego at this stage of her development, takes place under the auspices of her radical scepticism. Later in the novel when she leaves Rochester, Jane seems to have come round to Helen's position. She recommends to Rochester: '"Do as I do: trust in God and yourself. Believe in heaven. Hope to meet again there"' (p. 343). But it has always been hard for readers to believe that Jane believes this herself. Where in the story since then has Jane gained the faith that she lacked at Lowood School? Barbara Hardy asked this important question about the novel in her essay on 'dogmatic form'.[7] She pointed out that the narrative never does enact the transformation – that is to say, the conversion – of the sceptical, querulous child into the dogmatic, Christian adult. I think this is because we are to understand that such a transformation never really occurs. In a novel so dedicated to weighing the differences between this world and the hope of another – or between the authority of the self's desire and God's law – we have to see the omission of a conversion scene, not as a flaw, but as a choice.

God as radical other is always by definition the power elsewhere, and Jane's failure to comprehend (in the sense of internalise, as well as in the sense of understand) that radical otherness is a measure of her resolute commitment to the sanctions of the self and its worldly desires. The conversion scene is missing from the novel precisely in order to leave this an open question throughout the next episodes. The metaphorics of the novel carefully rationalise the Providential dimension of the plot by casting the beloved as 'idol' who stands between Jane and her God (pp. 302, 342); and Rochester himself voices this view when he admits that 'Providence has checked me' (p. 319). But Rochester's marriage to Bertha Mason threatens Jane's self-definition much more than it threatens her religious scruples, as the nightmarish mirror scene in chapter 25 makes clear. There Jane confronts the spectre of the other woman who is at once the obstacle between her self and its object and at the same time the disowned, angry self-reflection (pp. 311–12). This Gothic dimension of the plot reveals the internal aspects of the problem by externalising them; and one way to understand Jane's self-division is to sense the conflict between Gothic and Providential elements of the plot's logic.

God's law, in other words, is the ostensible but not the deepest reason for Jane's separation from Rochester. She never does adopt a belief in God's law as an end in itself; nor does she accede to His radical otherness. However, she does at this point in the plot learn to invoke His name, to produce Him as a figurehead in her text, to use the notion of God's law in her narrative as a means to an end. In this strategy she subscribes, not to Helen Burns's otherworldly interpretation of Providence, but to Grace Poole's practical and instrumental interpretation: 'A deal of people, miss, are for trusting all to Providence; but I say Providence will not dispense with the means, though He often blesses them when they are used discreetly' (p. 185). When Jane must find the means to separate from Rochester after her aborted wedding, she finds them in the name of the Father. But the pre-Oedipal, maternal environment grounds this symbolic transformation. In this crucial place in the narrative, Jane projects first the figure of the Father, then the Mother, then the Father again to rationalise and heal over the break from Rochester, and to generate more narrative.

After first invoking the Father's law, she leaves Thornfield Hall under the auspices of the Mother. The maternal symbology of the red-room scene has often been noted, not only for the most obvious reasons (the whole range of uterine analogies) but also because of the presiding moonlight, and because it is the scene of Jane's threat to starve herself to death.[8] Since the novel opens with this scene, one could say that the whole articulated text literally emerges from this quintessentially pre-Oedipal place. The novel's subsequent structure bears this out: the ghastly mirror scene which again expresses Jane's self-division and prefigures her break from Rochester (through Bertha Mason's tearing the wedding veil in two) is explicitly drawn as a parallel of the mirror scene in the red-room; and the moonlight on the night after Jane's departure from Thornfield is explicitly reminiscent of the moonlight in the red-room (pp. 312, 346). After Jane's farewell to Rochester, the moon breaks through vaporous clouds to whisper: 'My daughter, flee temptation.' And Jane answers, 'Mother, I will' (p. 346). She wanders away, entertaining the idea that she can figure nature as a benevolent mother, who will feed and lodge her freely: 'I have no relative but the universal mother, Nature: I will seek her breast and ask repose. ... Nature seemed to me benign and good; I thought she loved me, outcast as I was; and I, who from man could anticipate only mistrust, rejection, insult, clung to her with filial fondness. To-night, at least, I would be her guest, as I was her child: my mother would lodge me without money and without price' (pp. 349–50). But the fantasied 'good mother' has its other, darker side; in the sequence that follows in chapter 28, Jane almost starves to death on this cold hillside, explicitly figured as a female landscape.[9]

In Margaret Homans's interpretation, the mother threatens to betray her daughter by leading her into the silence, objectification, and death of 'the literal', starving her of actual food and depriving her also of the sustenance of narrative: that is, language and figuration. But Jane evades the literal and figures her way back into narrative.[10] I substantially agree with Homans, but I would like to read the scene in another way simultaneously. For this is the only place in the novel where the text opens itself fully to another kind of story altogether, a story as yet untold and perhaps, in its purest sense, untellable (the story of Nature as opposed to Culture, the Lacanian Imaginary as opposed to the Symbolic, the pre-Oedipal as opposed to the Oedipal). This story would be by definition untellable in the sense that it is the story of the prelinguistic, undifferentiated plenitude. But our imagination of the pre-Oedipal itself is necessarily always figurative, since we have no access to the undivided world before language except through language. Jane does quite soon return to the world of culture; but it is the Mother as much as the Father who facilitates her return. Chapter 28 is the scene of new plot in the process of generation. Mother Nature holds Jane as she strips down to her bare bones to generate another chance from within the visionary rigours of starvation. Jane's fantasmatic shift from 'good mother' to 'bad' might itself be read as a kind of figuration, as the infant imagines that the mother will punish aggressivity and separation and thus projects a betrayal *by* the mother to cover its imagined betrayal *of* the mother. Thus the heath, despite its barrenness, may paradoxically be understood in its aspect as the Kleinian 'good mother' as well as 'bad' – or as the 'holding mother' Jessica Benjamin describes, who gives her child the sense of being figuratively held so securely that the child can risk individuation, can wander away, secure in the feeling (the memory, the figuration) of plenitude and immediacy.[11]

It is reductive to excavate the text for signs of the pre-Oedipal without also looking for the route that discourse takes as it re-enters and interacts with the Oedipal plot. For it is neither the one nor the other, but the crossings and junctures of the two – pre-Oedipal and Oedipal models – through which the generation of narrative plot and voice may be described. Jane does reproduce the figure of the Father here, turning her prayer away from Nature and toward God.[12] She explicitly names 'Providence' as the interventional force which both regenerates figuration and renews the plot. In other words, she writes herself back into the plot of culture, and the struggle with the Father. Jane spots a small light on the hillside, which materialises many pages later as her cousins, and this coincidental sighting of her earthly family may be called 'Providential', after all, because the plot here is ostentatiously represented as coming from beyond the world of the self.[13] This providential intervention is, in the final analysis, not so very different from the externalisations of the Gothic plot, as we will see very clearly when we come soon to an examination of the 'call' scene. Jane's inheritance from this Father is wish-fulfilment figured as the answer to prayer – the self's own wishes externalised – for Providence provides her at this point in the story with an earthly family, which leads later to her financial as well as her psychological 'independence'.

Just as dangerous as the apparent plotlessness of Mother Nature, however, is the overdetermined plot of God the Father. Under His auspices, the female 'I' also reaches an impasse, as we are soon to see. 'Providence', which may be projected as a beneficent force when Jane is in control of the naming and figuration, becomes a threatening force in the hands of another character plotting her life for her. Jane names God as the principle of separation from Rochester, only to find that she must contradict or circumvent the category 'God' when it is being wielded by St John Rivers as an indicator of his will. Even God as radical other is no exception to the dynamics of contradiction in this text. But a further act of internalisation will be necessary in order for Jane to neutralise the compelling otherness of the God she has invoked. Jane will then be able to use Him as an internal marker from which to swerve away, and she can then push His words to the intertextual edges of her narrative.

With God as her Father and Nature as her Mother, Jane is caught in a very old story. To write from the position of the separating daughter is endlessly to be caught in an oscillation between two different ways of not being able to speak. Mother Nature seemed to deprive her daughter of voice and plot. But a providential Father offers language already spoken by another, and too much plot, already written for her. In this archetypal version of the family romance, the only mode of daughterly speech is 'contradiction'. Jane must differentiate herself from both figurative parents to become a narrating subject. After her separation from Rochester, Jane's oscillation from Father to Mother to Father again serves to heal the rift in the plot, as well as to do the work of mourning Jane's separation from her romantic alter ego.

At the point in the plot through which we will now enter the text, she imagines that she has successfully allied herself with the Father, but now comes the struggle with God's earthly representative. Jane 'knows no medium', but St John claims to be God's 'medium'. Her struggle with him represents the struggle with the Father and with the voice of God he presumes to convey. She has evaded the vastation of the cold breast. But now she faces cold phallic compulsion and the words of another substituted for her own.

VOCATION AND VOICE

Jane's separation from Rochester is difficult indeed, but the separation from St John is more difficult still – in terms of its narrative logic. For Jane finds herself in the apparent position of having to contradict God's will. That is essentially her dilemma, since St John convincingly claims to be a 'medium', to convey God's will and God's voice transparently. In solving this problem, Jane finds it more difficult to transform St John than to 'retransform' – the word is Jane's – her notion of God. This section of my argument will end by discussing the 'call' from Rochester, which gives Jane her vocation. But in order to understand that call, we have to know more about the circumstances of its occurrence. I will discuss these circumstances in terms of plot, theme, and intertextual grounding.

In chapter 34, Jane is under duress from St John's proposal of marriage. He claims to speak both for Nature and for God when he enjoins her to his service:

> 'And what does your heart say?' demanded St John.
> 'My heart is mute – my heart is mute', I answered, struck and thrilled.
> 'Then I must speak for it', continued the deep, relentless voice. 'Jane, come with me to India: come as my helpmeet and fellow labourer.'
> The glen and sky spun round: the hills heaved! It was as if I had heard a summons from Heaven – as if a visionary messenger, like him of Macedonia, had enounced, 'Come over and help us!' But I was no apostle – I could not believe the herald – I could not receive his call.

'Oh, St John!' I cried, 'have some mercy!'

I appealed to one who, in the discharge of what he believed his duty, knew neither mercy nor remorse. He continued: – 'God and nature intended you for a missionary's wife. ... you are formed for labour not for love. A missionary's wife you must – shall be. You shall be mine: I claim you – not for my pleasure, but for my Sovereign's service.'

'I am not fit for it: I have no vocation', I said.

(pp. 427–8)

Recent feminist theory makes clear the sense in which St John's words may be illuminated by the pornography of sadomasochism. This scene shares several features with that tradition, including Jane's ritually formalised pleas for mercy with no hope of mercy forthcoming; the melodrama of St John's chilly debasement of her physical person; his intention to turn her over to another man superior to himself in status, that is, his 'King'; and even including Jane's momentary thrill at the possibility of relinquishing her life to a will other than her own, through which she can hope for transcendence.[14] The titillation of St John's attempt to get Jane into the missionary position is in part a result of the fact that his words have a primary, innocent, and even sacred import. Jane feels momentarily as if she had heard a summons from Heaven, as if a visionary messenger were promising her a part in sacred history, in a latter-day, typological re-enactment of St Paul's mission to the Macedonians (Acts 16:9). She wants her 'vocation' to be authorised by a blinding call like Paul's. But she cannot recognise St John's call on her service; she swerves almost immediately into the stance of contradiction, of antithetical self-definition: 'I was no apostle ... I could not receive his call ... I have no vocation.' On the other hand, St John will not let her go, and he holds her with the very sanction she has recently invoked as a rationale for leaving Rochester: the representation of God's will, the aspiration to be His 'medium'.

The phallic character of St John's physiognomy has often been re-marked; and he has been compared to the Reverend Brocklehurst as a 'pillar of patriarchy'.[15] But St John's most ostentatiously patriar-chal characteristic is his pride of access, his altogether sure sense of already having the keys to the kingdom. He does not hesitate to threaten Jane in the name of God:

'I shall be absent a fortnight – take that space of time to consider my offer; and do not forget that if you reject it, it is not me you deny

but God. Through my means, he opens to you a noble career; as my
wife only can you enter upon it. Refuse to be my wife, and you limit
yourself for ever to a track of selfish ease and barren obscurity.
Tremble lest in that case you should be numbered with those who
have denied the faith, and are worse than infidels! ... I had thought I
recognised in you one of the chosen. But God sees not as man sees:
His will be done.'

(pp. 434, 440)

A rough translation of this threat might run: 'Do what I want you
to do, or be damned'.

In St John's scheme, the glories of access to God's voice and authority are not equally available to all. St John is very explicit about
this: 'I claim you – not for my pleasure, but for my Sovereign's
service' (p. 428). Marriage according to St John's terms is very
clearly the institutionalised symbol of a hierarchical chain of mediation, patrilineally organised with Jane as its last term. She can
briefly imagine a missionary's life for herself, but not for a moment
can she imagine being a missionary's wife under these conditions.
She is ready to go with him to India if she might be allowed to go
'free' (p. 430), unmarried, as his 'sister', in which role she could
imagine them both as equal siblings of one Father. It is marriage
that puts her in the subservient position, not St John's lack of love
for her in and of itself. This is all very explicit in the text; St John
wants a wife not a sister, he says, so that he can 'influence [her]
efficiently' and 'retain [her] absolutely till death', and he uses here,
appropriately enough, the language neither of romantic love *nor* of
vocation, but that of wage service (p. 431). He says 'I know my
Leader, ... and while He has chosen a feeble instrument to perform
a great task, He will, from the boundless stores of His providence,
supply the inadequacy of the means to the end. Think like me, Jane
– ' (p. 428). In St John's plot, Jane would be the means to his end; as
he figures himself an instrument of God, so she would be his instrument. Jane is fully aware of the dynamic at work here, which puts
her in the position, as Adrienne Rich has pointed out, of Milton's
Eve: 'He for God only, she for God in him'.[16] She asks St John's
sister Diana, in a fury of rebellion: 'Would it not be strange ... to be
chained for life to a man who regarded one but as a useful tool?'
(p. 441). But though St John tries to make Jane 'adequate' to his
end, she in turn makes him a means to her 'end' instead, as we are
in the process of seeing.

We are close now to the staging of Rochester's call in the night, that deus ex machina as romantic ESP which resolves the plot in place of Providence. Interestingly enough for our purposes, this call takes place just after a scene of family Bible-reading in which St John reads from none other than 'the twenty-first chapter of Revelation', in which is recorded St John the Divine's 'vision of the new heaven and the new earth'. St John's voice is compelling as he reads of this vision: '[N]ever did his manner become so impressive ... as when he delivered the oracles of God', Jane acknowledges. In this scene, St John Rivers uses St John's vision of the other world, Jane feels sure, as a pre-text to frighten her with the threat of eternal damnation if she does not go with him.

> 'He that overcometh shall inherit all things; and I will be his God, and he shall be My son. But,' was slowly, distinctly read, 'the fearful, the unbelieving ... shall have their part in the lake which burneth with fire and brimstone, which is the second death.'
> Henceforward, I knew what fate St John feared for me.
>
> (p. 442)

She comments to her readers that St John 'believed his name was already written in the Lamb's book of life'. He believes himself already to be a figure in God's plot, a character in His Book. But is Jane's name written there? The son 'shall inherit all things'. But the daughter? In this tensely evocative scene, St John presumes to pray for Jane, hoping for her salvation and, as its precondition, her agreement to his plot. Jane was 'touched by [his prayer], and at last awed' (p. 443). If only she could feel his will as the will of God, speaking directly to her! But the trouble is – and the subtlety of the novel's feminist critique is here – the trouble is that the means are not adequate to this end. God's will, mediated through St John, still feels like St John's will. God's voice mediated through St John sounds like St John's voice.

When we return to the final paragraphs of the novel, it will be important to remember that St John reads, in this scene, the chapter of *Revelation* directly preceding the one from which the last words of the novel are taken. This scene establishes for us the association of St John's threatening coercion, his pride of access, and his vision of the new heaven and the new earth. It will also be important to remember that Jane is angry in this scene – she says so – though her anger is soon blocked and covered over by her conviction of

St John's sincerity, his apparent success at figuring himself as a 'medium' for the words of the other.

It is at this very point that Jane almost agrees to go with St John. 'I could decide if I were but certain ... that it is God's will I should marry you', Jane tells St John, who instantly cries 'My prayers are heard!' – so sure is he that his wishes correspond exactly with God's will (p. 444). But Jane now makes a prayer of her own, which is answered instead – and answered in such a way that her deepest wishes, not St John's, are expressed as correspondent with God's voice. The answering call from Rochester comes, in other words, as the result of a prayer to Heaven to know God's will. And like the last two paragraphs of the novel, it is patterned on the last words of the *Revelation*. Here is the scene (and incidentally, the Mother's moonlight presides here over this crucial invocation of the Father):

> 'Show me, show me the path!' I entreated of Heaven. I was excited more than I had ever been; and whether what followed was the effect of excitement the reader shall judge....
>
> All the house was still. ... The one candle was dying out: the room was full of moonlight. My heart beat fast and thick: I heard its throb. Suddenly it stood still to an inexpressible feeling that thrilled it through. ... The feeling ... acted on my senses as if their utmost activity hitherto had been but torpor, from which they were now summoned and forced to wake. They rose expectant: eye and ear waited while the flesh quivered on my bones.
>
> 'What have you heard? What do you see?' asked St John. I saw nothing, but I heard a voice somewhere cry –
>
> 'Jane! Jane! Jane!' – nothing more.
>
> 'O God! what is it?' I gasped.
>
> I might have said, 'Where is it?' for it did not seem in the room, nor in the house, nor in the garden; it did not come out of the air, not from under the earth, nor from overhead. I had heard it – where, or whence, for ever impossible to know! And it was the voice of a human being – a known, loved, well-remembered voice – that of Edward Fairfax Rochester; and it spoke in pain and woe, wildly, eerily, urgently.
>
> 'I am coming!' I cried. 'Wait for me! Oh, I will come!'
>
> (pp. 444–5)

I want to make several points about this scene, before we return to the novel's intertextual closure.

First and most simply, the call from Rochester is produced as an instance of contradiction, of Jane's antithetical self-definition, as she makes clear when she says, I 'fell on my knees; and prayed in my way – a different way to St John's, but effective in its own fashion' (p. 445). The last paragraphs of the novel, then, by extension – because they too involve a response to the same biblical intertext – may also be read as a part of this sweeping gesture of contradiction, even though they seem in the end so peaceful. Here in the call scene Jane's frustration produces an explosion, not of anger, but rather of conviction, an inner voice that provides her with a way out of this impasse, a return in the plot, and a vocation antithetical to St John's otherworldly one. In the language of vocational service, they will serve different 'Masters'. (I refer of course to the fact that Jane continues to call Rochester her 'Master'.) Jane's discovery of her 'vocation' has been figured here as a vocalised 'call'. After her prayer to know God's will for her life, she feels she knows His will, and it is her own.

Of course, the voice she hears in answer to her prayer to Heaven is not the voice of God, but the voice of Rochester. This is an extra-ordinary trope of secularisation, no matter how often we consider it. The secularisation turns on the substitution of a human for a divine respondent, and the internalisation of the radical other as Jane's own 'inner voice'. 'I recalled the voice I had heard', Jane writes. 'Again I questioned whence it came, as vainly as before; it seemed in me – not in the external world' (p. 446). Jane surrounds the call scene with these questions, prompting us to read Rochester's call as a chiasmic figure of voice, an exchange between figuratively external (God's) and internal (Jane's) voices. In the double-crossing of this chiasmus, the voice of God is internalised as Jane's own desire and at the same moment Jane's desire is exter-nalised as Rochester's voice, the romantic alter ego projected away from the self again. Jane's narrative voice is generated in the figural play across this boundary.[17] Indeed, the call scene produces the last turn in the plot, its resolution, and thus – according to the logic of first-person retrospective form – the achieved voice which generates the entire narration. This brilliant figure – the chiasmic exchange of voices in the call scene – wraps together the voice of Jane's roman-tic alter ego, the Protestant 'inner voice', and the narrative voice. Jane has heard the voice of her conscience, of God's will, of her own wish-fulfilment, and of her lover's need all in one. Invocation generates both vocation and voice in this dramatised call to service.

It has always been puzzling – here again, in terms of narrative logic – that Jane doesn't tell Rochester about hearing his 'call'.

During the scene in Ferndean garden in the penultimate chapter of the novel, Rochester tells Jane the story of calling to her and hearing her voice on the wind answering: 'I am coming! Wait for me!' He had prayed to die, to be taken from this life so that he might have some hope of meeting Jane again, in the other world, according to her promise at their parting. The answer to his prayer is Jane's voice, telling him to wait, here on this earth, for her return. The story of Rochester's prayer and its answer is of course the mirror image of Jane's prayer and its answer. I should say it is the 'echo', for in this scene the chiasmic figure of voice is given another twist, in the image of their disembodied voices crossing in the wind. Rochester's side of the story dramatises the call scene by giving us two equal human voices 'co-responding' on the wind, rather than the traditional hierarchy of prayer with its one human voice invoking a divine respondent. But this return to the call scene as a part of Rochester's story threatens to deflect its force away from its primary role as a turning point in the narrative of Jane's coming to voice. By keeping it a secret from Rochester, she keeps it as her story, the story of her call to voice and vocation.

Jane holds the story of her call within that figurative space between pure inferiority (or wish-fulfilment) and pure exteriority (or God). She confides it only to us, her readers, and thereby holds the secret there between us, as pure *narration*. And finally, she confides it in a figure: 'I listened to Mr Rochester's narrative, but made no disclosure in return. ... I kept these things then, and pondered them in my heart' (p. 472). In this typological figure, Jane positions herself as Mary after the Nativity (Luke 2:19), delivered of the Word. This time, however, it is not God's word, but her own name on the wind – 'Jane! Jane! Jane!' – that she keeps inside.

MEDIATION AND IMMEDIACY

When Jane claims that her heart is mute, St John instantly replies, 'Then I must speak for it'. It is against this threat of coercive mediation that Jane's heart speaks after all, and she replaces the voice of Heaven with the call of her lover and her own narrative voice, as we have seen. Aside from realising that she must produce a voice of her own or someone else will speak for her, Jane's move of contradiction at this point in the plot represents her rejection of a role in which she would become the merest 'useful tool', allowing – even wishing – St John to mediate the voice of authority to her, hoping to achieve transcendence through him. As Jane bluntly puts it: 'I was tempted to cease struggling with him – to rush down the torrent of his will into the gulf of his existence, and there lose my own. I was almost as hard beset by him now as I had been once before, in a different way, by another. I was a fool both times' (p. 443). That is Jane's explicitly formulated protest. But let us return now to the novel's intertextual closure, which reveals a deeper questioning of the traditional structure of apostolic mediation to a power elsewhere, a critique of the mediated access to authority and voice that seems too strictly reserved in the male line. I think each of the three strands of its intertextual web forms a covert protest against mediation, a protest that is at once Protestant, romantic, and feminist in its force.

Calling St John 'Greatheart', for example, is a double business. Greatheart appears only in the second part of *The Pilgrim's Progress*, as a guide for Christiana, the wife of the original pilgrim. The very structure of Bunyan's work, in other words, emphasises the patrilineality of apostolic succession and the inevitably mediated and secondary position of woman reading within that system. Christian begins his pilgrimage as the result of reading a book of his own, while she has only a letter to initiate her pilgrimage; and that letter is from her husband's king.[18] Several critics have written of Brontë's extensive use of *The Pilgrim's Progress* as a model for Jane's 'progress'.[19] But the important point here – which Barry Qualls has noted – is that Bunyan's work is also a negative model, finally positioned within this text in order to be contradicted. The allusion to Greatheart seems to me not to discredit St John, but to emphasise the fact that Jane has chosen not to be led by a 'guardian angel watching the soul for which he is responsible' (p. 443). She chooses to generate her own calling, rather than to be called, through her husband, by the letter from her husband's king.

The second intertextual reference reproduces the words of Christ as if hypothetically spoken by St John: 'His is the exaction of the apostle, who speaks but for Christ when he says "Whosoever will come after Me, let him deny himself, and take up his cross, and follow Me".' The objective pronoun 'Me' syntactically refers in this interpolated quotation both to Christ and to St John. Their voices are represented as if in unison. St John's apostolic 'exaction', then at once reminds us of its disciplinary rigour and of his belief that 'I John' and 'I Jesus' may be exactly fitted to one another, that he speaks 'but for Christ', and not also for his own will to power. The whole of *Jane Eyre* is written as a protest against this arrogant belief in the perfect substitution of one voice for another, this refusal to grant the overlap or excess that would signify the difference of individual voice.

And finally, the passage from *Revelation* also reproduces the figure of a chain of voices in apostolic succession, as we have seen. 'I John' speaks for and with 'I Jesus' in the text, which St John Rivers quotes, adding himself to the chain. His letter does not convey 'his own words', as Jane calls them, but the words of another, the words of radical otherness, of God. It should be said that Jane, too, places herself at the end of that chain, but ambivalently, in her customary mode of contradiction or negation. She appropriates the words of another as a means to her own end. Let us now consider the effects generated by this complex gesture of incorporation and simultaneous negation.

When Jane turns to St John in these last words, she honours his vocation from a safe distance, accepting and even admiring for another what is rejected for herself. These final words can be read as a 'sincere' tribute to St John's heroic vocation only if we also register the double edge, the angry refusals of the past, and her achieved safety in distance from his psychological and textual threat. In this gesture she reminds us, at the moment of closure, of her refusal to follow him (or Him). She can afford to be generous now, but this last verbal tribute is an act of altruism only in the strictly literal sense that it is expressed as a figure of otherness. According to the logic of incorporation and differentiation within, the gesture is appropriative, making a place for the other only to turn away from that place in closing her book. I am reading these last words, then, as Jane's culminating act of self-definition in the diction of contraries.

She turns the tables on the patrilineal principle of voice by pushing the insider outside, memorialising him at the edges of the text, anticipating his death, soon and far away. This is poetic justice, after all. Death was what, in a real sense, he yearned for, he who was 'inexorable as death' and whose aspiration for the other world amounted to 'an austere patriot's passion for his fatherland' (pp. 426–7). Meanwhile, we are to imagine Jane, Rochester, and their recapitulatory infant with his father's eyes, living on in their insular, domestic hum.

Representing the other world in a mode of negation, in other words, serves to focus the fiction of Jane's immediate, ongoing life 'here and now', in England. England, which would have been empty without Rochester, is now revalued as home, while St John waits for death on the 'Himalayan ridge' (p. 419). The fireside and the parlour were not his sphere. Here the difference between life and death is figured geographically, in the local colour of India as a way station between England and the grave.[20] The central value of domesticity posited here is not a new thing in the novel by any means, but it gains in authority and prestige as a result of this antithetical structure. This is an anti-apocalyptic closure, in that it focuses our attention on a domestic marriage through and against the language of the apocalyptic marriage.[21] Indeed, tropes of secularisation always work doubly this way: lending borrowed authority to forms of secular life and literature by analogy with the sacred forms they no longer quite represent, but still remember; carrying within themselves an implicit revision of the sacred text even as they borrow its authority for secular ends. *Jane Eyre* re-envisions marriage as a romantic institution of equal alter egos, a true alternative to marriage as an institution of male mediation, though it is certainly also the case that the novel notoriously fails to imagine a new society to contain this new vision of marriage.[22] The high value placed upon Jane's choice of romantic love and domestic marriage depends absolutely upon the hovering vision of the apocalyptic marriage, a vision entertained and then explicitly rejected. The novel uses the traditional force of the other world, the new heaven and the new earth, to mediate back to the fictive immediacy of this world, this earth, this domestic marriage.

The one thing an autobiographical narrator cannot do, after all, is to narrate her own death.[23] As we close this book, its closure deftly has us thinking about death without its being Jane's death, and thinking about the possibility of another world without its seeming to be Jane's idea. As we close her book, it is another Book that has us thinking about these last things, another voice invoking the apocalyptic marriage, the new heaven and the new earth. The only kind of eternal life that secular fiction can bestow is to leave Jane in the middle of her fictional life, and so her story ends in medias res, in the middle of worldly things, on this earth.[24] But of course immediacy is a fiction of language. The here and now can only be imagined through the mediation of figures that pretend to deny mediation. Contradicting the systematic mediation to the other world can work to imply the fictive plenitude of an immediate here and now, at home in England. Representing the voice of the other here at the end returns us to the remembered difference of Jane's particular narrative voice. Of course the ending of this novel does not sound like 'Jane Eyre'. But it serves graphically to mark the difference between received views and her own, between other voices and her own.

The figure of intertextuality works in this contradictory and double-binding way as well. The text in the mode of explicit inter-textuality is like the first-person narrative in the voice of another. Though in a mode of negation, Jane too joins the mediating chain as its last link, by making the last words of canonical Scripture the last words of her own text. In this bold gesture, she implies a rela-tion of apostolic succession between Christian Scripture and the lit-erary genre of autobiography. Her life story succeeds Scripture as the authoritative text, and in this sense Jane has the last word. But in this boldly *ambivalent* gesture, she poses a profoundly radical question about voice. This radical gesture puts her narrative closure at risk, destabilising her feminist position as well as the integrity of her narrative voice, and opening her text to the almost overwhelm-ing influx of the other just at the moment of attempting to close its frame. Her primary claim to speak for herself is threatened by the closing invocation of a patrilineally mediated structure of authority and voice. The integrity of her text almost dissolves into the tradi-tion she is writing (perforce) within and (by design) against. But her text has been produced from the first within these contradictions, as a sequence of transformations in which the figure of a gendered, in-dividual subject is generated against the background of traditional authority. This first-person narrator uses the patrilineal structure of tradition and its systematics of voice to write herself into the chain, without losing the radical position she would like to construct as its last link. This is, I think, the essential effect of closing with these words, but closing in the voice of the other, and not in the voice represented as her own narrating 'I'. She manages to preserve the code and its authority, making it a means to her end, while disown-ing – or at least distancing herself from – its affiliations with a power elsewhere.

As Jane is fearful and enraged at the structures of apostolic me-diation, so we may become conscious of the dynamics of canon-ical literary history which, like apostolic succession, has been structured as a chain of inherited authority, coded in just such intertextual references to power elsewhere. In closing her book, Jane closes with the other Book. I mean she 'closes with' the other

Book in a spirit of struggle, engages it, and maintains a strong sense of difference from it. And she 'closes with' the other Book in the sense of using it to her own contradictory ends. These 'ends' are never stable, but always mediate, involved in their means, generated only in the process of successive narrative transformations, as the female subject weaves its way between belated mediation to a power elsewhere and the silent plenitude of an impossible immediacy.

From Jerome McGann (ed.), *Victorian Connections* (Charlottesville, VA, 1989), pp. 60–3, 68–85.

NOTES

[Carolyn Williams' essay appears here in slightly abridged form. I have excluded a section entitled 'Contradiction' (immediately preceding the discussion of Jane as orphan) which discusses the ways in which Jane's narrative of separation and individuation works through 'comparison, contradiction, and negation' (p. 66). In the remainder of her essay, reprinted here, Williams considers how this dynamic might be related to questions of gender. Like Homans, Poovey and Bronfen, she draws on psychoanalytic theory in order to explore some of the most distinctive features of Jane's narrative. She is particularly concerned with tracing the way in which, within that narrative, 'the figure of a gendered, individual subject is generated against a background of traditional authority', through the 'crossings and junctures' of the 'pre-Oedipal and Oedipal plots'. In psychoanalytic theory, Oedipal ideas and feelings (first described as such by Freud, in *The Interpretation of Dreams* [1900]) are those which centre around the wish to possess the parent of the opposite sex, and the pre-Oedipal (with which, since the 1930s, psychoanalysis has been increasingly concerned) relates to that earlier stage of psychic life, in which the relationship to the mother is paramount. The term 'intertextuality', which appears in Williams' title, was introduced into French criticism in the late 1960s by Julia Kristeva, as an elaboration and development of the Russian critic M. M. Bakhtin's theory of the essentially 'dialogic' nature of the novelistic text. According to Bakhtin, every novelistic utterance is in 'dialogue' with other texts or utterances that exist outside it, and it is by being alert to such 'dialogue', in its historical specificity, that its import can best be grasped. It is on this theory that Williams draws, in her discussion of the quotations and allusions which mark the ending of *Jane Eyre*. Ed.]

1.   Charlotte Brontë, *Jane Eyre*, ed. Queenie Leavis (Harmondsworth, 1966), p. 477. Subsequent references in the novel will be to this edition and will be cited parenthetically in the text.

2. This romantic rhetoric is most graphic in the proposal scene of ch. 23 and is symbolised there and subsequently by the horse chestnut tree, split manifestly in two, yet unified underground, at the root.

3. M. Jeanne Peterson, 'Status Incongruence in Family and Society', in Martha Vicinus (ed.), *Suffer and Be Still: Women in the Victorian Age* (Bloomington, IN, 1972), pp. 3–19.

4. Harold Bloom, 'The Internalisation of Quest Romance', in *Romanticism and Consciousness: Essays in Criticism*, ed. Harold Bloom (New York, 1970), pp. 3–24.

5. This dimension of my argument is grounded in specifically feminist developments of object relations theory. The locus classicus for American critics is Nancy Chodorow, *The Reproduction of Mothering: Psychoanalysis and the Sociology of Gender* (Berkeley, CA, 1978). A recent volume of essays in psychoanalytic feminist criticism marks the attempt to theorise the relation between Oedipal and pre-Oedipal models in literary analysis and the attempt to theorise a relation between feminist uses of Lacan and feminist object relations: *The (M)other Tongue: Essays in Feminist Psychoanalytic Interpretation*, ed. Shirley Nelson Garner, Claire Kahane, and Madelon Sprengnether (Ithaca, NY, 1985).

    For analysis and critique of the position of the separating daughter within psychoanalysis and literature, see the editorial introduction to *The (M)other Tongue*, pp. 15–29; Susan Rubin Suleiman's contribution to that volume, 'Writing and Motherhood', pp. 352–77; Jane Flax, 'The Conflict between Nurturance and Autonomy in Mother–Daughter Relationships and within Feminism', *Feminist Studies*, 4 (June 1978), 171–91; and Jane Gallop, 'Reading the Mother Tongue: Psychoanalytic Feminist Criticism', *Critical Inquiry*, 13.2 (Winter 1987), 314–29.

6. Gilbert and Gubar have pointed out the relevance of this song to the 'patriarchal terrors of the red-room and ... patriarchal terrors to come – Lowood, Brocklehurst, St John Rivers', in *The Madwoman in the Attic: The Woman Writer and the Nineteenth Century Literary Imagination* (New Haven CT, 1979), pp. 342–3.

7. Barbara Hardy, 'Dogmatic Form: Defoe, Charlotte Brontë, Thomas Hardy and E. M. Forster', in *The Appropriate Form: An Essay on the Novel* (London, 1964), pp. 51–82.

8. On the moon as Mother, see Adrienne Rich, 'Jane Eyre: the Temptations of a Motherless Woman', in *On Lies, Secrets and Silence: Selected Prose 1966–1978* (New York, 1979), pp. 101–3; and Gilbert and Gubar, *Madwoman*, pp. 340–1, 363–4.

9. On the good object and the bad object (good mother and bad mother, good breast and bad breast), see Melanie Klein, 'A Contribution to

the Psychogenesis of Manic-Depressive States', in her *Love, Guilt and Reparation* (London, 1977), pp. 262–89; and chs 8 and 9 of *The Psycho-Analysis of Children, The Writings of Melanie Klein*, Vol. 2 (New York, 1984).

10. See Margaret Homans, 'Dreaming of Children: Literalisation in *Jane Eyre*', in *Bearing the Word: Language and Female Experience in Nineteenth-century Women's Writing* (Chicago, 1986), pp. 84–99 [Reprinted in this volume – see pp. 147–67. Ed.]

11. For Jessica Benjamin's specifically feminist extension of Winnicott's concepts of the 'holding mother' or 'holding environment', see 'A Desire of One's Own: Psychoanalytic Feminism and Intersubjective Space', in *Feminist Studies/Critical Studies*, ed. Teresa de Lauretis (Bloomington, IN, 1986), pp. 78–101.

12. Homans notes this turn in 'Dreaming of Children'. [See this volume, p. 160. Ed.]

13. On the providential plot in *Jane Eyre*, see Thomas Vargish, *The Providential Aesthetic in Victorian Fiction* (Charlottesville, VA, 1985), especially pp. 58–67.

14. See Rich, 'Jane Eyre: the Temptations of a Motherless Woman', pp. 103–4; Kaja Silverman, '*Histoire d'O*: The Construction of a Female Subject', in *Pleasure and Danger: Exploring Female Sexuality* (Boston, 1984), pp. 320–49; and Jessica Benjamin, 'Master and Slave: the Fantasy of Erotic Domination', in *Powers of Desire: the Politics of Sexuality* (New York, 1983), ed. Anne Snitow, Christine Stansell and Sharon Thompson, pp. 280–99. For another influential reading of the female as a signifier of a male–male transaction, see Eve Kosofsky Sedgwick, *Between Men: English Literature and Male Homosocial Desire* (New York, 1985).

15. Gilbert and Gubar, *Madwoman*, p. 366.

16. Rich, 'Jane Eyre: the Temptations of a Motherless Woman', p. 103.

17. My argument here is indebted to Barbara Johnson, 'Metaphor, Metonymy, and Voice in Zora Neale Hurston's *Their Eyes Were Watching God*', in *Black Literature and Literary Theory* (London, 1985), pp. 205–19. See also Ruth Bernard Yeazell, 'More True Than Real: Jane Eyre's "Mysterious Summons"', *Nineteenth-Century Fiction*, 29 (1974), 127–43.

18. Judith Wilt makes this point in 'Brava! And Farewell to Greatheart', a review of Gilbert and Gubar, *The Madwoman in the Attic*, in *Boundary*, 28:3 (Spring 1980), 285–99.

19. See Gilbert and Gubar, 'Plain Jane's Progress', in *Madwoman*, pp. 336–71 and Barry Qualls, *The Secular Pilgrims of Victorian Fiction* (Cambridge, 1982), pp. 43–84. On the figurative tension

between vocational service to different 'Masters' in Bunyan, see Michael McKeon, 'Romance Transformations II: Bunyan and the Literalisation of Allegory', in *The Origins of the English Novel, 1600–1740* (Baltimore, MD, 1987), pp. 295–314.

20. Thanks to my colleague David Suchoff, who has pointed out to me the critique of colonialism implicit in this closing view of St John Rivers.

21. On the secularised apocalyptic marriage as a figure of romanticism, see M. H. Abrams, *Natural Supernaturalism* (New York, 1971).

22. As Carol Ohmann argues in 'Historical Reality and "Divine Appointment" in Charlotte Brontë's Fiction', *Signs*, 2:4 (1977), 757–78.

23. Walter Benjamin, 'The Storyteller: Reflections on the Works of Nikolai Leskov', in *Illuminations* (New York, 1986), pp. 83–110.

24. 'In the middest', to use Frank Kermode's famous phrase from *The Sense of an Ending: Studies in the Theory of Fiction* (London, 1966).

Further Reading

Any serious student of Charlotte Brontë will want to know more of her life, and of the writings of her early years. The classic biography – one of the greatest biographies in the language – is that by her friend Elizabeth Gaskell (*The Life of Charlotte Brontë* [1857; rpt Oxford: Oxford University Press, 1974]). More recent biographical studies, which draw upon material unavailable to Mrs Gaskell, include Winifred Gérin, *Charlotte Brontë: the Evolution of Genius* (Oxford: Clarendon Press, 1967) and Juliet Barker, *The Brontës* (London: Weidenfeld & Nicholson, 1994).

Most of the surviving letters of the Brontë family are reprinted in T. J. Wise and J. A. Symington (eds), *The Brontës: Their Lives, Friendships and Correspondence*, 4 vols (Oxford: Shakespeare Head, 1932). This edition contains many inaccuracies: a new and definitive edition of Charlotte Brontë's letters is in the process of preparation by Margaret Smith. Of this, Vol. I, *The Letters of Charlotte Bronte 1829–1847* (Oxford: Clarendon Press, 1995) has so far appeared.

A good overview of Charlotte Brontë's juvenilia is offered in Christine Alexander, *The Early Writings of Charlotte Brontë* (Oxford: Basil Blackwell, 1983). Of her *Edition of the Early Writings of Charlotte Brontë*, the following volumes have so far appeared: Vol. I, *The Glass Town Saga 1826–1832* (Oxford: Shakespeare Head Press, 1987); Vol. II, *The Rise of Angria 1833–1835, Part 1: 1833–4* and *Part 2: 1834–5* (Oxford: Shakespeare Head Press, 1991). Five longer fictions, dating from the period 1836–9, are reprinted in Charlotte Brontë, *Five Novelettes*, ed. Winifed Gérin (London: Folio Press, 1971).

A useful selection of early criticism may be found in Miriam Allott (ed.), *The Brontës: The Critical Heritage* (London: Routledge & Kegan Paul, 1974).

CRITICAL STUDIES

Most of the works listed below were published during the last twenty years. For the benefit of students wishing to pursue further some of the issues raised in this New Casebook, I have grouped them roughly according to topic, though many in fact cannot be very neatly categorised. The following studies of Charlotte Brontë's works also contain much to interest the student of *Jane Eyre*:

Annette Tromly, *The Cover of the Mask: The Autobiographers in Charlotte Brontë's Fiction* (Victoria, BC: English Literary Studies, University of Victoria, 1982). Challenges the type of reading which looks to the novels for 'undigested traces of Brontë's experience' by examining Brontë's 'aesthetic transformation' of that experience through a sophisticated use of the first-person narrator.

John Maynard, *Charlotte Brontë and Sexuality* (Cambridge: Cambridge University Press, 1984). Offers a detailed account of Brontë's exploration of the complexities of sexual experience, in her published and unpublished fiction. Contains a useful bibliography of Victorian writings on sexuality.

John Kucich, *Repression in Victorian Fiction: Charlotte Brontë, George Eliot, and Charles Dickens* (Berkeley: University of California Press, 1987). Argues that in Charlotte Brontë's fiction the deliberate refusal of self-expression is not a tragic psychic compromise but plays a positive, empowering role in the construction of subjectivity and the engendering of desire.

Janet Gezari, *Charlotte Brontë and Defensive Conduct: the Author and the Body at Risk* (Philadelphia: University of Pennsylvania Press, 1992). A defence of the idea of self-defence, as it is embodied in Charlotte Brontë's fiction.

Carol Bock, *Charlotte Brontë and the Storyteller's Audience* (Iowa City: University of Iowa Press, 1992). Traces Charlotte Brontë's persistent concern with the reader's collaborative role in the storytelling experience from the juvenilia to *Villette*.

FORMALIST AND STYLISTIC STUDIES

David Lodge, 'Fire and Eyre: Charlotte Brontë's War of Earthly Elements', in *The Language of Fiction: Essays in Criticism and Verbal Analysis of the English Novel* (London: Routledge & Kegan Paul, 1966), pp. 114–43. A pioneering attempt to pay close attention to the language and imagery of *Jane Eyre*.

Karl Kroeber, *Styles in Fictional Structure: The Art of Jane Austen, Charlotte Brontë and George Eliot* (Princeton, NJ: Princeton University Press, 1971). Close formal analysis of such features as characterisation, setting, time and action in Charlotte Bronte's novels.

Margot Peters, *Charlotte Brontë: Style in the Novel* (Madison: University of Wisconsin Press, 1973). An attempt to 'reconcile the precision and objectivity of linguistic analysis with the more intuitive and interpretive discipline of literary criticism'.

Jerome Beaty, '*Jane Eyre* and Genre', *Genre*, 10 (1977), 619–54. Seeks to identify the differing generic expectations upon which *Jane Eyre* plays.

Hermione Lee, 'Emblems and Enigmas in *Jane Eyre*', *English*, 30 (Autumn 1981), 233–55. A suggestive discussion of the dreams, apparitions, pictures, tableaux, signs and emblematic figures of speech in *Jane Eyre*.

READING

For discussion of the significance of books and reading in *Jane Eyre*, see:

Mark M. Hennelly, Jr, '*Jane Eyre*'s Reading Lesson', *English Literary History*, 51 (1984), 693–717.

Carla L. Peterson, *The Determined Reader: Gender and Culture in the Novel from Napoleon to Victoria* (New Brunswick, NJ: Rutgers University Press, 1986), pp. 82–131.

Valentine Cunningham, *In the Reading Gaol: Postmodernity, Texts, and History* (Oxford: Basil Blackwell, 1994), pp. 341–62.

FEMINISM

The following classic feminist accounts of *Jane Eyre* date from the 1970s:

Adrienne Rich, 'Jane Eyre: the Temptations of a Motherless Woman', *MS*, 2 (October, 1973), reprinted in her *On Lies, Secrets and Silence: Selected Prose 1966–1978* (New York: W. W. Norton, 1979), pp. 89–106.

Maurianne Adams, '*Jane Eyre*: Woman's Estate', in A. Diamond and Lee R. Edwards (eds), *The Authority of Experience: Essays in Feminist Criticism* (Amherst, MA: University of Massachussetts Press, 1977).

Sandra M. Gilbert and Susan Gubar, *The Madwoman in the Attic: The Woman Writer and the Nineteenth-Century Literary Imagination* (New Haven, CT: Yale University Press, 1979).

More recent feminist studies include:

Cora Kaplan, in 'Pandora's Box', in *Sea Changes: Culture and Feminism* (London: Verso, 1986), pp. 170–4. A brief, suggestive discussion of *Jane Eyre's* radical association between political and gender rebellion.

Peter J. Bellis, 'In the Window-Seat: Vision and Power in *Jane Eyre*', *English Literary History*, 54 (1987), 639–52. Discusses the way in which *Jane Eyre* seeks to redefine and reverse masculine structures of power, by appropriating the gaze and the written word for the novelist and her heroine.

Patricia Yaeger, *Honey-mad Women: Emancipatory Strategies in Women's Writing* (New York: Columbia University Press, 1988). Draws on psychoanalytic and deconstructionist theory in order to explore the subversive multivoicedness of *Jane Eyre*.

Eugenia C. DeLamotte, *Perils of the Night: A Feminist Study of Nineteenth-Century Gothic* (New York: Oxford University Press, 1989). Discusses Charlotte Brontë's reworking of 'women's Gothic' in *Jane Eyre* and *Villette*.

Irene Tayler, *Holy Ghosts: The Male Muses of Emily and Charlotte Brontë* (New York: Columbia University Press, 1990). Examines issues of gender in the writings of both sisters by exploring their construction of what she calls a 'male muse'.

Susan Sniader Lanser, *Fictions of Authority: Woman Writers and Narrative Voice* (Ithaca, NY, and London: Cornell University Press, 1992), pp. 176–93. A historically informed analysis of *Jane Eyre's* attempt to present an authoritative female narrative voice.

Sharon Marcus, 'The Profession of the Author: Abstraction, Advertising, and *Jane Eyre*', *PMLA*, 110:2 (March 1995), 206–19. Draws on Marxist and Lacanian theory to explore the ways in which Brontë 'negotiated the conflict between the embodiment attributed to women and the increasing abstraction of the publishing, advertising, and professional identities she sought to assume'.

TEXT AND HISTORY

Terry Eagleton, *Myths of Power: a Marxist Study of the Brontës* (London: Macmillan, 1975; 2nd edn, 1987). A ground-breaking Marxist analysis of the novels of the Brontë sisters. Eagleton's volume appeared before the real burgeoning of feminist criticism, and paid little attention to questions of gender. His view of Brontë's heroines as 'asexual representatives of the upwardly mobile bourgeoisie' was stringently criticised by the Marxist-Feminist Literature Collective, in 'Women's Writing: *Jane Eyre, Shirley, Villette, "Aurora Leigh"'*, in *1848: The Sociology of Literature*, ed. Francis Barker et al. (Colchester: University of Essex, 1978). In a Preface to the second edition, Eagleton offers a critical account of the methodological assumptions which shaped *Myths of Power*, paying particular attention to the work's 'gender blindness' and to what he now sees as its other 'faults or exclusions'.

Nancy Pell, 'Resistance, Rebellion and Marriage: The Economics of *Jane Eyre*', *Nineteenth-Century Fiction*, 31 (1977), 397–420. A thoughtful account of the way in which the novel's romantic individualism is controlled and structured by a social and economic critique of bourgeois patriarchal authority.

Carol Ohmann, 'Historical Reality and "Divine Appointment" in Charlotte Brontë's Fiction', *Signs*, 2:4 (1977), 757–78. Discusses the tension between radical and conservative tendencies in Charlotte Brontë's fiction.

Igor Webb, *From Custom to Capital: the English Novel and the Industrial Revolution* (Ithaca, NY: Cornell University Press, 1981), pp. 70–86. Argues that *Jane Eyre* 'expresses the forces of its time in a triumphant merger of Romanticism and the individualist ethic of laissez-faire'.

Paul Schacht, '*Jane Eyre* and Self-Respect', *Modern Language Quarterly*, 52:4 (December 1991), 423–53. A historically informed discussion of the ways in which *Jane Eyre* contributes to a new conception of the self, 'which in Brontë's time was still emerging and developing against the background of a changing social order'.

Sally Shuttleworth, *Charlotte Brontë and Nineteenth-Century Psychology* (Cambridge: Cambridge University Press, 1996). Combines close textual analysis with historical specificity of reference in order to explore the ways in which Brontë's fiction 'actively encodes the language and preoccupations of mid-nineteenth-century social, psychological and economic thought'.

RACE

Gayatri Chakravorty Spivak, 'Three Women's Texts and a Critique of Imperialism', *Critical Inquiry*, 12 (1985), 243–61. An influential essay which uses the figure of Bertha Rochester to argue that the construction of 'feminist individualism in the age of imperialism' entails the exclusion of the '"native female" as such'.

Suvendrini Perera, *Reaches of Empire: The English Novel from Edgeworth to Dickens* (New York: Columbia University Press, 1991). Discusses the feminist appropriation of orientalist discourse in the early nineteenth century, and focuses on sati as *Jane Eyre's* 'central image'.

Joyce Zonana, 'The Sultan and the Slave: Feminist Orientalism and the Structure of *Jane Eyre*', *Signs: Journal of Women in Culture and Society*, 18:3 (1991), 592–617. Suggests that in systematically linking gender oppression to oriental despotism, *Jane Eyre* (like the writings of others in early Victorian England) in fact presses orientalism into the service of feminism.

Laura E. Donaldson, 'The Miranda Complex', in *Decolonising Feminisms: Race, Gender and Empire-Building* (London: Routledge and University of North Carolina Press, 1993). Draws on recent film theory in order to challenge readings such as Spivak's, which fail, she argues, to take account of the ways in which Jane, no less than the 'native' subject Bertha Rochester, is portrayed as a victim of oppression.

Deirdre David, 'The Governess of Empire: Jane Eyre Takes Care of India and Jamaica', in *Rule Britannia: Women, Empire, and Victorian Writing* (Ithaca, NY: Cornell University Press, 1995). Extends the familiar reading of *Jane Eyre* as an account of triumphant individual female subjectivity by arguing that 'the novel also imagines the ideal Victorian woman of empire, a figure who combines the selflessness of Little Nell and Florence Dombey with the complicated authority of the young Queen Victoria'.

RELIGION

Barry Qualls, *The Secular Pilgrims of Victorian Fiction* (Cambridge: Cambridge University Press, 1982), pp. 43–84. Discusses *Jane Eyre* as an attempt to reconcile a continuing tradition of spiritual autobiography dating from the seventeenth century and the more recent legacy of Romanticism.

Thomas Vargish, *The Providential Aesthetic in Victorian Fiction* (Charlottesville, VA, 1985), pp. 57–67. Argues that a central concern of *Jane Eyre* is to represent a divine order within the temporal world.

PSYCHOANALYSIS

Jean Wyatt, *Reconstructing Desire: The Role of the Unconscious in Women's Reading and Writing* (Chapel Hill, NC and London: University of North Carolina Press, 1990), pp. 23–40. In the light of recent psychoanalytic theory, examines the rather different messages *Jane Eyre* addresses to the unconscious and conscious registers of the reader's mind.

Michelle A. Massé, *In the Name of Love: Women, Masochism and the Gothic* (Ithaca, NY: Cornell University Press, 1992), pp. 192–238. Draws on contemporary feminist and psychoanalytic theory in order to explore *Jane Eyre's* dealings with issues of female masochism.

Notes on Contributors

Penny Boumelha holds the Jury Chair of English Language and Literature at the University of Adelaide. Her publications include *Thomas Hardy and Women* (Brighton, 1982) and *Charlotte Brontë* (Brighton, 1990). She is editor of the forthcoming volume on *Jude the Obscure* in the New Casebook series. She is currently working on gender and nationality in late nineteenth-century Irish writing and writing about Ireland.

Elisabeth Bronfen is Professor of English at the University of Zurich. She is the author of articles on nineteenth- and twentieth-century fiction, film, psychoanalysis, and literary and cultural theory. She is co-editor of *Death and Representation* (Baltimore and London, 1993) and author of *Over Her Dead Body: Death, Femininity and the Aesthetic* (Manchester, 1992) and *Dorothy Richardson's Art of Memory: Space, Identity, Text* (Manchester, forthcoming). She is currently working on a study on representations and interpretations of hysteria, entitled *The Knotted Subject: Hysteria and its Discontents.*

Karen Chase is Professor of English at the University of Virginia. She is the author of *Eros and Psyche: The Representation of Personality in Charlotte Brontë, Charles Dickens and George Eliot* (New York and London, 1984) and of *George Eliot: Middlemarch* (Landmarks of World Literature, Cambridge University Press, 1991). She is the co-author, with Michael Levenson, of a forthcoming book on domesticity in the age of Dickens.

Peter Allan Dale is Professor of English at the University of California, Davis. His publications include *The Victorian Critic and the Idea of History: Carlyle, Arnold and Pater* (Cambridge, MA, 1977) and *In Pursuit of a Scientific Culture: Science, Art, and Society in the Victorian Age* (Madison, WI, 1989), as well as numerous essays on Victorian literature and intellectual history. He is currently working on a study of late nineteenth and early twentieth-century Liberalism and the institution of literary culture.

Margaret Homans is Professor of English at Yale University, where she also chairs the Women's Studies Program. Her publications include *Women Writers and Poetic Identity: Dorothy Wordsworth, Emily Brontë, and Emily Dickinson* (Princeton, NJ, 1980) and *Bearing the Word: Language and Female Experience in Nineteenth-century Women's Writing* (Chicago, 1986): she has also written numerous essays on nineteenth-century literature and on feminist theory. She is currently working on a book about Queen Victoria and Victorian literature.

Susan Meyer is Associate Professor of English at Wellesley College. She is the author of *Imperialism at Home: Race in Victorian Women's Fiction* (Cornell University Press, forthcoming) as well as of a number of articles on Victorian women writers, American literature, and American photography, published in such journals as *Victorian Studies, ELH, South Central Review* and *Prospects,* and in various essay collections. She is co-editor of *The New Nineteenth Century: Feminist Readings of Underread Victorian Fiction* (Garland, forthcoming).

Jina Politi was a fellow of Churchill College, Cambridge, and is now Professor of English Literature at the Aristotle University of Thessaloniki, Greece. She is the author of *The Novel and its Presuppositions* (Amsterdam, 1976) and of numerous articles on English and modern Greek literature. She is currently working on Walter Scott and the historical novel.

Mary Poovey is Professor of English at Johns Hopkins University. Her publications include *The Proper Lady and the Woman Writer: Ideology as Style in the Works of Mary Wollstonecraft, Mary Shelley, and Jane Austen* (Chicago, 1984), *Uneven Developments: the Ideological Work of Gender in Mid-Victorian England* (Chicago, 1988) and *Making a Social Body: British Cultural Formation, 1830–1864* (Chicago, 1995).

Doreen Roberts is Lecturer in English at the University of Kent at Canterbury. She has published articles on Dickens, John Fowles, A. E. Housman and modern poetry, and is currently working on a book which investigates the interaction between literature and British empiricist philosophy in the period between Addison and Hazlitt.

Elaine Showalter is Professor of English at Princeton University. She is editor of *The New Feminist Criticism: Essays on Women, Literature and Theory* (New York, 1985) and of *Speaking of Gender* (New York and London, 1989), and author of *A Literature of Their Own: British Women Novelists from Brontë to Lessing* (Princeton, NJ, 1977), *The Female Malady: Women, Madness and English Culture, 1830–1980* (New York, 1985), *Sexual Anarchy: Gender and Culture at the Fin de Siècle* (New York, 1990), *Sister's Choice: Tradition and Change in American Women's Writing* (Oxford, 1991).

Carolyn Williams is Associate Professor of English at Rutgers University (New Brunswick, New Jersey), where she is also the Associate Director of the Center for the Critical Analysis of Contemporary Culture. She is the author of *Transfigured World: Walter Pater's Aesthetic Historicism* (Ithaca, NY, 1989) and of essays on various other Victorian writers. She is currently at work on a cultural study of the Savoy operas by Gilbert and Sullivan.

Index